The Political Economy of Spanish America in the Age of Revolution, 1750–1850

The Political Economy of Spanish America in the Age of Revolution, 1750–1850

Edited by Kenneth J. Andrien and Lyman L. Johnson

University of New Mexico Press
Albuquerque

To our mothers
Edith Andrien
Helen Johnson

Library of Congress Cataloging-in-Publication Data

The Political economy of Spanish America in the age of revolution, 1750–1850 / edited by Kenneth J. Andrien and Lyman L. Johnson. — 1st ed.
p. cm.
Includes bibliographical references and index.
ISBN 0-8263-1489-9
1. Latin America—Economic conditions. 2. Latin America—Politics and government—To 1830. 3. Latin America—Politics and government—19th century. I. Andrien, Kenneth J., 1951– . II. Johnson, Lyman L.
HC124.P65 1994
338.98—dc20

First edition.

Contents

Acknowledgments

This project grew out of conversations with colleagues at the American Historical Association meeting in 1986, concerning recent contributions to the history of late colonial and early national Spanish America. From our discussions it became clear that much of this new literature provided evidence of significant socioeconomic continuities over the period from approximately 1750 to 1850. This contrasted sharply with the conclusions reached in most other studies, which emphasized the importance of the dramatic political changes brought about by the independence movements. In fact, the findings of these newer works suggested to us that the traditional historical periodization and mainstream interpretations of the independence era needed revision. We decided, therefore, to bring together at the International Congress of Americanists in Amsterdam some of the principal scholars whose work was prompting this process of revision. The papers, commentaries, and discussions in Amsterdam covered a broad array of topics and geographic regions, beginning with the reign of Charles II (1759–1788) and ending in 1850. Our discussions of this transitional period made clear the importance of the colonial and early national states as economic actors. Following the meeting, we decided that a volume of comparative essays focused on the role of the state in the economic history of Spanish America had the potential to make a significant historiographical contribution and promote further research. We hope that our readers will agree.

As with all scholarly projects, we have benefited from the generous support and active collaboration of many colleagues. Jacques A. Barbier, Javier Cuenca Esteban, John R. Fisher, Charles Fleener, Allan J. Kuethe, Anthony McFarlane, Susan M. Socolow, and John J. TePaske all participated in the Amsterdam conference or subsequent discussions and have directly contributed to shaping this study. Others, too numerous to mention individually, have contributed to this project through their published work and presentations at scholarly meetings. Without their stimulation and encouragement, this volume could not have been completed. They, of course, bear no responsibility for any errors of fact or interpretation that remain.

The College of Humanities, the Department of History, and the Latin American Studies Program at Ohio State University, and the College of Arts and Sciences and the Department of History at the University of North Carolina at Charlotte provided needed financial support. We are particularly grateful to David V. Holtby, an editor at the University of New Mexico Press, for his active support, encouragement, and patience.

Anne Andrien and Sue Johnson have provided sympathy, support, and hospitality as we engaged in this collaborative effort. Their patience and good humor have sustained our efforts. Finally, we would like to dedicate this book to our mothers, Edith Andrien and Helen Johnson. We hope this volume can serve as a small expression of our love and gratitude for the innumerable ways that they have guided and enriched our lives.

Kenneth J. Andrien
Columbus, Ohio

Lyman L. Johnson
Charlotte, North Carolina

The Political Economy of Spanish America in the Age of Revolution, 1750–1850

I

Introduction

KENNETH J. ANDRIEN AND
LYMAN L. JOHNSON

This volume contributes to a growing body of scholarly literature focusing on the pervasive role of the state in the regional socioeconomic development of late colonial and early republican Spanish America.[1] Despite its relatively small size, the colonial state influenced the long-term growth of important social structures, labor systems, patterns of settlement, and religious practices. The state also maintained a tradition of intervening in the market economy, promoting some favored sectors, such as mining or export agriculture, while discouraging others—particularly most forms of manufacturing. Despite the disruptions of independence and the lapse into political disorder during the *caudillo* era, a pattern of state intervention in the economy continued well into the nineteenth century. As a result, we contend that the colonial and early republican regimes played a central role in shaping key elements of the political economy in Spanish America during the so-called "Age of Revolution" (from approximately 1750 to 1850).*

The colonial state played a particularly active role in regulating and directing the market economies of late colonial Spanish America. Through a complex network of commercial regulations, monopolies, and fiscal levies, the Spanish crown attempted to control the nexus between the international market and regional economies throughout the Indies. The links between the representatives of the state—high-level bureaucrats, local magistrates, and parish priests—and civil society extended throughout Spanish America even to the remote rural villages of the Amerindian peasantry.[2] In the Andean countryside, for example, state officials were able to extract millions of pesos in taxes and to help mobilize a large

*By *political economy* we mean the historical intersection of political culture, public policy, and economic performance (defined by economic production, the exchange of goods and services, and the distribution of wealth within a given polity).

Amerindian labor force for Spanish mining and agrarian enterprises. State policies also influenced the evolution of colonial cities, forcing miners and agriculturalists to subsidize distant administrative centers, like Lima or Buenos Aires. The long-term macroeconomic implications of these policies affected most sectors of the market economy to some degree. In fact, the state system of taxes, monopolies, and market regulations effectively established the context for many important commercial exchanges in the Indies.

Despite the downfall of the Spanish colonial regime, much of this legacy of state intervention in the market economy continued into the national period. The power of republican-era governments was limited by reduced resources and regional political instability, but there is still strong evidence of important continuities with the colonial era. The national regimes in Spanish America retained many colonial fiscal policies, including Amerindian tribute, commercial and manufacturing monopolies, protective tariffs, and many other restrictive trade regulations. Some historians now contend that essential elements of Spanish colonialism endured until the last quarter of the nineteenth century. As William Taylor has stated: "Of the two great structural changes . . . influencing the Europeanizing areas of the world after 1500—capitalism and state formation—the institutions of the state . . . had an earlier, more direct, and deeper impact on the central areas of Spanish America, at least until the last quarter of the nineteenth century."[3]

In recent years some influential studies have downplayed the importance of the state in the socioeconomic development of eighteenth- and nineteenth-century Spanish America. Among these, a minority persist in identifying studies of the state with older legal and institutional history. Others have disparaged much of the work in political economy as "statolatrous."[4] In part, this opposition to a reexamination of the state's economic role is a reaction against a few influential early studies that emphasized links between Bourbon state policies after 1765 and the onset of the independence wars in Spanish America.[5] It also represents, in many cases, a repudiation of social science literature focusing on the role of the state as a powerful "autonomous actor," capable of prompting profound changes, such as mass-based popular insurrections and revolutions.[6] A few Latin Americanists who examine elite and popular protest movements have condemned any purported "reification" of the state, emphasizing instead factors like popular ideology, community values, and political consciousness in provoking such violent upheavals. These revisionist historians picture the state as small, weak, fragmented, and incapable of serving as an instrument for important historical change.[7] In fact, Eric Van Young has argued in favor of "taking the state back out" of regional studies of nineteenth-century Spanish America.[8]

We find efforts to categorize the state as either a powerful "autonomous force" or a weak secondary actor unconvincing and extreme, particularly for the late colonial and early republican periods. Such formulations are symptomatic of the relatively early stage of research and theoretical exploration dealing with the political economy of Spanish America.[9] Instead, we believe that the colonial state's role—operating at the metropolitan, viceregal, and regional levels—as an economic actor must be defined in the broadest terms. The policies of the colonial government went beyond attempts to tax and regulate the market economy; in some cases, state policies (and the public officials empowered to enforce them) created the arena in which important commercial exchanges took place. As Brian Hamnett has demonstrated, mercantile elites and local *alcaldes* in Oaxaca collaborated to channel cochineal and other indigenous products through the public sector (using tribute exactions) to markets in Mexico City.[10] Agents of the colonial government in Oaxaca, and elsewhere, did not always serve the narrow interests of the crown or even reflect colonial administrative priorities. Instead, state policies most often arose from the complex interplay among self-interested metropolitan and colonial elite factions, later moderated by political pressures from local middle, laboring, and peasant classes.[11] Even after independence this pattern continued, as interest groups in Spanish America sought to control the policies of weaker national regimes whenever their sectoral interests were at stake. Exploring these themes can provide the context for understanding the link between the dramatic events of independence and the more gradual socioeconomic changes occurring over long- and medium-range time periods. An approach emphasizing changes in political economy can also furnish an important unifying element in studies comparing these basic structural changes across the varied regional landscapes of Spanish America.[12]

Our emphasis on the state's role in socioeconomic development also offers an alternative analytical framework for examining the issues raised in the historiographical controversy over the meaning of independence in Spanish America. Many dependency writers, social historians, and specialists in political economy have begun giving less emphasis to the vivid political changes accompanying independence, focusing instead on long-term continuities during the Age of Revolution.[13] Indeed, some historians argue that the framework of the ancien régime remained virtually unchanged—as demographic trends, systems of taxation, transport and communications networks, and the structures of rural life persisted well into the nineteenth century.[14] Many of these scholars also contend that both popular and elite ideological notions experienced few fundamental alterations after the region's incomplete assimilation of enlightenment ideas in the eighteenth century.[15] Even historians who see a sharp decline in political stability, economic performance, and social cohesion after independence trace these changes to the late colonial period, arguing that the period from approximately 1750 to 1850 represents "a coherent century."[16] In short, works representing several distinct historiographical traditions picture this era as a transition between the crisis of the ancien régime and the maturation of export economies in Spanish America after 1850.

Many scholars disagree with this revisionist position, regardless of its formulation, and maintain that the downfall of the colonial regimes transformed the development of Spanish America.[17] They argue that the colonial state played a central role in shaping socioeconomic changes through price controls, monopolies, tariffs and taxes, economic subsidies, and policies that defined many important racial, ethnic, and gender relationships.[18] From this perspective, the decline and fall of this pervasive colonial system necessarily produced severe economic and social crises that disrupted the existing order. Out of the resulting chaos, a new society evolved. Advocates of this view maintain that this clear break with the past warrants the traditional periodization of Spanish American history into the colonial, independence, and national periods.

This controversy continues unabated, mainly because so few monographic studies actually span the entire period 1750–1850. Although some works dealing with the late colonial or early national period do address longer term continuities, few historians trace such changes systematically across the traditional chronological divide of independence. Those few empirical studies that do engage the period from 1750 to 1850 usually deal with limited geographical regions and delimited, or focused, historical themes.[19] Larger comparative issues simply have not been engaged. In addition, no published monographic studies emphasize the role of the state as an economic actor—a historical theme common to both the colonial and republican eras.[20] As a result, the colonial, independence, and early national periods are commonly studied by three separate groups of scholars, often interested in very different historical issues.

We believe that a comparative examination of the state as an agent of socioeconomic change will provide a coherent analytical framework for assessing the meaning of independence in Spanish America. All the essays in this volume focus on the enduring importance of the state as an economic actor during the transitional period from 1750 to 1850 in important regions of Spanish America. Moreover, each contribution deals with a specific topic crucial to understanding the nature of the political economy of this transitional era—the persistence of a colonial political culture (Timothy E. Anna) and business practices (John E. Kicza); the long-term trends in the political economy of different regions in Spanish America (Brian R. Hamnett, Lyman L. Johnson, and Jerry W. Cooney and Thomas L. Whigham); the importance of state-run enterprises (Susan Deans-Smith and Kendall W. Brown); and finally, the role of state fiscal and commercial policies on economic development (Richard J. Salvucci, Linda K. Salvucci, Aslán Cohen, and Kenneth J. Andrien).

Despite inherent difficulties, this comparative perspective allows us to identify more complex periodizations, modify or overturn existing hypotheses, clarify the salient historical issues involved, identify how the continuity of basic socioeconomic structures helped shape the impact of independence, and encourage much-needed additional research into this relatively neglected era. Finally, this book also explores some of the *similarities* and the salient historical *differences* between the experiences of territories in Mexico and South America between 1750 and 1850. Until other works of synthesis emerge using a broadly comparative approach, we hope these essays can unite the diverse strands of inquiry dealing with the political economy of Spanish America during this vital transformational epoch.

The State and Socioeconomic Change, 1750–1850

Studies of the independence era often emphasize the sharp break in the political culture of Spanish America, as the new nations discarded their traditional adherence to monarchy and embraced republican forms of government. Timothy E. Anna, however, demonstrates that the persistence and vitality of a colonial political culture contributed to the creation of a constitutional monarchy in Mexico by Agustín de Iturbide. After the failure of the mass-based movements begun by Hidalgo and Morelos, diffuse regional insurrections motivated by local grievances still threatened the colonial order. But they lacked coherent goals and a national leadership. Divided creole elites generally shunned these movements, favoring "order" over the uncertain benefits of political autonomy. Iturbide temporarily overcame these divisions by offering a program that protected traditional elites and offered a form of government well established in the popular imagination, a monarchy. Anna asserts that this fragile political consensus ultimately failed because Iturbide feuded with a jealous and independent congress over efforts to resolve the fundamental problem of nineteenth-century Mexico—the pressures of regionalism.

Brian R. Hamnett's study of the southern Mexican state of Oaxaca identifies the ways in which the state influenced patterns of socioeconomic change during the long transitional period from 1750 to 1850. During the late colonial period, trade in cochineal and cotton textiles dominated the regional economy. Outside merchants and the local alcaldes manipulated traditional state policies, especially tribute collection and the *repartimiento de mercancías* (forced distribution of merchandise to Amerindians by the *corregidor de indios* or his agent), to compel the exchange of European and colonial products for indigenous dyes and textiles. Reform efforts by metropolitan authorities altered but failed to eliminate these commercial patterns, which then persisted until the disruptions of the independence era. Without the public sector's ability to compel these ongoing commercial relationships, Oaxaca might have evolved into either a subsistence economy or one in which indigenous communities, not mercantile elites and alcaldes, controlled and profited from a more limited integration into the Mexico City market.

By the early nineteenth century, the erosion of these traditional political and economic relationships led to significant reorientations. Mining replaced the dye and textile trades at the center of a diminished state-sponsored economy, and Oaxaca's leading creole families supplanted peninsular Spaniards in government and church administrations. Despite these changes, elite factions and indigenous communities continued their squabbles over tax policies and landownership within the well-established patterns inherited from the colonial era. Amerindian taxes continued as a principal prop for the state political apparatus, which redistributed these public revenues to rebuild the economy and maintain the power of regional elites long into the nineteenth century. In short, patterns of change and continuity coexisted throughout the century in Oaxaca.

Susan Deans-Smith uses the government-owned tobacco industry to examine the relative economic fortunes of the colonial and early national states in Mexico between 1765 and 1850. By the 1790s the tobacco monopoly employed more than 50 percent of Mexico City's manufacturing work force, and its profits ranked second to silver mining as a source of the colonial government's revenue. The monopoly regulated the production, supply, and price of tobacco itself, and controlled the manufacture and sale of cigarettes and cigars. Monopoly managers also attempted to organize a regimented labor regime in the factories. Although the industry's management structure remained highly centralized, the factory workers brought their own agenda to the work place. Labor sought control over income, working hours, job security, employment benefits, and working conditions. In the resulting conflicts between workers and management, labor achieved some of its objectives and played a major role in the evolution of this public-sector enterprise.

Despite efforts to abolish the monopoly after 1821, it endured into the national period in a more decentralized form. Over time individual states and private entrepreneurs came to control the tobacco industry. Nevertheless, the production side of this important enterprise was characterized more by continuity than by change. Technology remained primitive, labor disputes persisted, and political and fiscal issues continued to determine management decisions.

Richard J. Salvucci, Linda K. Salvucci, and Aslán Cohen explore the underlying economic continuities shaping Mexican tariff policy in the late colonial and early national periods. The eighteenth-century mining expansion provided the capital to buy cheap, European cloth. This, in turn, damaged Mexican textile production and encouraged the flow of scarce investment capital to silver producers. Although republican leaders initially lowered tariffs and promoted the export of those commodities where Mexico had a comparative advantage, this policy proved impractical. Trade liberalization had few powerful advocates. Silver producers, for example, were few in number, geographically remote, and economically weakened by the disruptive wars of independence. Mexican agricultural interests were also too diverse, geographically dispersed, and dependent on domestic markets to provide an effective lobby for lower tariffs. As a result, leadership in the tariff debate passed to those groups, such as urban textile producers and their labor force, most heavily dependent on protected domestic markets. In the end, these well-organized protectionist lobbies dominated the political debate over trade policies, ensuring that high tariffs prevailed.

In chapter 6, John E. Kicza traces the continuities of business practices by examining the fortunes of an important Basque mercantile family, the Iturbe e Iraeta. Despite the turbulence of the transitional period from 1750 to 1850, this prominent family of international wholesale merchants retained its economic position and political influence. The Iturbe e Iraeta developed a diversified commercial network with other established elite families, specializing in the Pacific and Caribbean trades—particularly in cacao, Chinese goods from Manila, cochineal, indigo, and local manufactures. Their only important surviving ties to Spain were cultural and familial, not economic. Although they supported conservative political factions during the instability of the independence and early national periods, the Iturbe e Iraeta remained key lenders to all governments in Mexico and prominent financiers of private business concerns. The family continued to use marriage, business, ethnic, religious, and political connections with other merchant families in traditional ways to survive in the changing political and economic environment of Mexico.

Kendall W. Brown demonstrates statistically that increased mercury supplies and lowered prices combined with other state-sponsored reforms to promote the eighteenth-century mining booms in Peru and Mexico. Mexican miners benefited from cheaper mercury imports from Europe, while their Peruvian counterparts were compelled to rely on supplies of mercury from the increasingly inefficient and expensive Huancavelica mines. In both colonies, however, the slow collapse of the imperial trading system from the mid-1790s led to mining crises. The transition to a free market in mercury after independence proved difficult, and despite adequate supplies and lowered prices, by 1850 structural damage to the mines, the loss of skilled workers, and reduced capital resources combined to undermine production. Despite its obvious inefficiencies, the Bourbon state had the territorial scale, political authority, and administrative cohesion to provide the stable supplies of mercury needed by American silver producers.

Kenneth J. Andrien traces the links between state fiscal policies and economic dependency in late colonial and early republican Ecuador. As a result of Bourbon fiscal reforms in the 1780s, tax receipts skyrocketed. The colonial state used this burgeoning income to remit ever larger amounts to the metropolis and to increase outlays for public administration and defense. Although the coastal cacao economy flourished during this period, the overall stagnation of the highland textile industry meant that the crown increased revenues by exploiting diminished regional economies more effectively. Per-capita tax rates soared compared to those achieved in other European colonies in the Americas. This system suffered during the disruptions of the independence era, however, and the income levels of the late Bourbon period were not attained again until 1850. Nevertheless, there were important continuities: Amerindian tribute still yielded large sums until its abolition in 1857, taxes on trade remained high after independence, and capital flowed out of the national economy, although it went to repay foreign loans, rather than as tax remittances to metropolitan Spain. These predatory fiscal policies continued to disrupt business, trade, capital accumulation, and autonomous economic growth from the late colonial era through the early republic in Ecuador.

Lyman L. Johnson analyzes probate inventories from 1800, 1829–30, and 1854–55 to discover changes in the pattern of wealth distribution in the province of Buenos Aires. Johnson finds that wealth inequality declined after independence and then increased significantly during the dictatorship of Juan Manuel de Rosas. The greater wealth equality found by Johnson for 1829 apparently resulted from the loss of wealth by urban elites (through the abolition of commercial monopolies and the confiscation of Spanish holdings), the property destruction caused by war and civil unrest, and the disruptive impact of foreign imports on artisan manufactures. Thereafter, urbanization and commercial concentration promoted greater inequalities. The relative stability of the Rosas period—along with land, tax, and monetary policies favorable to the grazing interests—promoted both economic growth and more disparities in the distribution of wealth. Despite its political populism, the economic policies of the Rosas regime actually reduced the share of wealth held by the provincial middle and poor groups and elevated the province's inequality above that of the colonial period.

Jerry W. Cooney and Thomas L. Whigham's study of Paraguay's export trade provides a sophisticated view of the structural changes taking place between 1750 and 1850. Although the powerful state of José Gaspar de Francia altered the workings of the colonial economy, there were also important continuities with the late Bourbon period. During his dictatorship, traditional colonial exports continued to flourish, and new markets in Brazil partially compensated for the loss of the Buenos Aires connection. After the fall of Rosas in 1852, however, the new government in Buenos Aires recognized Paraguay's independence, and the old patterns of trade reappeared. Changes in political leadership and military events could alter but not destroy the established colonial trade routes. In the long run, this nation's relative competitiveness and external market demands supported export agriculture and the reemergence of the Paraguay-Paraná commercial links.

Each of the essays in this volume demonstrates the role of the state in promoting socioeconomic changes in the late colonial and early national periods. The pervasive influence of the colonial state, however, meant that its slow-motion collapse between the 1790s and 1825 had a decided impact on the character of many long-term trends, often altering their configuration and heightening social tensions, political disorders, and economic fragmentation. Nevertheless, as Mario Góngora has stated, "the monarchial state may have disappeared in 1810, but not the notion of a *dirigiste* state, an active and decisive state."[21] The chapters in this volume indicate that the colonial and republican states played a central role in shaping the long-term patterns of conflict, transition, and coherence present in the century from 1750 to 1850.

Notes

1. Two of the pioneers in reexamining the role of the state in the financial and economic life of colonial and early republican Spanish America are John J. TePaske and Herbert S. Klein. For a review of their contributions and the burgeoning literature on the state and public finance, see Herbert S. Klein and Jacques A. Barbier, "Recent Trends in the Study of Spanish American Colonial Public Finance," *Latin American Research Review,* 23:1 (1988): 35–62. For another review of the literature of the state and socioeconomic change, see William B. Taylor, "Between Global Process and Local Knowledge: An Inquiry into Early Latin American Social History, 1500–1900," in Olivier Zunz, ed., *Reliving the Past* (Chapel Hill, NC, 1985), 115–90. See also Peter Guardino and Charles Walker, "The State, Society, and Politics in Peru and Mexico in the Late Colonial and Early Republican Periods," *Latin American Perspectives,* 73 (Spring 1992): 10–43.

2. Taylor, "Early Latin American Social History," 147–51. A collection of essays exploring the responses of indigenous peoples to the Spanish market economy in the Andes is Olivia Harris, Brooke Larson, Enrique Tandeter, comp., *La participación indígena en los mercados surandinos: Estrategias y reproducción social: Siglos XVI a XX* (La Paz, 1987).

3. Taylor, "Early Latin American Social History," 141.

4. Following a position outlined by Allan Knight in his study of the Mexican Revolution, Eric Van Young has termed any "preoccupation" with the state as an instrument of profound social change as "statolatry." See Allan Knight, *The Mexican Revolution* (Cambridge, Eng., 1986), 1:559, n. 386; and Eric Van Young, "The Raw and the Cooked: Elite and Popular Ideology in Mexico, 1800–1821," in Mark D. Szuchman, ed., *The Middle Period in Latin America: Values and Attitudes in the 17th–19th Centuries* (Boulder, CO, and London, Eng., 1989), 94.

5. The conclusions of this literature are concisely presented in an influential synthesis of the period by John Lynch. According to Lynch, these interventionist state policies sought to "increase the colonial status of America and heighten its dependency." Lynch finds that metropolitan authorities were more, not less, imperialistic between 1760 and 1808, and crown policy aimed at nothing less than a "second conquest of America." John Lynch, *The Spanish American Revolutions, 1808–1826* (New York, 1973), 1–37. This viewpoint is also presented in D.A. Brading, *Miners and Merchants in Bourbon Mexico* (Cambridge, Eng., 1971), 33–92; and Brading, "Bourbon Spain and Its American Empire," in Leslie Bethell, ed., *Colonial Spanish America* (Cambridge, Eng., 1987), 112–62. This position has

been sharply criticized in many studies examining metropolitan policies during the reign of Charles III and his son, Charles IV. According to Allan J. Kuethe, colonial policy under Charles III was never consistent over time, and factional conflicts at court led to the formulation of imperial policies with markedly different objectives for different regions of the empire. See Allan J. Kuethe, *Cuba, 1753–1815: Crown, Military, and Society* (Knoxville, TN, 1986); and Kuethe, "La desregulación comercial y la reforma imperial en la época de Carlos III: los casos de Nueva España y Cuba," *Historia Mexicana,* XLI (Octubre–Diciembre 1991): 265–92. In his published articles, Jacques A. Barbier contends that the seeds of colonial independence were planted during the reign of Charles IV, when the political and military events in Europe forced the Madrid government to sacrifice long-term political and economic goals in its desperate attempt to drain fiscal resources from the colonies to meet the exigencies of war. See Jacques A. Barbier, "The Culmination of the Bourbon Reforms, 1787–1792," *Hispanic American Historical Review,* 57:1 (February 1977): 51–68; Barbier, "Peninsular Finance and Colonial Trade: The Dilemma of Charles IV's Spain," *Journal of Latin American Studies,* 12:1 (May 1980): 21–37; Barbier, "Venezuelan 'Libranzas', 1788–1807: From Economic Nostrum to Fiscal Imperative," *The Americas,* 37:4 (April 1981): 457–78; Barbier and Herbert S. Klein, "Revolutionary Wars and Public Finances: The Madrid Treasury, 1784–1807," *Journal of Economic History,* 41:2 (June 1981): 315–37; Barbier, "Indies Revenues and Naval Spending: The Cost of Colonialism for the Spanish Bourbons, 1763–1805," *Jahrbuch für Geschichte von Staat, Wirtschaft und Gesellschaft Lateinamerikas,* 21 (1984): 171–88; Barbier, "Imperial Policy Toward the Port of Veracruz, 1788–1808: The Struggle Between Madrid, Cádiz, and Havana Interests," in Nils Jacobsen and Has-Jürgen Puhl, eds., *The Economies of Mexico and Peru During the Late Colonial Period,* 1760–1810 (Berlin, 1986), 240–51; Barbier, "Comercio Neutral in Bolivarian America: La Guaria, Cartagena, Callao, and Buenos Aires," in Reinhard Liehr, ed., *América Latina en la épocha de Simón Bolívar* (Berlin, 1989), 363–77; and Barbier, "Comercio secreto: The Economic and Political Significance of a Fiscal Expedient, 1800–1808" (unpublished paper presented at the International Congress of Americanists, 1987).

6. This is especially true of studies of popular riots, insurrections, and revolutions. For an influential social science formulation of the importance of the state in popular upheavals, see Theda Skocpol, *States and Social Revolutions* (Cambridge, Eng., 1979).

7. Much of this recent literature has drawn its inspiration from an early article by James Lockhart, "The Social History of Colonial Spanish America," *Latin American Research Review,* 7 (Spring 1972): 6–46. A recent exponent of this position has been Eric Van Young. See Van Young, "The Raw and the Cooked," 94; Van Young, "Quetzalcoatl, King Ferdinand, and Ignacio Allende Go to the Seashore: or Messianism and Mystical Kingship in Mexico, 1800–1821," in Jaime E. Rodríguez O., *The Independence of Mexico and the Creation of the New Nation* (Los Angeles, 1989); 109–27. For a different viewpoint, which highlights the role of the state in popular upheavals in Mexico during this same period, see John Tutino, *From Insurrection to Revolution in Mexico: Social Bases of Agrarian Violence, 1750–1940* (Princeton, NJ, 1986), 367 and passim.

8. Van Young, "The Raw and the Cooked," 94.

9. This point is made with clarity and force by Taylor, "Early Latin American Society History," 145.

10. Brian R. Hamnett, *Politics and Trade in Southern Mexico, 1750–1821* (Cambridge, Eng., 1971), especially chap. 2.

11. The colonial state never functioned as an autonomous actor, removed from societal pressures. For a discussion of the basic literature dealing with this issue, see Guardino and Walker, "The State, Society, and Politics in Peru and Mexico," 14–15.

12. The importance of the state in Spanish American development during the late colonial and early republican periods has been examined directly or indirectly in several important works. See, for example, Miles L. Wortman, *Government and Society in Central America, 1680–1840* (New York, 1982); John Coatsworth, "The Limits of Colonial Absolutism: The State in Eighteenth-Century Mexico," in Karen Spalding, ed., *Essays in the Political, Social, and Economic History of Colonial Latin America* (Newark, DE, 1982); 25–51; Coatsworth, "Obstacles to Growth in Nineteenth-Century Mexico," *American Historical Review*, 83 (February 1978): 80–100; Tutino, *From Insurrection to Revolution*, passim; and Tulio Halperín Donghi, *Guerra y finanzas en los orígenes del estado argentino (1791–1850)* (Buenos Aires, 1981). Two fine studies of the early national states that establish links with the late colonial period are Barbara Tenenbaum, *The Politics of Penury: Debts and Taxes in Mexico, 1821–1856* (Albuquerque, NM, 1986); and Paul Gootenberg, *Between Silver and Guano: Commercial Policy and the State in Postindependence Peru* (Princeton, NJ, 1989). Some interesting recent essays that touch on these themes are: Charles Walker, "La violencia y el sistema legal: Los indios y el estado en el Cusco después la rebelión de Tupac Amaru," in Henrique Urbano, comp. and Mirko Lauer, ed., *Poder y violencia en los Andes* (Cusco, Peru, 1991); 125–48; Víctor Peralta Ruíz, "Fiscalidad y poder regional en el Cusco a fines de la colonia e inicios de la república: El caso de los iquichanos realistas: Ayacucho 1825–1828," *ibid.*, 165–188.

13. This chronology is only approximate. It reflects the general periodization of European historiography on the "Age of Revolution." See, for example, R. R. Palmer, "Social and Psychological Foundations of the Revolutionary Era," in A. Goodwin, ed., *The New Cambridge Modern History: The American and French Revolutions, 1762–1793* (Cambridge, Eng., 1965), passim; and Jacques Godechot, *France and the Atlantic Revolution of the Eighteenth Century* (London, 1971), 3. It also represents the period from 1750 to 1850 in Spanish America as a time of transition, beginning with the crisis of the colonial order—from the escalation of the Bourbon Reforms between approximately 1750 and 1765—to Spanish America's incorporation into the global economy between approximately 1850 and 1900. Historiographical articles emphasizing this periodization are: Woodrow Borah, "Discontinuity and Continuity in Mexican History," *Pacific Historical Review*, 48 (1979): 1–25; Eric Van Young, "Mexican Rural History since Chevalier: The Historiography of the Colonial Hacienda," *Latin American Research Review*, 18:3 (1983): 5–61; Van Young, "Recent Anglophone Scholarship on Mexico and Central America in the Age of Revolution (1750–1850)," *Hispanic American Historical Review*, 65:4 (November 1985): 725–43. Dependency and world-system advocates who trace long-term continuities from the colonial period

into the republican era are: Immanuel Wallerstein, *The Modern World-System, III: The Second Era of Great Expansion of the Capitalist World-Economy* (New York, 1989), 191–256; Stanley J. Stein and Barbara H. Stein, *The Colonial Heritage of Latin America: Essays on Economic Dependence in Perspective* (New York, 1967); Fernando Henrique Cardoso and Enzo Faletto, *Dependency and Development in Latin America* (Berkeley, CA, 1979, 1971); and Andre Gunder Frank, *Capitalism and Underdevelopment in Latin America* (New York, 1967). One book presenting an array of different perspectives on dependency and its chronology is Christopher Abel and Colin M. Lewis, eds., *Latin America, Economic Imperialism and the State: The Political Economy of the External Connection from Independence to the Present* (London, 1985). See also Tulio Halperín-Donghi, *The Aftermath of Revolution in Latin America* (New York, 1973). For differing chronological breakdowns of this period, see Tutino, *From Insurrection to Revolution*; Enrique Semo, "Acerca de la periodización," in Semo, *Historia mexicana: Economía y lucha de clases* (Mexico City, 1978); Szuchman, *The Middle Period in Latin America,* 11–13; and Franklin W. Knight and Peggy K. Liss, eds., *Atlantic Port Cities: Economy, Culture, and Society in the Atlantic World, 1650–1850* (Knoxville, TN, 1991), 3–5.

14. The most important recent empirical studies that self-consciously trace long-term continuities from the late colonial through the early republican eras are: Brian R. Hamnett, *The Roots of Insurgency: Mexican Regions, 1750–1824* (Cambridge, Eng., 1986); Wortman, *Government and Society;* Tutino, *From Insurrection to Revolution;* Halperín, *Guerra y finanzas;* Miguel Izard, *El Miedo a la Revolución: La lucha por la libertad en Venezuela (1777–1830)* (Madrid, 1979); Brian R. Hamnett, "Popular Insurrection and Royalist Reaction: Colombian Regions, 1810–1823," in John R. Fisher, Allan J. Kuethe, and Anthony McFarlane, eds., *Reform and Insurrection in Bourbon New Granada and Peru* (Baton Rouge, LA, 1990), 292–326; and Christine Hünefeldt, *Lucha por la tierra y protesta indígena: Las comunidades indígenas del Perú entre colonia y república* (Bonn, Ger., 1982). Some recent studies that establish links between late colonial changes and the independence and early republican eras are: Christian I. Archer, "Where Did All the Royalists Go? New Light on the Military Collapse of New Spain, 1810–1822," in Jaime E. Rodríguez O., ed., *The Mexican and Mexican American Experience in the Nineteenth Century* (Tempe, AZ, 1989), 24–43; Archer, "La Causa Buena: The Counterinsurgency Army of New Spain and the Ten Year's War," in Rodríguez O., ed., *The Independence of Mexico,* 85–108; Tenenbaum, *Politics of Penury;* and Gootenberg, *Between Silver and Guano.*

15. Borah, "Discontinuity and Continuity," 18; and David Bushnell, *Reform and Reaction in the Platine Provinces, 1810–1852* (Gainesville, FL, 1983).

16. Jaime E. Rodríguez O., "Down from Colonialism: Mexico's Nineteenth-Century Crisis," in Rodríguez O., ed., *The Mexican and Mexican American Experience,* 7–23; and Rodríguez O., *The Independence of Mexico,* 15.

17. William B. Taylor has questioned "the idea that long-term continuities make the years from roughly 1750 to 1850 a decisive period in Latin American social history" and makes "the preliminary case for returning one series of events—the Independence Wars—to a prominent place in the chronology of Latin American social history." See Taylor, "Early Latin American Social History," 122–23.

18. Two recent collections on the socioeconomic history of Spanish America that embody this more traditional periodization are Jacobsen and Puhl, *Economies of Mexico and Peru;* and Liehr, *América Latina en la época de Simón Bolívar.*

19. For some recent monographs and articles exemplifying this trend, see the following: Linda Arnold, *Bureaucracy and Bureaucrats in Mexico City, 1742–1835* (Tucson, AZ, 1988); D. A. Brading, *Haciendas and Ranchos in the Mexican Bajío: León, 1700–1860* (Cambridge, Eng., 1978); Jonathan C. Brown, *A Socioeconomic History of Argentina, 1776–1860* (Cambridge, Eng., 1979); Maurice P. Brungart, "The Economy of Colombia in the Late Colonial and Early National Periods," in Fisher, Kuethe, and McFarlane, eds., *Reform and Insurrection,* 164–93; Bushnell, *Reform and Reaction;* Tulio Halperín Donghi, *Reforma y disolución de los imperios ibéricos, 1750–1850* (Madrid, 1985); Margaret Chowning, "The Management of Church Wealth in Michoacán, Mexico, 1810–1856," *Journal of Latin American Studies,* 22:3 (October 1990): 459–96; Malcolm Deas, "The Fiscal Problems of Nineteenth-Century Colombia," *Journal of Latin American Studies,* 14:2 (November 1982): 287–328; Juan Carlos Garavaglia and Juan Carlos Grosso, "Mexican Elites of a Provincial Town: The Landowners of Tepeaca (1700–1870)," *Hispanic American Historical Review,* 70:2 (May 1990): 255–93; William Paul McGeevey, *An Economic History of Colombia, 1845–1930* (Cambridge, Eng., 1971), 19–66; Carlos A. Mayo, "Landed But Not Powerful: The Colonial Estancieros of Buenos Aires (1750–1810)," *Hispanic American Historical Review,* 71:4 (November 1991): 761–79; Jaime E. Rodríguez O., *The Emergence of Spanish America: Vicente Rocafuerte and Spanish Americanism, 1808–1832* (Berkeley, 1975); and Guy P. C. Thomson, *Puebla de Los Angeles: Industry and Society in a Mexican City, 1700–1850* (Boulder, CO, 1989).

20. For an important alternative approach to integrating the state and social history, see Taylor, "Early Latin American Social History," 140–73.

21. Simon Collier, "Interview with Mario Góngora," *Hispanic American Historical Review,* 63 (November 1983): 668.

2

Iturbide, Congress, and Constitutional Monarchy in Mexico

TIMOTHY E. ANNA

One of the characteristics of Mexican historiography, as represented in the writing and teaching of both Mexicans and foreigners, is that it denies credit to the nation's liberator, Agustín de Iturbide. As a direct consequence, there is little discussion or even recognition of the meaning and purpose of the moderated constitutional monarchy that Mexico adopted as its first government in the wake of the separation from Spain. The inherent assumption is that monarchy was a false step, unrepresentative and mistaken, while a federal republic was the inevitable first choice of Mexicans. Such an assumption is inaccurate and misleading. One does not need to be an apologist for Iturbide to recognize that ignoring him and his empire does a disservice to him, to Mexican history, even to Spain and its legacy, for the creation of a constitutional monarchy in Mexico is one of the foremost early examples of the continuity of Spanish influence in that country.

The argument so frequently encountered in the historiography, often stated explicitly, is that Iturbide created a monarchy so that he could seize the throne for himself. This argument, however, completely ignores the fact that monarchy was natural, normal, and appropriate to the needs of a vast nation facing a transition period of undetermined duration in the wake of separation from Spain. It was inherent in the process of independence in Mexico and met the needs of the new state. It was a solution, not an absurd imposition. That is, it solved the immediate problem of 1821. Monarchy failed because it did not solve the next great problem the nation had to face, the pressure of regionalism.

The immediate problem of 1821 was how to unite the divergent strains of creole and elite dissatisfaction toward Spanish imperial policies. This dissatisfaction coalesced behind two schools of thought, what might be called the radical and the moderate. The radical strain was the tradition of lower class rebellion against what was perceived as Spanish tyranny.

Remember, however, that every dissident Mexican in 1820 knew that this tyranny was directed from Spain but implemented in Mexico by creole and domestic collaborators. Policy directives came from Madrid (or Cádiz) and from the viceroy and other Spanish authorities and officers in Mexico. But it was implemented by loyal Mexicans. Spain could not have resisted the breakaway of Mexico if Mexicans themselves had not provided the armed resistance to rebellion.

Of greater impact in the long run was the fact that those Mexicans who fought to oppose Hidalgo, Morelos, and many other rebel leaders and their forces, also came to have serious complaints of their own against the effects of Spanish policy. Take Iturbide himself. In his own memoirs (a startling document usually dismissed as merely an apologia) he perfectly encapsulates the mixed motives of elite and aspiring Mexicans toward the rebellions and the civil war they launched. "Hidalgo, and those who came after him and who followed his example, desolated the country, destroyed the fortunes of the people, . . . sacrificed millions of victims, . . . and far from obtaining independence, increased the obstacles that opposed it. . . . If I took up arms in that time, it was not to make war on Americans, but on those who infested the country."[1] To follow Brian Hamnett's recent distinction, the Mexican War of Independence started out under Hidalgo as an insurrection but rapidly deteriorated into a series of regionally based and weakly grounded insurgencies.[2] Iturbide's explanation that to preserve order he fought for Spain and that in so doing he was also saving Mexicans and their fortunes is the fundamental explanation of why so many Mexicans also fought for Spain.

The acceptance of the need for independence was motivated by the same desire for order. With the restoration of the Constitution in 1820 the crisis was renewed. "Great revolutions were on the point of breaking out, my country was being deluged in the blood of its inhabitants, I thought myself able to save it from ruin, and ran once more to fulfill such a sacred duty." Of course, protests of altruism are suspect; for Iturbide self-interest was the primary motive, as it was for most other participants. As Bulnes put it: "If we must knock Iturbide off his pedestal for being ambitious for power, we have to knock down all the heroes of independence except for two, Morelos and Matamoros."[3] We know, at any rate, that because his regime implemented several of the reforms issued originally by the Cortes in Spain, his rebellion was not, as many claim, a mere counterrevolution aimed at resisting those reforms.

What to do? Iturbide correctly summed up the fundamental problem: "The Americans wished independence, but did not agree upon the method of acquiring it, nor upon the system of government that ought to be adopted." The objective of a republic, with implied regional powers, as proposed by some of the earlier rebels, had obviously not swept the nation before it. The "old" rebels had never agreed on what form of government to adopt, and most had never even proposed one.

Demonstrably, the rebellions lacked an agreed-upon set of objectives. At any rate, the fact that politically active Mexicans were frightened away by the rebellions' threat to status and property indicates that these earlier rebels did not provide grounds for consensus. Most of the rebel leaders were unschooled politically and totally inexperienced. None had a truly national vision or agenda. There are no valid grounds to assume that the automatic aspiration of all rebels was a republic, much less a federal one. As Hamnett has argued, many of the rebels were not even fighting for independence.

Indeed, this was not even a "war of independence"—if that term is interpreted as meaning a united action with a cohesive purpose, a set agenda, a national consciousness, and a series of leaders. Rather, it was a congeries of regional insurrections, motivated by myriad grievances, exploding in a thousand directions at once with a bewildering range of different motives and led by local *caciques*. Historians often reflect this fact by calling them "wars of independence," but that term still implies a common purpose that did not exist.

There was, indeed, no such thing as "Mexico." The word itself was resurrected from the popular culture of neo-Aztec movements in the wishful hope that one could create a nation merely by declaring it so. The pamphleteers of 1821 rarely used the term *Mexico*; they called the area América Septentrional or Anáhuac. Iturbide's Plan of Iguala (1821) called it the kingdom of New Spain or America Septentrional. It was not until the Treaty of Córdoba (1821) that Iturbide declared that the entity was to be called *imperio mexicano*. Iturbide chose to call it an empire precisely because he knew that it would be, at best, a coalition of many peoples and many states (New Spain, New Galicia, the Eastern and Western Interior Provinces, the Californias, the South, Yucatán, and, as it happened, even the kingdom of Guatemala). Based on the tradition of three centuries, could the central elite's aspirations not extend so far as to recreate the imperial sway of Mexico City over the regions subject to the authority of the Spanish viceroy of the north (minus Cuba and minus the Louisiana territories and the Floridas, which had only recently been transferred to the United States)? Is it not past time to abandon the assumption that somehow Mexico was a self-conscious and united nation in 1821 merely by virtue of achieving separation from Spain?

So what was Iturbide's accomplishment? He produced a political principle around which to rally the interests and needs of all, a minimum not a maximum that corresponded to the traditions and political culture of Mexico and provided a base for future development. For the first time since the insurrections began, he provided a program, an agenda that was acceptable to a wide range of Mexicans.

He declared as a fundamental principle the protection of the Spaniards living in Mexico, few in number but vital to the economic life of the country and its hopes for diplomatic recognition from Spain and the European powers. That point is far more critical than the historiography usually recognizes. It actually played much the same role in the subsequent rejection of Iturbide as defense of the Portuguese living in Brazil played in the fall of that country's liberator-emperor, Dom Pedro I.[4] During the period he served as president of the regency and then as emperor, Iturbide stalwartly protected any Spaniard who chose to remain in Mexico, even suggesting the need to attract new Spanish immigrants to the country. The rising tide of anti-Spanish sentiment among Mexicans meant that Iturbide would ultimately be accused of servilism, even though his guarantee of the defense of the Spaniards had made the consensus of Iguala possible.

Iturbide also guaranteed the status and privilege of the church and the clergy. This point required little cunning: the consensus was undoubted, but in the context of the restored Spanish Constitution of 1812, it needed to be affirmed.

Iturbide guaranteed that everyone born or settled in Mexico, of whatever ethnic background (American, African, European, or indigenous) was a Mexican. Even the Spanish Constitution of 1812 had denied citizenship to blacks: that is, to persons whose parents on both sides had not derived from the Spanish dominions. This guarantee instantly united the insurrectionary and the liberal, the conservative and the fearful, the *letrado* and the peasant, the rural and the urban, the Yucatecan and the Chihuahuan. It was not a recognition of nationhood, only of the hope for union, but none of the insurrections, based as they were on class or caste demands or regional aspirations, had done as much. This was not announcing the existence of a nation; it was the first step in building a nation.

The Plan of Iguala was not, as the historiography almost universally implies, a cretinous throwback designed to prevent change or pander to the antisocial interests of inherited privilege. It was merely the declaration of fundamental principles around which all could see, as Iturbide himself put it, that the child had outgrown its father's house. The moment everyone agreed on that, political separation from Spain became an accomplished fact. Iturbide's comment to Viceroy Juan Ruíz de Apodaca that "any nation is free that wants to be free,"[5] was a statement of the profound consensus that Mexico had previously lacked.

What government system could all agree on? Again, the purpose was to create consensus. A monarchy, deriving from the traditions of three hundred years and the universal prestige of that form, but modified by the advanced principles of the Spanish Constitution of 1812, provided the solution. Iturbide was not a brilliant man; his schooling was profoundly traditional, and he represented no avant-garde of ideology or party. That is not a criticism, for there were very few advanced thinkers among the men active in 1821. In the choice between Servando Teresa de Mier's advocacy of a foreign model of republicanism or Iturbide's declaration of a moderated constitutional monarchy in the Hispanic tradition, there was no contest. Furthermore, the chronology of events must be remembered. On 24 February 1821, when Iturbide released the Plan of Iguala, Mier was in exile in the United States and his writings were known only to a small coterie of advanced intellectuals in Mexico, Bolívar's republic of Colombia was still struggling for life, the viceroyalty of Peru was still under Spanish imperial control, and the new states at Santiago de Chile and Buenos Aires had not yet reached consensus on what form of government to establish. The United States provided a model, but for most Mexicans it was English, Protestant, and alien; only in 1823 would they begin to perceive its relevance to a country like Mexico. The French republic had led to terror, irreligion, and the greatest war of modern history. The proposal to create in Mexico a moderated constitutional monarchy copied whole from the mother country was both logical and appropriate.

The Plan of Iguala did contain real anomalies, but they are not those on which historians of Mexico normally focus. It is necessary to clarify this point, because these anomalies help explain the failure of Iturbide's program.

The first anomaly was the call for Ferdinand VII to take the throne of Mexico. The Plan of Iguala said that if Ferdinand did not agree, the throne would be offered to other members of his dynasty or to a member of some other reigning house; the Treaty of Córdoba added that if none of them accepted, the Mexican Cortes (Congress) could choose its own candidate. It makes no sense to assume that Iturbide honestly expected the Spanish king or a relative to come live in Mexico; nor did the Mexican deputies to the Spanish Cortes, when they joined other deputies in 1821 to propose the division of the American territories into three states presided over by members of the royal family; nor did Juan O'Donojú, when he signed the

Treaty of Córdoba. Some historians have concluded that if Iturbide did not expect Ferdinand VII to take the throne in Mexico, it must have been part of a conspiracy to engineer himself onto the throne. The real point is that the call for a Mexican throne under a member of the Spanish Bourbon dynasty is a sign of the monarchy's prestige, an inconvenient fact for Mexican writers who wish to assert that a republic was the goal all along. What opposition there was to a monarchy in the Plan of Iguala revolved around the reluctance of some to contemplate having Ferdinand VII as king in Mexico. Only Mier, in a published message sent from Philadelphia, argued against both the idea of having Ferdinand VII and the idea of monarchy itself.[6]

No one had a clear idea of what relation Spain and Mexico would have as a result of calling on Ferdinand VII. Was Mexico to become some sort of partner in a Spanish commonwealth of nations, would it head such a commonwealth with Spain as a junior member, or would the king give up the throne of Spain? There were far too many unanswered questions, and this may just as likely explain why Iturbide came to feel that a Mexican should take the throne. Iturbide's own popularity primarily explains why most other published expressions of sentiment written by Mexicans assumed Iturbide was destined to the throne all along.

A second fundamental anomaly is that the Plan of Iguala did not comment in any way on what the powers of the monarch were to be. Presumably, the Spanish Constitution then in effect would determine the king's powers in Mexico as in Spain, but what sort of specific adjustments would be made to meet the needs of Mexico? The Plan of Iguala did not even specify the extent of the national territory. There was as yet no Mexican nation. The viceregal administration had not controlled the far north, the far south, Yucatán, or Central America; New Galicia was a separate *audiencia*. It is unacceptable to assume that the invisible hand of national identity was at work in the process of separation from Spain. The Plan of Iguala seemed to assume that an elected congress would dominate whoever became emperor. The emperor would submit to this domination while the congress would somehow work in serene harmony to pursue its goals.

A third basic anomaly is that the Plan of Iguala was clearly designed to make room for, indeed to encourage, provincial status. It did this by retaining the Constitution of 1812, which—in a clause that had not yet been implemented in Mexico—called for the creation of a provincial deputation (and thus, recognition as a province) in each intendancy that did not yet have one. This was a giant step forward for the peripheral provinces, and even for the provinces closer to the center—indeed for any region that was itself the hub of a geographical zone of influence that aspired to provincial status. It was the secret behind the universal acceptance of the Plan of Iguala. Yet Iturbide and the members of his administration were sons of Bourbon unitarism and did not endorse regional self-government.

The greatest anomaly of the Plan of Iguala was that some Mexicans, Iturbide foremost among them, assumed that the Plan of Iguala, once accepted by the expressed consent of Mexican opinion, was fundamental law. There is no doubt that a consensus existed (though Iturbide's opponents rewrote history after his abdication to contest the point), but there was no agreement on whether the consensus of Iguala made the Plan and the Treaty of Córdoba fundamental law.[7]

Iguala was the act of one person, but was it a simple political project or a fundamental code for a nation? One of Iturbide's leading contemporary enemies, Vicente Rocafuerte, argued that Iturbide should have created the *junta* called for in the Plan of Iguala, or even a congress, before the arrival of Juan O'Donojú and the signing of the Treaty of Córdoba. Córdoba would then have had the status of an agreement between the Mexican nation and the Spanish superior political chief rather than between Iturbide alone and the political chief.[8] Iturbide's view, however, is best summed up in his speech after closing the Constituent Congress: "Since [Iguala] my voice has . . . constituted the single organ of the general will of the inhabitants of this empire." In his memoirs he expressed the same idea in similar ways. Referring to his triumphal entry into Mexico City in September 1821: "When I entered Mexico my own will was the Law." Referring to the universal acceptance of the Plan of Iguala: "I was the depository of the will of the Mexicans."[9]

Was Iturbide merely giving vent to his powerful ego when he made that astounding assertion? Consider the evidence of Javier Ocampo, who, in studying the pamphlets published in the weeks immediately following Iturbide's triumphal entry in the capital on 27 September 1821 found overwhelming and universal support for him, support strong enough to be called a mandate.[10] Consider the recent work of Eric Van Young, who in tracing the motif of messianism and monarchism in Mexico during the insurrections found repeated evidence of a primitive and mystical messianism and monarchism among the Mexican Indians and peasants.[11] Could anyone other than Iturbide lay claim to the right to rule and speak for the nation in the wake of the triumph of 1821? Is a successful revolution not a powerful mandate in its own right?

The nineteenth-century historiography, upon which almost all later histories have been based, has planted a profoundly inaccurate view of the triumph of Iturbide and his election as emperor. It must be remembered, as I have argued elsewhere,[12] that this historiography is based on the works of Carlos María Bustamante, Vicente Rocafuerte, Lorenzo de Zavala, Anastasio Zerecero, José María Bocanegra, Lucas Alamán, Joel R. Poinsett, and Henry George Ward. Every one of them denigrated the life and career of Iturbide, and every one of them except perhaps Alamán and Ward was a leading political opponent of Iturbide in 1821–23. They won, and they write the history. If we allow ourselves to criticize our sources—looking at the political axes they had to grind and not permitting the nineteenth-century historiography to set the agenda and formulate the questions—it becomes obvious that, as Iturbide put it in his memoirs, his enemies had internal contradictions of their own.

Suffice it to say that I am prepared to make two important assertions that the historiography has led us to overlook. First, the monarchy, as long as it was a moderated constitutional and liberal monarchy, was an entirely logical and appropriate choice for Mexico's first autonomous government following political separation from Spain, and Iturbide had the most right to claim the throne. Second, the Spanish Constitution of 1812 was fundamental to the new government because it provided both a means of transition and a mechanism for the rapid creation of a functioning government. But Iturbide's enemies, in their campaign to destroy him and his monarchy, would ignore the Constitution and misuse it.

The first assertion is implicit in what I have said so far. In 1821 Iturbide was the "Savior of the Nation," the "Immortal Liberator," the "Hero of Iguala," among the many titles by which the writers of contemporary pamphlets hailed him.[13] He had promised at Iguala to make Mexico free, and on 27 September 1821 that promise was fulfilled. Furthermore, he achieved this result by a peaceful victory that took as its fundamental basis the union of all Mexicans, no matter what their origin, and the protection of the Spaniards living in Mexico. In addition, he was the protector of the church. As the bishop of Sonora wrote Iturbide in November 1821: "To you alone belongs the glory because you alone were chosen by God."[14]

Iturbide had promised in the Plan of Iguala that Mexico would become a moderate constitutional monarchy because monarchy was the form of government Mexicans were used to, and because he and others believed that a republic would lay the country open to factionalism and discord. They believed that the legitimacy of the Spanish Constitution of 1812 was so universal that the Mexican monarchy must be a liberal one operating under the precepts of the Constitution. In a manifesto of October 1821 Iturbide declared that at the time of Iguala and Córdoba he had fixed the political base of the new country as a constitutionally moderated monarchy, not because monarchy was the best form of government, but because monarchy modified by a constitution was.[15] Clearly he was not in the avant-garde; his object was to preserve the best of Spanish traditions as modified by the Cádiz Constitution. As Luis Villoro points out, this was an organic transformation, an example of evolution rather than revolution. Villoro believes it was the abdication of Iturbide in March 1823 that was the revolution.[16]

No issue more clearly points to the bias of the contemporary chroniclers followed by the historiography than the question of Iturbide's election as emperor. The universal view is that he was illegitimately elected by a Congress that had no choice and that lacked a quorum. The fact, pointed out by only one historian that I know of (José Bravo Ugarte), is that according to the Constitution of 1812, then in effect provisionally in Mexico, a quorum did exist. While Congress was certainly pressured to elect Iturbide emperor, it did so legally, and the pressure was an expression of overwhelming popular sentiment.[17] Article 139 of the Spanish Constitution declared that a quorum was "at least one half plus one of the totality of the deputies who should compose the Cortes." The Constituent Congress that elected Iturbide emperor was supposed to have 178 members in May 1822, while the official Acts of Congress declared that enough members were present on the day it elected him emperor "because they exceeded ninety." One half plus one is exactly ninety. Of that number, a clear majority of sixty-seven deputies voted for the immediate proclamation of Iturbide as emperor.[18]

It was after Iturbide's abdication that the myth of his having been illegally elected by a Congress that lacked a quorum was instilled. This process started with the statement in April 1823 by a commission of Congress called to consider whether Iturbide, who had abdicated a few days before, had been named emperor legitimately in the first place. The commission declared that the events of 18 and 19 May 1822 that led to Iturbide's election were the result of the violent actions of the "insolent people," urged on by an "imbecile portion" of the populace, who had terrorized the peaceful residents of the capital. "The doors that served to hide the mysteries of government were forced, and the dike was broken that ought to separate the simple citizens from the representatives of a great nation." The commission concluded: "This act of violence . . . could in no manner legitimize the acclamation of Iturbide as emperor, because the vote rendered by the deputies so deprived of liberty was under law null."[19] The same commission recommended that Congress declare the Plan of Iguala and Treaty of Córdoba invalid on the grounds that no one had the right to oblige the nation to subject itself to any law or treaty that its representatives had not debated. The fact that a commission of Congress—the body that had just triumphed over Iturbide in the Casa Mata revolt—declared his election invalid does not, of course, mean that it necessarily was.

Obviously the elite members of the Constituent Congress held the common people in low regard and were signaling, among other things, that the simple citizens must not be permitted a voice in choosing a government. In a similar vein a few days later another commission of Congress—whose report was written by Carlos María Bustamante, the leading anti-Iturbide writer—argued that because the people were divided by class and engaged in earning a living, only those persons who had the leisure to study law and philosophy were prepared by their moral capacity and knowledge to undertake the duties of governing. "Such is the origin and such the principles of representative government."[20]

Addressing issues in this way helps clarify that it was actually Iturbide, rather than his enemies in the Constituent Congress, who possessed popular support. Why would the elite deputies in Congress be so agitated—as they were throughout this period—by the threat of the mob if they did not perceive that the mob sided with Iturbide? They insisted that the mob had made him emperor. Just before his abdication it was the mob that unhitched his carriage and refused to let him retreat to Tacubaya;[21] it was the mob that caused widespread disquiet and unrest in Mexico City in the last days of the uprising of Casa Mata;[22] it was the mob that conducted general demonstrations that prevented Congress from meeting during much of March 1823 as the emperor was about to abdicate; and it was the mob that demonstrated against the army of Casa Mata when it entered Mexico City on 26 March 1823, causing a skirmish that led to the death of seven along with thirty people injured and fifty jailed.[23] This was hardly the joyous deliverance of a downtrodden people that the anti-Iturbide historiography would have us believe. On Iturbide's trip overland to the coast and to exile it was the people who demonstrated in support of the ex-emperor, leading the government to order the commander of Iturbide's escort, General Nicolás Bravo, to arrest members of Iturbide's party and to avoid entering the towns.[24]

The evidence clearly indicates that among the common people, no doubt because they were susceptible to his charisma, Iturbide was popular, both before and after his time as emperor. Zavala argued that the only people who supported Iturbide to become emperor were "the clergy, the miserable nobility of the country, the army in its greater part, and the common people who saw in that chief nothing more than the liberator of their country." This led Bulnes to comment: "That is to say, the immense majority of the nation were for the empire of Iturbide."[25] Is the support of the clergy, the nobility, the army, and the people not enough, by traditional standards, to constitute legitimacy?

It was clear at the time that the throne was Iturbide's just reward for the incalculable gift of independence. It was only logical that a native son become emperor rather than a foreigner. As José Joaquín Fernández de Lizardi wrote in a pamphlet two days after Iturbide's triumphal entry in Mexico City, "The most common, and even most general, opinion, was no other but that Sr. Iturbide should be crowned." On the day of Iturbide's election Fernández de Lizardi pointed out that if Iturbide had not accepted the throne, no other faction could have garnered enough support for another candidate, and Mexico would have fallen into civil war. "If Your Excellency is not emperor, our independence will be damned."[26]

Intertwined with the personal appeal of Iturbide to Mexicans was the promise of constitutionality. The third article of the Plan of Iguala was the creation of a monarchy tempered by a constitution, while the Treaty of Córdoba declared the creation of the Mexican empire with a constitutional monarchy. All existing Spanish laws that were not contrary to Iguala would remain in power. Most important, the Spanish Constitution of 1812 would remain provisionally the constitution of Mexico until the Congress could write a new one. This was a fundamental and inherent part of the program of independence, which, as one pamphleteer put it, "was formed with the presumed will of the Nation [and] has been confirmed with the express will of the Nation."[27]

Iturbide's opponents would soon try to argue that only some parts of the Plan of Iguala represented a national consensus, and the historiography has repeated that line, generally decreeing that the choice of Iturbide as emperor was not part of the package. This constitutes a misinterpretation of the real point of controversy. The choice of Iturbide as emperor was not what his opponents resisted on theoretical and philosophical grounds. The real sticking point involved the Constitution. Why? Because the Constitution of 1812 assumed a centralized state system. Iturbide also assumed a centralized state system. Some of Iturbide's opponents came to equate Iturbide and the monarchy with a centralized state. Others, primarily the leaders of the Plan of Casa Mata, could live with Iturbide and the monarchy (Casa Mata, it must be remembered, specifically guaranteed the continuation of Iturbide on the throne); but none of his opponents in 1823 could live with centralism combined with monarchy. So in general, the problem was centralism versus regional power (self-government for the states in a federal system).

At independence, Mexico became the only Latin American country formally to declare the Spanish Constitution as its provisional constitution. This should be the critical focus of historical attention, but the constant preoccupation with Iturbide and the propounding of artificial dichotomies (such as monarchy versus democracy, which absolutely was never the issue) has misled scholars. For that matter, since the call for a republic was a muted part of the program of Antonio López de Santa Anna's uprising at Veracruz, not at all a part of the rebellion of Nicolás Bravo and Vicente Guerrero in the south, and not at all a part of the Plan of Casa Mata, we can conclude that the creation of a republic was not the primary object of the rebellions that broke out against Iturbide. Obviously, the object of the rebellions was restoration of an independent Constituent Congress following Iturbide's closure of the Congress and its replacement with the Junta Nacional Instituyente at the end of October 1822. That is what each of the three rebellions declared as its object.[28]

The struggle was over sovereignty—whether it should be central or regional. In late 1822, particularly, what historians summarily characterize as a struggle between Congress and Iturbide was really something else. As Bravo Ugarte states: "More than anti-Iturbidism, this was the picturesque spectacle symptomatic of the disease of sovereignty."[29]

The first Constituent Congress had been elected in early 1822 on a defective formula set by the Sovereign Provisional Governing Junta. This formula created representation on the basis of both population and class or profession. Since the number of deputies per province was based on the number of *partidos* in each province, any attempt at proportionality was abandoned, and peripheral provinces—where partidos had been created under the Spaniards for the defense or administration of frontiers—ended up with greater numbers of deputies than some heavily populated core areas. Thus Durango, with 200,000 inhabitants, got 23 deputies, while Guanajuato with more than 400,000 inhabitants, got only 7 deputies.[30] Since elections were indirect and held in three different stages—the local, district, and provincial levels—local and municipal interests intervened decisively to elect deputies sympathetic to regional demands. This meant that deputies representing the interests of peripheral provinces outnumbered those from central Mexico, opening the door for the first time to peripheral and regional dominance.

The Constituent Congress met for the first time on 24 February 1822. The deputies' first act was to swear to uphold the fundamental principles of the Plan of Iguala: they would support religious intolerance, create a moderated constitutional monarchy, call to the throne those persons designated in the Treaty of Córdoba, and see that all free inhabitants of the empire possessed equal civil rights. The members of Congress endorsed each one of the articles of Iguala. Congress's second act was to declare that the national sovereignty resided in itself.

These two acts were inherently contradictory. According to the Plan of Iguala, the Constituent Congress was to be free to determine what form the government should take, and the Congress's right to exist lay in the fact that the Plan of Iguala created it; but by virtue of swearing to uphold the precepts of the Plan of Iguala, the Congress could only opt to create a monarchy.[31] By declaring that national sovereignty resided in itself, the Congress created a situation of dual sovereignty, for Iturbide believed that sovereignty resided in the people and that he was the only true voice of their will. As the Spanish commander of the fortress of San Juan de Ulúa, General José Dávila, pointed out in a letter to Iturbide: "The political existence of yourself is in contradiction with that of the Cortes."[32]

Further, because it was Congress that elected Iturbide emperor, it was Congress that set the terms of his oath of office. On 21 May 1822 Iturbide took the carefully crafted oath written by Congress. In it he declared that if he did not observe the Constitution and the laws, if he dismembered the empire, if he took property away from anyone, and if he did not respect the liberty of every individual, he ought not to be obeyed; whatever he did contrary to his oath was to be null and void. In essence, therefore, he recognized that he was inferior to Congress. As generalissimo of the army and president of the regency, Iturbide in some ways had more clear-cut powers than as emperor.

These two fundamental disagreements led to the destruction of Iturbide and to the failure and later collapse of the first Constituent Congress. The legalistic ties between them were so constructed that neither could have the upper hand. If Iturbide acted against Congress, he would nullify his right to be obeyed. If Congress acted against Iturbide (that is, against the creator and creature of Iguala), it would erase its own legitimacy. Quite literally, both Iturbide and the Congress were caught in this trap and it destroyed them, but the urge toward regional power was greatly strengthened.

The attitude of the most extreme wing of Congress, as focused primarily on Servando Teresa de Mier, was that the Plan of Iguala, the Treaty of

Córdoba, the acts of the Sovereign Provisional Governing Junta, and even the Spanish Constitution itself were all interim and that Congress had more than enough power to alter any or all of them. According to this argument, the nation had delegated sovereignty to the Constituent Congress; as a Constituent Congress it had the power to ignore any existing law. Therefore all powers belonged to Congress, not just legislative but also executive and judicial powers. Congress had subdelegated executive power to the emperor; he was its creature. He did not represent the nation, Congress did. In this view, using the words of Joel Poinsett, Congress had reserved to itself the power of passing all necessary laws, "even such as were in contradiction to the constitution they had adopted temporarily. That instrument [the Constitution] could not therefore confer any powers upon the emperor in opposition to the will of the Cortes [Congress]."[33]

The argument of an Iturbidist, on the contrary, would have been that the Plan of Iguala was supreme in that it provided the only clearly agreed-on elements of consensus. By virtue of that fact, the Spanish Constitution was fundamental law, and the Constituent Congress, while it could certainly replace the Spanish Constitution, could not write into the new constitution anything contrary to the system created by Iguala. Until such time as the new constitution was promulgated, the Congress could not deny the emperor the powers the Spanish Constitution allowed the king to have. This argument was based on the idea that all developments since Iguala were evidence that the political system created by Iguala had been confirmed by the express will of the nation.

In the latter half of 1822 a series of concrete disagreements gave substance to these theoretical perspectives, making any attempt to create a workable government impossible. The struggle of Congress to exert its powers would have made the task of any executive difficult, laying whoever held the executive office open to the charge (universally accepted by later historiography against Iturbide) of despotism and tyranny.

Three basic disputes over powers occurred. One was the decision of Congress, arrived at after long debate in the period from May to August, not to allow the emperor the veto power. The second was the question of who was to appoint the members of the Supreme Tribunal of Justice that the emperor created. On 31 May Congress declared these appointments to be within its powers. The emperor refused to accede to this, having decided to create the tribunal and appoint its members as an attribute of executive power. Congress voted no fewer than three times that the judges must be appointed by itself. The third point of contention was the government's wish to set up military commissions to try suspected traitors and ordinary criminals in the absence of a complete national judiciary. Congress strongly opposed these military commissions on the grounds that they were aimed at attacking Iturbide's enemies.

It should be emphasized that the Spanish Constitution gave all three of these powers to the monarch. Articles 144–49 said that the king could veto enactments of the Cortes, in all matters except those involving taxation, by denying his royal sanction to new laws. The royal veto could be overridden only if the Cortes passed the same item a second and a third time in successive years. Article 131 gave the Cortes the power to create tribunals, but Article 171 gave the king the power to name magistrates to those tribunals. Article 308 permitted the suspension of judicial formalities in times of need and for a period of six months. Consequently, Congress had to ignore the Constitution.

In August 1822 the discovery of a conspiracy against Iturbide, and the complicity of some deputies in it, caused him to order the arrest of many people, among them several deputies of Congress.[34] Congress, at first outraged, soon realized its credibility with the people was not strong enough to take energetic action.[35] By this point, Congress had lost most public support. That is why the September 1822 mutiny—Felipe de la Garza, military commander of Nuevo Santander, calling for the liberty of the imprisoned deputies and removal of the cabinet—failed to attract a following.

Throughout the crisis, Iturbide supported the idea of a constitutional monarchy with national representation. He rejected the attempt to compare him to Ferdinand VII of Spain, who had annulled the Cortes in 1814, arguing that Ferdinand VII had overthrown a congress while he himself had given life to one. He was convinced, however, that the Constituent Congress had been improperly constituted, and he argued that public pressure from the people was demanding a new representation, in other words, a new Congress. He wrote to Congress: "I have sworn to the nation to govern it under a constitutional system, I will be loyal to my word respecting [the system] that actually exists as far as the good of the empire permits me. But if, through the vices of its organization or the passions of its agents, it wants to convert itself into an instrument of anarchy, the nation itself in use of its sovereign rights will give a new representation, and I will be the first to invoke it."[36]

Hot on the heels of these disputes, the proposal of Lorenzo de Zavala to reduce the size of Congress became the main focus during September and October 1822 and thoroughly paralyzed the ability of Congress to proceed with vital business. As a member of Congress himself, Zavala had argued all along that the convocation of the Congress was flawed; it was too large, and there was no proportional representation. He blasted Congress for its unbridled use of the doctrine of national sovereignty, its restraints on the emperor's powers, and its attempt to seize excessive powers. Citing Montesquieu and Benjamin Constant, he argued that the executive power must have the ability to restrain the actions of the legislature, otherwise the legislature would itself become despotic. The proposal by Zavala has the historical merit of making it clear that Congress had fallen into great discredit by making the emperor subject to the Constitution while acting as if it were exempt itself. Indeed, Zavala even pointed out that Congress had lost its quorum and was proceeding illegally.[37]

A furious debate followed, during which a commission of Congress recommended that it accede to pressure and declare that all parts of the Spanish Constitution were provisionally in effect. That would allow the emperor to sanction or veto laws, to proceed to the naming of the Supreme Tribunal of Justice, and to prosecute conspiracies directly. Iturbide, however, was no longer in a mood to compromise and refused this proposal, having already decided what he would do. Iturbide told Zavala that after eight months of existence Congress had still not proposed a constitution, which was its primary purpose, nor had it come up with a single law on the national finances or the army. At the same time Congress had occupied itself in attempting to humiliate him and present him to the public as a tyrant. "The nation is tired of this fight and wants a remedy," said Iturbide.[38] At his house he convened a meeting of members of Congress, the cabinet, and army officers to discuss the crisis. During the meeting, he called Bocanegra aside and showed him the many letters from various provincial deputations, corporations, communities, generals, and army corps, all asking for the dissolution of Congress.[39] With that, according to Alamán, the dissolution of Congress became inevitable.[40]

In light of the deep crisis between the emperor and Congress, it is possible to see that Iturbide had good reasons to believe that the Constituent Congress, as it was then organized, stood in the way of national unity and the creation of a functioning government. By the end of October 1822 Mexico had gone thirteen months without its own constitution. Not a single law was passed by Congress dealing with the fiscal crisis facing the new country. Mexico had its own emperor, but further institutional development was stymied. As a consequence, Iturbide dissolved Congress on 31 October 1822 and selected forty-five of its members to compose a Junta Nacional Instituyente. In the months ahead the Junta proceeded to draft a provisional constitutional proposal, new fiscal legislation, the convocation of a more representative Constituent Congress on the basis of proportional representation (which it did not have time to implement), and other basic enactments.

Iturbide's dissolution of the Constituent Congress, however, also led to his abdication, since it provoked the rebellions—most notably that of Casa Mata—which took as their purpose the restoration of national representation, either through reinstallation of the dissolved Constituent Congress (as Santa Anna advocated in his rebellion) or through election of a new one (as Casa Mata advocated). In early March 1823 Iturbide gave in to the pressure and called the old Constituent Congress back into session although it still did not possess a quorum and therefore could not legislate. On 19 March 1823 Iturbide submitted his abdication to Congress.

The victory of the Plan of Casa Mata constituted the victory of the regions over the center. The Plan of Casa Mata did not call for the overthrow of the monarchy, only for the restoration of a representative Congress. It included, however, a clause calling for executive control of the province of Veracruz to be vested, during the uprising, in the provincial deputation of Veracruz. This was exactly what the provinces wanted: provincial self-government. This clause opened the floodgates to provincial power and was the reason most of the provinces declared their support for it in less than six weeks. It had the effect of destroying the central government by assuring each provincial deputation that it could take over administrative control of its respective province. As Benson wrote, "By the middle of March, 1823, Mexico, instead of being a united country, was broken into virtually autonomous provinces," which neither the emperor, nor for that matter the army or Congress, could control.[41] The rapid achievement of regional autonomy, though undoubtedly meeting the demands of regional elites, would greatly complicate the task of nation building. Hamnett cites the dictum of Bulnes that federalism, which would soon be formally decreed, signified the institutionalization and apogee of the cacique system.[42]

It is not surprising that the constitutional problems that had characterized the empire remained unresolved. As soon as the "liberating army" of Casa Mata occupied Mexico City on 26 March 1823, the reinvigorated Constituent Congress finally had a quorum. Its first major item of business was to create the Supreme Executive Power, an interim executive of three men. The most significant question it had to address was Iturbide's abdication and the proposal that it declare invalid the Plan of Iguala and Treaty of Córdoba. In early April a commission of Congress stated that

Iturbide's election as emperor was invalid all along and recommended that Congress declare the Plan of Iguala and Treaty of Córdoba invalid.

Zavala, a member of that commission, wrote that several members of Congress privately put to him the view that since the provinces had named their deputies on the basis of Iguala and Córdoba, therefore an invalidation of Iguala and Córdoba constituted invalidation of the Congress. Had the deputies not, in fact, been elected to create a constitutional monarchy and choose an emperor? In Zavala's opinion, the Congress then existing did not have the right to create a republic because it had not been elected on that premise.[43] On 8 April the Congress voted on the recommendations, with people in the galleries shouting down those deputies who tried to explain why they had voted for Iturbide as emperor. In the end, it voted that the election of Iturbide was null and that Iguala and Córdoba were the work of Iturbide alone and thus were not binding on the nation.

Congress thus nullified Iguala and Córdoba, which had been accepted with universal applause by the nation and solemnly sworn to, and also declared that its own decree of 24 February 1822, in which it accepted the principles of Iguala, was invalid. Alamán points out that in this way Congress not only nullified Iguala but also declared that on 24 February 1822 it had not possessed the right to speak for the nation and had not legally represented the nation in so doing.[44] José María Becerra, a member of the congressional commission that drew up the recommendations about Iturbide and the Plan of Iguala, issued a dissenting vote that made this same point. He argued that while the Treaty of Córdoba was clearly null, since Spain had refused to accept it, the Plan of Iguala could not be nullified by Congress because it did not possess the power to nullify a fundamental document upon whose basis Congress itself had been created.[45]

That Congress had denied its own legitimacy led immediately to another commission to discuss whether the present Congress should be dissolved and a new one convoked. It recommended against dissolution in a long and convoluted report, written by Carlos María Bustamante, that convinced no one.[46]

It should come as no surprise that a Congress that denied its own legitimacy would soon lose credibility, while the provinces were left to create the form of government they most desired. In the next few months the demand for a federation would be forcefully voiced by many provinces. The only option was to give in to provincial pressure and convoke a new Constituent Congress. The first Constituent Congress, which in April 1823 had so enthusiastically congratulated itself for overcoming, in the name of the "gente decente," the threat posed to its members, had effectively committed suicide. It had declared itself unworthy of the confidence of its constituents and of the great struggle it had waged against Iturbide.[47] If the Plan of Iguala had contained within it the seeds of its own destruction, the instrument of its nullification—Congress—also tied itself in untenable and legally unacceptable contortions in its zeal to be rid of the plan and its author.

The center could not hold, and federalism rapidly followed. Whether the center was conceived of as Iturbide and his Plan of Iguala, whether it was the first Constituent Congress and its claim to represent national sovereignty, or whether it was the army of Casa Mata as the de facto protector of the national will, each lost to the forces of regionalism in the wake of the collapse of a national government, a national Congress, and a national army.

The story of the rise and fall of the constitutional monarchy in Mexico might be paraphrased as follows: The nation endorsed it when it endorsed the Plan of Iguala; Iturbide's enemies in Congress destroyed it when they destroyed him; Iturbide dissolved Congress but had to abdicate because of it; Congress overwhelmed Iturbide but in the process committed suicide. Since it was Iturbide's enemies in Congress who wrote the history of these events, the confusions and contradictions that characterized their thinking have been glossed over while Iturbide has, on all counts, emerged as a tyrant.

Notes

1. Agustín de Iturbide, *Memoria de Livorno,* 27 September 1823, draft of the English translation by Michael Joseph Quin, Benson Latin American Collection, University of Texas at Austin (hereafter cited as BLAC), Hernández y Dávalos collection (quotations following from same work).

2. Brian R. Hamnett, *Roots of Insurgency: Mexican Regions, 1750–1824* (Cambridge, Eng., 1986), 47–59.

3. Francisco Bulnes, *La guerra de independencia: Hidalgo-Iturbide* (México, 1910), 396.

4. Neill Macaulay, *Dom Pedro: The Struggle for Liberty in Brazil and Portugal, 1798–1834* (Durham, NC, 1986).

5. Iturbide to Apodaca, Iguala, 24 February 1821, Archivo General de Indias, Seville, Mexico, 1680.

6. Servando Teresa de Mier, "Memoria político-instructiva, enviada desde Filadelfia en agosto de 1821 a los gefes independientes del Anáhuac" (México, 1822), BLAC, Garcia collection.

7. Tadeo Ortiz de Ayala, *México considerado como nación independiente y libre,* 2 vols. (rpt., Guadalajara, 1952), 1:10.

8. Vicente Rocafuerte, *Bosquejo ligerísimo de la revolución de Mégico* (Philadelphia, 1822), rpt. as vol. 2 of *Colección Rocafuerte,* prologue and notes by Neptalí Zúñiga (Quito, 1947), 61.

9. "Acta de instalación de la Junta Nacional Instituyente conforme al decreto imperial de 31 del ultimo octubre" (México, 1822), BLAC, García collection; Iturbide, *Memoria de Livorno.*

10. Javier Ocampo, *Las ideas de un día: El pueblo mexicano ante la consumación de su independencia* (México, 1969), 66–82.

11. Eric Van Young, "Quetzalcoatl, King Ferdinand, and Ignacio Allende Go to the Seashore; or Messianism and Mystical Kingship in Mexico, 1800–1821," in Jaime Rodríguez O., ed., *The Independence of Mexico and the Creation of the New Nation* (Los Angeles, 1989), 109–28; Van Young, "Millennium on the Northern Marches: The Mad Messiah of Durango and Popular Rebellion in Mexico, 1800–1815," *Comparative Studies in Society and History,* 28 (1986): 385–413; and Van Young, "Who Was that Masked Man, Anyway?: Popular Symbols and Ideology in the Mexican Wars of Independence," in *Rocky Mountain Council on Latin American Studies, Annual Meeting, Proceedings,* two vols. (Las Cruces, NM, 1984), 1:18–35.

12. Timothy E. Anna, "The Rule of Agustín de Iturbide: A Reappraisal," *Journal of Latin American Studies,* 17:1 (May 1985): 79–110.

13. Ocampo surveyed 505 pamphlets written in the weeks following the triumph, *Las ideas de un día,* 331, n. 58.

14. Bishop of Sonora to Iturbide, Culiacán, 5 November 1821, Archivo Histórico de la Biblioteca Nacional de Antropología e Historia Eusebio Dávalos Hurtado, Mexico City (hereafter cited as BNAH), Colección Antigua.

15. Iturbide, "Breve manifiesto del que subscribe" (Mexico City, 1821), in Sutro Branch, California State Library, *Catalogue of the Mexican Pamphlets in the Sutro Collection, 1632–1822* (San Francisco, 1939), 229–32.

16. Luis Villoro, "The Ideological Currents of the Epoch of Independence," in Mario de la Cueva, et al., *Major Trends in Mexican Philosophy* (Notre Dame, IN, 1966), 185–219.

17. José Bravo Ugarte, *Historia de México: Independencia, caracterización política e integración social,* 2nd ed. rev. (México, 1953), 134–35.

18. *Actas del Congreso Constituyente Mexicano,* four vols. (Mexico: Alejandro Valdés, 1822), 1:282, 286–301; List of Deputies, Mexico City, about 24 February 1822, Archivo General de la Nación, México (hereafter cited as AGN), Governación, Leg. 11, exps. 25, 26.

19. "Dictamen de la comisión especial encargada por el soberano congreso de examinar los puntos de abdicación de la corona" (México, 1823), BLAC, García collection.

20. "Dictamen de la comisión especial de convocatoria para un nuevo congreso" (México, 12 April 1823), BLAC, Hernández y Dávalos collection.

21. Lucas Alamán, *Historia de Méjico desde los primeros movimientos que prepararon su independencia en el año de 1808 hasta la época presente,* 5 vols. (1849–1852; rpt., Mexico, 1942), 5:463, 465; Carlos María Bustamante, *Continuación del cuadro histórico: Historia del emperador D. Agustín de Iturbide hasta su muerte, y sus consecuencias, y establecimiento de la república popular federal,* vol. 6 of the original *Cuadro histórico* (México, 1846), 6:104–5.

22. Council of State minutes, 27 February, 1 and 4 March 1823, AGN, Gobernación, Leg. 13, exps. 22, 23.

23. Alamán, *Historia,* 5:467–69.

24. William Spence Robertson, *Iturbide of Mexico* (Durham, NC, 1952), 251–262.

25. Lorenzo de Zavala, *Ensayo crítico de las revoluciones de México desde 1808 hasta 1830,* 2 vols., rpt. in *Obras* (México, 1969), 1:121; Bulnes, *La guerra de independencia,* 349.

26. *El amigo de la paz y de la patria,* 19 May 1822.

27. "Derechos convincentes para elegir emperador americano," (México, 1821), BLAC, García collection.

28. Anna, "Rule of Iturbide," 79–110. See the program of Santa Anna's rebellion: "Proclamas del Brigadier Santana a los habitantes y tropa de Veracruz," Veracruz, 2 December 1822, BLAC, Santa Anna papers; "Plan del pronunciamiento en Veracruz y reformas que se le hicieron," Veracruz, 2 and 6 December 1822, BLAC, Hernández y Dávalos collection. See also the program of Guerrero and Bravo: Proclamation of Guerrero and Bravo, Chilapa, 13 January 1823, in Carlos María de Bustamante, *Diario histórico de México,* 2 vols. (México, 1980–81), 1:131; and the program of Casa Mata: Acta de Casa Mata, Cuartel General de Casa Mata, 1 February 1823, BNAH, T-2, 10, Colección Antigua.

29. Bravo Ugarte, *Historia de México,* 141.

30. "Estado que manifiesta los Diputados proprietarios y suplentes que se han de nombrar para el Congreso constituyente del Imperio Mexicano" (México, 1821), BLAC, W. B. Stephens collection.

31. Rocafuerte, *Bosquejo ligerísimo,* 80; Joel Roberts Poinsett, *Notes on Mexico Made in the Autumn of 1822* (New York, Praeger, 1969), 274; Raymond Estep, *Lorenzo de Zavala, profeta del liberalismo mexicano,* trans. Carlos E. Echánove Trujillo (México, 1952), 75.

32. Dávila to Iturbide, San Juan de Ulúa, 23 March 1822, BLAC, Hernández y Dávalos collection.

33. Poinsett, *Notes on Mexico,* 274, 269.

34. Horace V. Harrison, "The Republican Conspiracy Against Agustín de Iturbide," in Thomas E. Cotner and Carlos E. Castañeda, eds. *Essays in Mexican History* (Austin, TX, 1958), 142–65.

35. José María Bocanegra, *Memorias para la historia de México independiente, 1822–46,* 2 vols. (México, 1892–97), 1:79–81.

36. "El oficio que la comisión del soberano congreso presento a S.M.I., y su contestación" (México, 1821), BLAC, García collection.

37. Zavala, "Proyecto de reforma del congreso" (México, 1822), BLAC, García collection; Zavala, *Ensayo crítico,* 1:140.

38. Zavala, *Ensayo crítico,* 1:141.

39. Bocanegra, *Memorias,* 1:92.

40. Alamán, *Historia,* 5:418–19.

41. Nettie Lee Benson, "The Plan of Casa Mata," *Hispanic American Historical Review,* 25:1 (February, 1945): 45–56.

42. Hamnett, *Roots of Insurgency,* 197.

43. Zavala, *Ensayo crítico,* 1:170–71; Bocanegra, *Memorias,* 1:207–8.

44. Alamán, *Historia,* 5:471–72; Bravo Ugarte, *Historia de México,* 156.

45. "Dictamen de la comisión . . . de la abdicación de la corona," BLAC, García collection.

46. "Dictamen de la comisión especial de convocatoria para un nuevo congreso" (México, 12 April 1823), BLAC, Hernández y Dávalos collection.

47. Bocanegra, *Memorias,* 1:216–18.

3

Between Bourbon Reforms and Liberal Reforma: The Political Economy of a Mexican Province—Oaxaca, 1750–1850

BRIAN R. HAMNETT

Bourbon reforms and Liberal reforms in Mexico responded to distinct problems and operated in different contexts. It is important not to view the latter as foreshadowed by the former. The principal differentiating factor was the imperial context of the Bourbon reforms. New Spain's political economy during the colonial era remained subordinated to the broader metropolitan and imperial interests. After 1821, the canvas was much reduced. Many of the linkages of the late colonial period unraveled under the impact of changes in the direction of translatlantic trade, disaggregation of the imperial organism, and disruption of the networks of business constructed by the merchant-financiers of Mexico City and the main provincial capitals. A national context was quite different from an imperial system with its center in Europe. Furthermore, the political disintegration of the former viceroyalty of New Spain provided the opening for provincial elites to assert their control over revenues and resources through the medium of federalism. Elite perceptions altered considerably between the Bourbon era and the Liberal Reforma of the mid-nineteenth century.

In Oaxaca, the elites mainly consisted of merchants rather than great landowners because Indian land retention remained a pronounced phenomenon in the province. Many provincial merchants were closely connected with their capital-city counterparts through business arrangements involving the marketing of high-demand produce from the principal Indian villages. Some of them, notably in the Mixteca, had become sugar planters on lands rented from Indian communities, for instance in Tlaxiaco. Several merchants owned haciendas in the central valleys, though these were rarely of great extent or value. Some played an active role in the attempted revival of the Oaxaca mining industry in the last decades of the colonial era. Many were of Spanish origin, through resident in Oaxaca and often married to local women.

The late colonial elite may be regarded as a homogeneous entity, regardless of geographical provenance. Its members controlled the city council of Antequera de Oaxaca, the provincial capital, and the consular and mining deputations. By and large the colonial district administrators, the *alcaldes mayores,* were their collaborators, at least until the establishment of the intendant system in New Spain in 1786. Members of this business elite also provided the leading figures in the ecclesiastical institutions of the province, though they did not control the office of bishop, which was a crown appointment sanctioned by the papacy.

Political Economy in the Late Colonial Era

The Bourbon state sought to transform the commercial relationships of the province of Oaxaca as part of a generalized imperial restructuring. The method was to alter the institutions through which policy would be implemented. The objective was to respond to the perennial problem of Spain's failure to draw maximum benefit from its vast and wealthy American empire. Ministerial policy saw the root of this drastic failure in traditional economic organization and commercial practices.

Changes of direction within Spain were reflected in policy decisions regarding the Americas. Above all, these policies affected the American elites, which consisted of creoles and resident Spaniards with far-ranging business and family interests in the American territories. Metropolitan policy remained erratic, subject to constant shifts of interest and objective within the Madrid government itself, and the attempts of visitors, viceroys, magistrates, and ecclesiastics to alter the balance of power within each of the American territories provoked opposition and outrage among the elites. The elites had been the principal supporters of imperial rule. During the second half of the eighteenth century, however, a clear disengagement on the part of important sectors of the elites could be discerned. Government policy could no longer depend on the cooperation of influential elite groups for its implementation.[1]

The late Bourbon state operated through a series of distinct institutions and at several different levels—metropolitan, viceregal, provincial, and local. Competing interest groups and political factions sought to use state institutions to promote their own objectives. Bureaucratic agencies often challenged one another's authority, and interest groups at one level subverted policies at another level. As a result, the characteristics of the Bourbon state varied according to context. The further state authority moved downwards into the provincial and local environment, the more its weaknesses became apparent. These weaknesses enabled provincial interest groups to recover part of the area of maneuver previously available to them. In effect, elite recovery during the course of the 1790s imposed a de facto compromise on the viceregal state at the provincial level.[2]

The expansion of bureaucratic organs during the eighteenth century formed a vital aspect of metropolitan Spain's attempt to take advantage of the demographic and economic recovery of New Spain. The Bourbon Reforms were, in this respect, essentially reactive, even though certain aspects of state policy, such as the reduction of the price of mercury, were designed to accelerate expansion in the mining sector. The province of Oaxaca participated in this recovery, but in its own characteristic ways. The principal economic activities in Oaxaca were neither cereal cultivation nor mining but commerce in dyes and cotton textiles conducted from Indian villages. Current research points to population recovery and to the reassertion of a sense of identity among the Indian communities of Oaxaca (and elsewhere in Spanish America, most notably the Andean zones) during the eighteenth century.[3]

Increased mercantile penetration of the Indian economy represented the attempt by private interests to tap these developments and direct them into lucrative commercial channels. The collaboration of the local royal administrators, the alcaldes mayores, with the merchant-financiers provided the latter with an instrument of coercion in the district with which to enforce commercial monopolies. In some provinces, notably Puebla and Tlaxcala, merchants organized the supply of commodities, which were distributed on credit usually by the *teniente,* the official subordinate to the alcalde mayor. In Oaxaca, the repartimiento de mercancías took several forms. Merchants, generally from Mexico City, provided the funds to be used in the financing of village dye or textile production on an increased scale. Because dyes were among New Spain's principal exports—with strong demand in the textile industries of Europe—investors could expect large profits in good years from a sector that was operated at its production base by the Indian communities.

Similar practices also extended into other spheres, such as the cultivation of cotton in the Pacific coastal or Gulf lowland districts and indigo in the Isthmus of Tehuantepec. In the case of the cotton textile industry of Villa Alta, the repartimiento consisted of the supply of raw material for the spinners and weavers (mainly women) and the collection of the final product for distribution through the principal markets of New Spain. The alcalde mayor and his financial backer purchased from the producers at the lowest price and sold at the highest. Accordingly, this sector also could yield large profits. These commodities distinguished the repartimiento in Oaxaca from that in other provinces.[4]

Through such practices, merchants incorporated Oaxaca's indigenous communities into wider commercial networks that extended across the length and breadth of New Spain and beyond. Textiles from Villa Alta or Teotitlán del Camino went to the north-central mining zones; cotton went to the artisan textile industries of Puebla; and dyes went across the Atlantic, mainly to Great Britain or France. In other words, a private commercial superstructure was built over and above existing Indian networks of local markets. This private intervention indicated the degree to which Indian villages were already participants in the commercial activities of New Spain. They did not live in complete isolation from the market and the money economy. On the contrary, they needed to earn surplus revenues in order to finance their own religious confraternities (*cofradías*) dedicated to particular cults, official ecclesiastical dues, and tribute payments to the crown. The cofradías, furthermore, acted as custodians of community properties, which the *república de indios* (Indian governments) had transferred to them during the course of the eighteenth century. The governments transferred the properties to prevent their appropriation by the alcaldes mayores as payment of debts to the tribute-revenue or to the repartimiento.[5]

Considerable sums were invested by merchants in the Oaxaca trades, and the great names of Mexico City commerce became involved. Several local business families expanded their interests and prospered through these trades, chiefly in the period from the 1760s to the 1790s. These networks were impressive and far-ranging. Many of the merchants were also officers in the colonial militia and members of the city council of Oaxaca. Some owned land, and others were deeply involved in the mining industry. The breadth of their activities meant that they did not depend exclusively on any particular activity, covering themselves in difficult times.[6]

One of the most important Mexico City merchants investing in Oaxaca was Francisco Ignacio de Yraeta, a Spanish immigrant (born in 1732) from the Basque Province of Guipúzcoa. He had first arrived in New Spain in 1744 but had lived for ten years in the Philippines before returning to Mexico in 1758. Marrying in Mexico City in 1763, Yraeta inherited from his father-in-law and *consulado* member, Pedro de Ganuza, a large fortune and trading interests that extended to Manila, Guatemala, Guayaquil, and Peru. One of Yraeta's daughters married another wealthy merchant, Isidro Antonio de Ycaza, in 1782. Ycaza, from time to time a member of the city council of Mexico, joined the Yraeta company. He was elected consul to the consulado in 1801 and 1802. Another daughter married Yraeta's nephew, Gabriel de Yturbe y Yraeta, in 1784. Yturbe became the company's principal partner. A militia officer and member of the Mexico City council, he was consul from 1805 to 1806. Yraeta's agent in Oaxaca was Alonso Magro, one of the most important members of the city's mercantile community in the last decades of the eighteenth century and a member of the municipal council. Magro supplied him with indigo. In Villa Alta, Yraeta dealt with Bernardino de Bonavía, subdelegate from 1790 to 1795, and distributed the town's cotton textiles through the northern mining camps and haciendas.[7]

Oaxaca's intimate connection with the business networks radiating out of Mexico City is evident at all points. Colonel Victores de Manero y Pinedo, for example, had been a commercial contact of Yraeta's father-in-law. One of the leading merchants and *alcalde ordinario de primer voto* of the city council in 1763, he dealt principally in the cochineal of Miahuatlán and was a dependent of the alcalde mayor, Fausto de Corres, and his partner, Juan María García. Manero's son, Captain Victorés de Manero y Embides, who died in 1820 when he was *alcalde de segundo voto,* married Rafaela Ramírez de Aguilar, who came from an old family of entailed estate owners in Oaxaca. During his career as a merchant, Manero dealt with Veracruz merchants in the cochineal dye of Jamiltepec in the coastal Mixteca. His brother, Vicente, became a deputy for Oaxaca in the Federal Congress of 1833.[8] Tomás López Ortigoza was not only a major local trader but also the Oaxaca agent for businessmen such as Yturbe in Mexico City and the Marqués de Aycinena in Guatemala. He was also an importer in his own right from Veracruz to his home province. He sent Puebla cottons and glassware to Aycinena and cochineal from Jamiltepec to Juan José Urcullo in Veracruz. He imported large stone hammers for the mines of Ixtepejí in the Oaxaca sierra, and iron for his own haciendas, San Antonio and Tlanichico. His son, José López Ortigoza, held the governorship of Oaxaca four times between 22 June 1830 and 18 September 1841.[9]

Bourbon administrative and commercial measures appeared to threaten powerful commercial interests in New Spain. At first, though, the relationship between the metropolitan government and the merchant-financiers of the repartimiento remained ambiguous. Conflicting legislation and continuing practice blurred the line between legality and prohibition. The crown seemed to be saying that abuse of the Indian population remained an offense but that repartimientos could continue for recognized commercial purposes. The prime objective of the repartimientos, however, was to channel the produce of indigenous communities into the coffers of powerful merchants. Metropolitan recognition of consequent tax losses did not prevent the existence of a tacit collaboration from approximately 1720 between the state at the highest levels and the beneficiaries of the repartimiento. Since commercial monopolies and coercion of the Indian producers were its most pronounced features, reformers viewed the continued survival of the repartimiento as a major scandal. Metropolitan-government legislation in 1754 sought to impose order on the district-level trade. Nevertheless, the government shrank from outright confrontation with private interests, and confined itself, instead, to challenging monopolies and outlawing abuses. Both, however, continued.[10]

The turning-point came with the official visitation of New Spain by José de Gálvez in the period 1765–71. A clear change in direction resulted from Gálvez's discovery of the extent of resident penetration of the senior bureaucratic organism, the audiencia of Mexico, and mercantile subversion of the local district administration. Even so, resistance in Spain and Mexico City to the implementation of the Plan de Intendencias of 1768 delayed Gálvez's most sweeping proposals of reform for nearly twenty years. Powerful commercial interests both within state organs and in the consulado of Mexico struggled to prevent the proposed reforms from damaging their traditional networks. The Bourbon state at this point appeared willing to sanction a profound alteration in the relationships between public policy and private interest. This alteration, moreover, affected the condition of indigenous producers and their relationship both to the state and to the market. The central aim of Gálvez was to separate the local administration from the merchant-financiers by abolishing the office of alcalde mayor and instituting a new tier of officials, the intendants, at the provincial level and a subordinate *subdelegado* at the district level. In this way, Gálvez strove to harness the authority of the colonial state to enforce a change in the nature of the economy at the local level. His objective was to free the Indian producer communities from the constraints of private monopoly. Competing merchants could thereafter supply the communities and trade freely in their products. Gálvez's policy, however, involved strict prohibition of advance financing such as had characterized the repartimiento.[11]

The colonial state intended to complement commercial liberalization in the transatlantic trade with a similar policy in the districts. Both struck severe blows at established interests. The consulado of Mexico City, in particular, moved increasingly into opposition to official policy, a highly disestablishing situation at the apex of the political hierarchy. The expansion of bureaucratic agencies within the viceroyalty enabled an initial implementation of reform policy. Gálvez, appointed minister of the Indies in 1776, managed to secure the introduction of the intendant system to New Spain during 1786 and 1787. Oaxaca became one of the eleven intendancies. Article 12 of the Royal Ordinance of Intendants (1786) prohibited repartimientos outright, as the principal means of attacking private trade monopolies in the districts. In practice, these aspirations were subverted not only in the localities but also in the central bureaucratic organs of the viceregal state. Above all, the crown never found a successful method of paying the new district subdelegates, with the result that they fell into arrangements with private merchants just as their predecessors had done.[12]

At the level of the provincial capital cities, the Bourbon reforms transferred power from local elites to crown servants—the intendant and his immediate administration. The Royal Ordinance of Intendants entrusted them with the implementation of a new type of economic policy. The objective of this policy was to free local commerce from the monopolies enforced on behalf of the merchant-investors by the alcaldes mayores. Although the reforms undermined the de facto political gains made by Mexican elites during the near-century of metropolitan weakness, they broke down at the local level. With the failure of the subdelegations, government authority, and therefore its ability to influence economic relations, remained considerably less effective in the pueblos. Traditional merchant-investors began to revive their interest, though they were less able to establish monopolies than in the pre-1787 era. This situation did not necessarily relieve the pressures on producing communities, because the new subdelegates were paid a percentage of the Indian tribute, the collection of which they supervised. Nevertheless, the entry of other merchants, such as those from Veracruz after the incorporation of the consulado in the Gulf port in 1795, introduced greater competition into local trades. At the same time, Spain's deepening involvement in the French Revolutionary and Napoleonic wars led to a British blockade of Cádiz and a severe interruption of the transatlantic trade. That, in turn, stimulated home production of textiles in the viceroyalty, and the demand for cotton and dyes within the Mexican textile industry grew for a time, until the entry of foreign manufactures through the neutral trades after 1797 acted as a curb.[13]

The impact of the Bourbon reforms at the pueblo level remains one of the least understood aspects of the period. The Bourbon attack on trade monopolies may have stimulated closer integration into market network bases on the village *tianguis* (indigenous marketplace) and also encouraged a closer integration into the broader, viceregal market. Even so, traditional merchant-investors repeatedly claimed the reverse: without enforced repartimientos Indians were lapsing, as they put it, into idleness. Such views were countered by the intendant of Oaxaca, Antonio Mora y Peysal, a *malagueño* and hence compatriot of Gálvez, and one who shared his vision of the overall purpose of the reform. Mora's remarks suggest an Indian capacity to respond to the opening of trades. Traditional vested interests were unwilling to recognize this and remained determined to subvert the reforms. The break-up of the merchant–alcalde mayor nexus, even allowing for a partial reconstruction of the old relationship during the 1790s, seems to have weakened outside authority at the village level. Given the weakness of the subdelegates, effective authority in the localities would have reverted to the Indian governments themselves or to the local caciques. Exactly what happened in the two most lucrative districts of Villa Alta and Jicayán remains to be explained. Did indigenous authorities and merchants enjoy a stronger hand in their dealings with outside powers and merchants from the late 1780s? To what extent had their relationship with the former alcaldes mayores and the investors behind them been one of shifting pressures and counterpressures, resistance, and reaction? Finally, did the producing communities discover a broader area of political space in the aftermath of the intendancy reform, during the twenty years before the outbreak of the revolutionary movement for independence in 1810?[14]

Oaxaca was not a region in which major insurgency flourished. Its economic problems and social structure were strikingly different from those of the Bajio, the central lakes area of Guadalajara, or the principal mining zones. Nevertheless, insurgency affected certain Oaxaca districts, namely the Mixteca Alta (where it attracted support mainly among creoles and *mestizos*), the Oaxaca continuation of the Costa Chica, the Isthmus, and the northern sierra. These were the geographically peripheral zones of intensified economic activity during much of the eighteenth century. Again, the connection between the socioeconomic relationships resulting from district trades and the outbreak of insurgency remains unclear. At a provincial level, however, the struggle for control of these zones after the autumn of 1810 was surprisingly intense and prolonged. Three significant engagements of the War of Independence were fought in Oaxaca: the siege of Huajuapan, the capture of Oaxaca City, and the defeat of the Guatemalan royalists on the Isthmus of Tehuantepec. The struggles in the Oaxacan outlying districts point to a local assertion of independence in opposition to the integrating power of the commercial elite of the provincial capital, itself seriously weakened by the assault on the European merchant-financiers at the national level during the Hidalgo insurrection. There were two aspects to this assertion: on the one hand, it involved Indian communities; on the other hand, it provided opportunities for local figures of prominence to establish control over their areas of influence independent of the commercial networks in which they had formed the lower echelons.[15]

Late colonial expansion generated sufficient surplus capital to encourage revived interest in Oaxaca's mineral resources. From the late 1770s into the early 1810s commercial capital attempted a revitalization of the mining industry. In 1776, the crown established the Mining Tribunal in order to accelerate this process. Scattered documentation tells us something of Oaxaca's participation. Still awaiting resolution is the problem of whether merchants' perceptions of the imminent decline of the dye trade—especially at a time of projected government reform of its conduct—influenced a transfer of capital to the mining sector. Several of the same merchants, such as brothers Colonel Juan Francisco and Captain Juan Felipe de Echarri, the Marroquín brothers, López Ortigoza, Fausto and Matías de Corres, Pedro de Iturribarría y Urquijo, Adrián de Ceráin, and Pedro José de la Vega (whose family had owned the important Hacienda del Vergel in Ejutla since 1735), were involved in the dye trades or the textiles of Villa Alta and in mining ventures. Several of them were at various times members of the Oaxaca mining deputation dependent upon the tribunal in Mexico City. The name Miguel Benito Meijueiro first appeared in that body during the mid-1800s. In the Bourbon era, both Villa Alta and Ixtepejí were administrative and commercial centers of considerable importance, in spite of the small number of their European inhabitants.[16]

Silver production continued to be regarded as New Spain's propeller of economic expansion from Rosario and Bolaños in the north to Taxco and Real del Monte on either side of the central valleys. It may have been that Oaxaca businessmen, faced with diminishing returns in the dye and textile trades, sought to cut their losses by attempting to stimulate mine production. The chronology certainly corresponds to such a suggestion. If that interpretation is correct, then it may have also been the case that merchants strove thereby to emancipate themselves from Indian village control of dye and textile production and to integrate Oaxaca's economy more completely into the international market by contributing to New Spain's overall silver output. The merchants were overtaken by the contraction of imperial trade during the first two decades of the nineteenth century.

Political Transformation: From Colony to Federation

Initially, Oaxaca did not participate in the Cádiz constitutional system, since insurgent forces occupied the provincial capital from 25 November 1812 until 15 March 1814 and occupied large parts of the Intendancy for longer periods. Insurgent occupation, however, altered the political structure of the region. The flight of Bishop Antonio Bergoza y Jordán, a central figure in the counterrevolution; the execution of the three principal royalist commanders; and the break-up of the merchant-financiers' networks of credit and distribution in the villages undermined Spanish peninsular hegemony. During the years of restored absolutism between 1814 and 1820, it became clear that this hegemony would never be reconstructed. By 1820, several prominent Spanish merchants long identified with Oaxaca, such as Manuel Solar del Campero, returned to the peninsula. Even though others remained through Mexican independence in 1821, their role was never as strong as before 1812. Political prominence passed to their Oaxacan associates and relatives. At the core of the postcolonial elite, then, were the sons and business partners of the great merchants of the late Bourbon era. Prominent among them was José López Ortigoza, son of Tomás López Ortigoza. This newer elite, however, could no longer depend either on the powerful support of the Mexico City merchants and their consulado or on a central government of unassailable legitimacy. On the contrary, the provincial elite, in the aftermath of the collapse of the Bourbon viceregency and the First Empire, seized the political initiative.[17]

After 1823, with a weakened central government, the provincial elites, notably in Guadalajara, Zacatecas, Puebla, and Oaxaca, asserted their control over regional policy. Their objective was to impose their own vision of political economy—doubly emancipated, in their perception, both from metropolitan Spain and from Mexico City, or "Tenochtitlán," as Guadalajara regionalists preferred to call it. The authorities in Oaxaca, however, faced diminished fiscal resources, in clear contrast to Zacatecas, which was passing through a postinsurgency revival in its silver-mining sector. At the same time, the range of Oaxaca's trades significantly contracted. This is evident from any comparison of the 1830s and 1840s to the 1770s and 1780s. Integration into the broader world market through the dye trade had in the latter period contributed to the rise of a circle of provincial-level plutocrats with varied economic activities within Oaxaca and wide-ranging contacts beyond it—from Cádiz to Havana, Veracruz, and Acapulco, and from the northern mining zones to Guatemala. Internal crisis in Oaxaca's trades during the 1790s and 1800s, accompanied by the revolutionary struggles of the 1810s, transformed an international market orientation into an interprovincial network.[18]

Underlying difficulties of technology, capital shortage, and inadequate labor supply threatened to plunge the struggling mining sector into deep recession. From the mid-1820s, foreign interests, encouraged by the governments of early independent Mexico, began to enter the economy, and interest in Oaxaca's mining sector revived. The Mexican Mining Company and the United Mexican Mining Company hoped to revive the Oaxaca sector as part of a general attempt to revitalize the whole silver economy. Mexican ministers argued that rehabilitation of the mining sector would provide a basis for national prosperity. Such a view underlined the continuities of political economy between the First Federal Republic and the Bourbon era, regardless of the disparities within the political order. The fundamental difference was that the investors were mainly British rather than Spanish. By the end of the 1820s, nevertheless, the new ventures encountered the same impediments as the colonial investors had several decades previously, though this time in a deteriorating political environment.[19]

Some foreign mine operators, notably British and German, did remain in Oaxaca, chiefly in Ixtlán and Yavesía. These were the territories where a number of local Oaxacan families were building up their own mining concerns. Chief among them was Miguel Castro, who had studied with Benito Juárez at the state's secular Institute of Science and Arts, founded in 1827. Castro married Jacinta Meijueiro, daughter of Miguel Benito Meijueiro. Castro and the Meijueiros worked closely with resident British investors for the rehabilitation of their mines. The alliance between Juárez, Castro, and the Meijueiros would form the mainstay of Oaxacan liberalism from the 1840s to the 1870s. Castro had broad interests across the sierra mining sector and a growing political influence in the state from the late 1840s, but he was never a rich man and certainly not a plutocrat. The decline of Villa Alta's once lucrative textile trade turned local hopes to mining. Oaxaca's mining industry remained potential rather than actual, rich in resources but deficient in exploitation. Juárez, as state governor (1847–52), sought to remedy that state of affairs, though with little success. He pointed to an inadequate infrastructure, capital shortage, and a general lack of entrepreneurial spirit in Oaxaca.[20]

Oaxaca's new political institutions reflected the interests and ambitions of a provincial elite formed during the second half of the eighteenth century. Although the peninsular merchant-financiers, the royal bureaucracy, and the Spanish episcopate disappeared in stages between 1812 and

1829, the native-born element within the elite remained to take control of political life. This was not an old colonial elite of large estate owners with noble titles, but a relatively new and open group of families that needed the cooperation of well-educated members of the nonelite social groups in order to serve the new institutions. The contraction of the economy reduced the income of this elite. With the decline of the dye and textile trades and prolonged recession in mining, the farming economy of the central valleys could offer few alternative opportunities for the creation of wealth. Similarly, the breakdown of the colonial fiscal structure reduced the sphere of influence of the state-level institutions established after 1825.[21]

After independence the provincial elite was no longer able to sustain its position through the traditional institutions or by appeals to monarchical and episcopal legitimacy. The elite did not remain a united political entity, and internal factions had recourse to informal, private power to pursue their objectives. A constant interweaving of constitutional politics and extra-legal interventions took place. This had not occurred before 1810, and it represented a fundamental change in the nature of politics. The Rebellion of Tulancingo in 1827 began this process when Vice President Nicolás Bravo attempted to subvert the federalism established under the Constitution of 1824. The seizure of power by Lorenzo de Zavala and Vicente Guerrero, following the latter's electoral defeat in 1828, ruptured the constitutional process altogether. Vice President Anastasio Bustamente removed Guerrero at the end of 1829 and between 1830 and 1832 established a neo-Bourbon conservative regime in collaboration with Lucas Alamán. The intervention of General Antonio López de Santa Anna, at the invitation of moderates, terminated the conservative regime. Santa Anna's intervention in 1834 similarly terminated the first Liberal experiment of 1833–34 under Vice President Valentín Gómez Farías. As a result of these political changes, government economic policies remained destabilized and inconsistent.[22]

Such events greatly frustrated the attainment of some durable form of constitutional government, desired in different ways by both liberals and conservatives alike. They also delayed the implementation of a coherent economic policy at national and state levels. Commercial recession in the late 1840s and continued failure to work out a nationally acceptable tax structure accompanied these repeated changes of regime. The first peaceful transfer of political power did not take place until 1851, when José Joaquín Herrera handed over power to Mariano Arista; the second transfer did not occur until 1880.[23]

The Political Economy of Recession and Revival

Oaxaca passed through a long recession from the 1790s to the 1880s. Elite assessments of the roots of the problem and the solutions to it focused on two dimensions: the introduction of export agriculture and the survival of indigenous corporate landownership. Even so, areas existed where the local economy continued to be buoyant. During the first three-quarters of the nineteenth century, the sugar zone of the Mixteca Alta, particularly in the vicinity of Tlaxiaco, remained the clearest example. In precisely this zone, the Guergué and Esperón families had made their wealth. They formed part of a group of Spanish merchants who had begun to rent lands from the Indian community of Tlaxiaco, particularly in the Yosotiche area, from the 1710s. From early plantings sizeable sugar-refining units arose during the second half of the century. In the mining districts of the sierra, Castro and the Meijueiros and a variety of English investor-operators continued to hope for the awaited breakthrough in the mining sector. The peasant base of the Oaxacan economy, however, encouraged political and business leaders within the state to argue for export-led growth as a means of overcoming what they increasingly regarded as stagnation.[24]

Throughout the nineteenth century most observers concluded that the three great hopes for Oaxaca's recovery were the construction of an interoceanic canal or railway, the revival of the mining industry, and the cultivation of tropical products, such as sugar, coffee, and cotton. In the meantime, attempts were made to revive the dye trade. To promote the trade, several major Mexican business houses, such as the Martínez del Río, invested in cochineal dye, and British merchants—such as Roberto Smith, Diego Innes, and Constantino Rickards—took up residence in Oaxaca from the 1830s or 1840s. National governments supported these efforts, above all during Alamán's tenure as director of national industries in the early 1840s under the centralist regime. Little came of these efforts. Oaxaca's registered dye production fell from a value of 1,695,375 pesos in 1819 to 419,248 pesos in 1831. Although a brief recovery in price and production levels took values to 480,647 pesos in 1834, this figure still represented only a quarter of late colonial values. Even so, cochineal dye remained Mexico's second export after silver. Demand for it in the European textile industry continued to be robust. This was indicated by the company formed in 1839 by the Martínez del Río brothers with Cotesworth, Prior & Co. to ship Oaxacan dye, purchased at source, from

Veracruz to London via New York. Although up to 50,000 pesos were invested in the first consignment, the contract fell down because of the continuing price decline in London.[25]

Oaxaca's dye sector could not compete with Guatemala, new producer of the postindependence era. This factor, more than any other, accounted for Oaxaca's failure to recapture traditional markets. As early as 1823, cochineal, valued at 2.5 million pesos, accounted for nearly a quarter of the exports of the Central American Federation, with indigo dye from San Salvador valued at 2 million pesos. The peak period of Guatemala's cochineal trade corresponded to the conservative hegemony under Rafael Carrera. The most successful harvest was that of 1854, when 2,587,000 pounds of dye were exported, valued at 1,757,300 pesos. The discovery of aniline dyes in 1856, however, led to regular declines in prices and imports on the London market. This factor contributed to the extinction of Oaxaca's prospects as well.[26]

Deficient communication, furthermore, held back Oaxaca's contact with the world market and prevented the province from responding to evident demand for products such as coffee in the way that the small republic of Costa Rica was able to do. With only 180,000 inhabitants, considerably fewer than Oaxaca's near half million, Costa Rica in the 1830s became closely integrated into the world market for coffee. Guatemala followed from the 1850s, finding in coffee an even more lucrative product than cochineal dye. The opening of Oaxaca's ports, first Huatulco and then La Ventosa (near Tehuantepec), had few positive results. Hardly anyone lived in Huatulco: the main town lay a few miles inland, and the "port" consisted of a deserted beach with no unloading facilities. Foreign merchants were still liable to be accused of contraband trading if they tried to discharge their produce in Huatulco or in nearby Puerto Escondido. This was the case of the British house of Montgomery and Nicod in the early 1830s. Since customs duties, anchorage fees, importation charges, and transportation costs were so high, prospective traders found they had to travel laden with ready cash. In any case these ports were located on the Pacific, while the market lay in Europe or the eastern seaboard of the United States. This location initially delayed Guatemala's entry into the coffee economy. It reinforced the need for direct access to the Atlantic by means of an interoceanic route.[27]

The state government tried but largely failed to encourage the development of an adequate road network across Oaxaca. Governor Juárez, for instance, convened in the late 1840s a committee of significant persons in the district of Ejutla, situated between the central valley and the coast, in an attempt to stimulate road construction. He was hoping for private enterprise to take over the project in view of state government fiscal constraints, but he encountered indifference. Failure to construct roads left all hopes fixed on the dream of a transoceanic canal across the Isthmus of Tehuantepec. Attention in the United States and Europe also fixed on this route, along with the route across the Nicaraguan lakes and the route through the Isthmus of Panama, as one of three possibilities. The Spanish Cortes in April 1814, a few weeks before its dissolution, had authorized construction of a Tehuantepec canal. Nothing had materialized. The Santa Anna regime revived the project in 1842, entrusting it to a controversial financial backer, José de Garay. Again nothing resulted. Pressures from the United States for transit rights across the isthmus and across northern Mexico mounted during the 1850s. The idea of a Tehuantepec canal inspired Louis Napoleon Bonaparte and became a motive for the French intervention in Mexico during the following decade. However, the idea proved elusive in reality. Oaxaca's dream of a miraculous deliverance from isolation and underdevelopment proved to be a chimera.[28]

Although Oaxaca's economy remained in recession, its population continued to grow. From an estimated 411,336 in 1793, it reached 521,187 by 1844. Of this total 90 percent was classified as Indian. There were only twenty-eight haciendas in the entire Department of Oaxaca in 1844, half of them located in the Central District, which included the fertile valleys of Etla, Oaxaca, and Zimatlán. Most of these haciendas were small and yielded little if any profit. One of the largest in Oaxaca, the Hacienda del Vergel in Ejutla, had frequent changes of owners during the nineteenth century. Oaxaca was certainly not a province in which a powerful territorial elite dominated political and economic life. On the contrary, there were 939 Indian pueblos and a further 525 *ranchos*, which belonged to various socioethnic groups. Indian communities retained control over the bulk of the land for much of the century.[29]

State governments identified Indian land retention as a root cause of backwardness. Governor José Ignacio Morales drew attention in 1827 to what he described as the irrational form of land use in the state. Morales called for a state land-reform law. Existing land distribution remained, in his eyes, absurd: "Some villages have extensive lands which are left for the most part uncultivated; other villages did not even possess enough for their own subsistence; yet others have scarcely anything but useless lands. As a result, the state is consumed by a plague of lawsuits, which not infrequently result in outright conflict between villages. . . ." Attempts to formulate a land-reform law, however, came to nothing. The obstacles proved too great. Villagers viewed this outside interest in their affairs as another pretext for imposing taxes, and they refused to cooperate.[30]

More than fifty years later, Matías Romero, minister of finance under both Juárez and Porfirio Díaz, argued that in his native state of Oaxaca, Indian land retention delayed the transition to coffee cultivation. Although the province had, he believed, sufficient land and population to transfer to large-scale production, obstruction in the villages frustrated the outcome. For that reason, Oaxaca proved unable to join the ranks of the major producers in Veracruz, Chiapas, Guatemala, or Costa Rica, not to mention Colombia and Brazil. Romero was, in effect, searching for a substitute commodity for cochineal, much as the Liberal elite of western Guatemala had been doing from the 1860s, when it successfully went over to large-scale coffee cultivation. He remained pessimistic—perhaps too much so—with regard to the mining sector. Yet the prospects for the expansion of coffee in Oaxaca were themselves hardly encouraging. Brazil, a major producer since the 1830s, already accounted for two-thirds of world consumption, and the rest of the market had been cornered by other Latin American and Asiatic producers. Romero, however, remained optimistic about the prospects for coffee. After a tour of the coffee zones of Veracruz-Cordoba in particular, he concluded in 1879 that coffee would be the best means of regenerating the Oaxacan economy.[31]

Oaxaca's tentative recovery did not begin until the 1870s, and even then it was distinctly regionalized. The periphery, rather than the central valleys, took the lead in the development of coffee, tobacco, cotton, sugar, and livestock raising. Again, there was no one supreme product. The late nineteenth-century recovery in Oaxaca was not tied—as it was in Yucatán, another state with an Indian majority—to the rapid expansion of a monoculture, such as henequen, oriented toward a defined market in the United States. In Oaxaca, however, Indian land loss was never as great as in either Yucatán or highland Guatemala. More than twenty years after the implementation of the Ley Lerdo of 25 June 1856 for the disamortization of corporate landownership, Romero still found it necessary to point out that "those who know the attachment the Indians have for their lands and the resistance they show towards any establishment among them of persons of Hispanic or mestizo race, will understand the difficulties coffee planters of Miahuatlán encounter when they try to acquire these lands. This is most especially the case when lands belong communally to the villages of different districts."[32]

Romero believed that peasant cultivators in Oaxaca could themselves grow coffee without the need of large outlays of capital, a conclusion based on his studies of production methods in Asia and Central America. He envisaged peasants growing coffee in addition to their customary maize planting and trading activities, without threat to their traditional way of life. Evidently peasant defense of land rights, combined with lack of adequate infrastructure, inhibited the development in Oaxaca of the type of plantation system, with heavy Indian land loss, which was taking shape in Guatemala from the 1850s. Romero's overriding concern, however, was to stem labor migration from the state into Veracruz and other regions. On the Veracruz cotton plantations, for instance, laborers received a daily wage of 50 centavos, twice the average wage in the Oaxaca sierra. At the same time they paid no capitation tax and performed none of the community duties or *tequios* usually required of village inhabitants.[33]

Elite Aspirations and Socioeconomic Realities

The leading families in control of institutions after 1823 repeatedly strove to introduce the forms and practices of the nineteenth-century state. They soon encountered widespread popular opposition to their project. Well before the Liberal regime's post-1856 assault on corporate property ownership at the national level, state authorities in many regions conducted their own campaigns to bring community land under private control. The states of Jalisco and Veracruz adopted no such measures in the decades before the Ley Lerdo. The explanation lay in the precarious nature of elite political power in the state in the aftermath of the wars of independence. This proved to be especially the case with regard to the southern isthmus, which remained largely beyond the control of the state authorities at least until the 1880s. The continued predominance of Indian landownership, moreover, and the resilience of communities in defending their corporate and ethnic identities acted as the most effective deterrents of all.[34]

Nevertheless, the postindependence political order imposed fundamental changes in the legal structure of the state. The Laws of the Indies, and with them official recognition of the separate and protected status of the Indian, lapsed after 1821. Although new civil codes were still only in the process of formulation during the first Juárez governorship of 1847–52, the administration sought to make it clear to Indian communities that they could expect no corporate exemptions from state laws. Under the state Constitution of 1825, every inhabitant of the state became a "citizen" in a republican system of government. Accordingly, the legal distinctions upheld during the colonial period no longer applied, with the result that every man owed obligations of tax payment and militia service to his state. The clear aim was to impose a new set of loyalties upon the majority ethno-cultural groups of Oaxaca. Their prime allegiance should be to the "Mexican nation," the republic, and the state in which they lived. Such required loyalties were to supersede traditional identification with village, linguistic or ethnic group, locality, and customary religious practices. The main fiscal burden of sustaining these new superstructures fell precisely upon this same majority through the direct contribution and the capitation.[35]

Communities strove to retain their separate identities and to defend traditional practices. What survived of the old legal order did so largely because state authorities lacked the financial means to substantiate their developing political ideology. Above all, they could rely only sporadically upon instruments of outright coercion. Projects for the establishment of a state militia dated from the spring of 1823. These first attempts provoked a riot in Tamazola and noncooperation in Tehuantepec. Villagers claimed exemption under colonial law. It had to be explained to them in their native language that they were now citizens equal before the law and with equal civic obligations. In Miahuatlán, the recruiting officer complained that local Indians were "lacking in civilization, and for that reason viewing with horror service to the Nation in its armed forces." In Ixtepejí in 1825, villagers expelled recruiting officers. In view of such opposition (which was by no means confined to these examples), projects for the formation of a state militia of 4,562 men had to be abandoned until 1828. Political upheaval in the city, with the arrival of Santa Anna's rebel forces, created havoc with the small force already in existence. Attempts had to begin anew in 1830. Santa Anna's defeat of the civic militia of the state of Zacatecas in 1835 presaged the end of the First Federal Republic (1824–36). The Centralist Republic (1836–46) sought instead to reconstruct a unified national army, though with little success due to factionalism and politicization.[36]

With the restoration of federalism in August 1846, intensified efforts were put to the organization of a national guard in each of the states of the republic. The aim was twofold: to protect state institutions from the central government and to maintain order within the states. President José Joaquín Herrera's Ordinances of 15 July 1848 provided for compulsory militia service for men between eighteen and fifty-five years of age, again with specific exemptions according to occupation. Juárez implemented this law in Oaxaca. Immediately, however, militia forces were caught up in the escalating conflict between the state authorities and the towns of the isthmus over control of salt deposits and lands.[37]

Parallel attempts to recruit the state quota of 1,709 soldiers for the regular army also led nowhere. By mid-1831, the state of Oaxaca still had not complied. Military service of any kind remained notoriously unpopular in Oaxaca: recruits hardly knew any Spanish and fled home at the first opportunity. Resistance to taxation and recruitment exposed the lack of consensus in the formation of the new republican institutions. Without roots in society, they remained isolated structures imposed upon an uncomprehending, resisting peasant-artisan majority. Outright confrontation, however, was prevented in most instances by the weakness of the postcolonial order. As peasant communities struggled to retain what had been to their advantage in the colonial system, state politicians found they had to compromise all along the line if day-to-day administration were to continue. Although local elites sought to shape events by taking control of state-level institutions, they rapidly discovered that Oaxaca's complex ethno-cultural inheritance would oblige them to adapt to realities. Bereft of revenue and armed power, they had to formulate a working relationship with community leaders through the medium of the district administrators or subprefects.[38]

The single most significant factor influencing the relationship between government and society was the capitation tax. This potentially lucrative tax applied to all males between sixteen and sixty years of age who had not been specifically exempted on account of occupation. The levy came to 12.5 centavos a month. Because the bulk of the levy in Oaxaca fell on the Indian population, it seemed to resemble the colonial tribute levy instituted in the 1540s, a head tax on both men and women. The tribute, abolished in 1810, had been a major revenue of the viceregal state. Its loss was a serious blow to the political authorities in heavily indigenous areas. Consequently, they sought substitutes. In March 1823, Oaxaca's provisional governing junta established a monthly capitation tax for the maintenance of troops, with the object of defending provincial autonomy from the central power.[38]

With the consolidation of federalism, state authorities began after August 1824 the process of institutionalizing this new tax. Between August 1824 and October 1826, a new postcolonial fiscal structure took shape. By 1829 and 1830, the direct contribution yielded 200,000 pesos annually, a figure that compared well with the total customs receipt of 150,000 pesos in the latter year.[40]

Trade recession made the state government all the more reliant on the head tax. Efforts were made to compile more accurate statistics—never an easy task, in view of Indian suspicions of government objectives. According to estimates of wealth compiled by the centralist regime from 1843 to 1844, the total number of eligible contributors in what is now the Department of Oaxaca came to 117,662, 40 percent of the population. The subprefects collected the tax. Herrera's decree of 6 August 1845 prepared the way for the restoration of federal institutions by specifying revenues pertaining to the departments. His law of 28 October regulated the capitation tax, by then the basis of Oaxaca's financial system.[41]

After the final restoration of federalism in August 1846, collection of the capitation tax continued to be the responsibility of the subprefects and collectors below them. In accordance with the federal structure established in 1824–25, Oaxaca was once more divided into departments under governors. The subprefects reverted to the role of officials subordinate to the department governors. Juárez informed the state congress that the average annual revenue from the capitation came to 167,250 pesos between 1849 and 1851. Village alcaldes, however, were unable to collect the tax in 1849 and 1850 in the mining districts of Ixtlán, Ixtepejí, and Capulalpan, with the result that the subprefect appealed to the state government to enforce collection by the dispatch of troops. None were available for that purpose because of the deepening crisis in the isthmus. There, the subprefect of Juchitán reported that hardly one-quarter of the tax had been collected by November 1849. In the case of Zaachila, near the state capital, the authorities were only able to enforce payment in 1853 by the use of troops. Revenue still reached only 193,788 pesos in 1877–78 out of a total state income of 630,866 pesos.[42] As in the colonial period, the weight of taxation in Oaxaca fell upon the indigenous population, which remained sensitive to any alteration in quotas. The capitation, however, was not a simple restoration of the tribute. It was conceived with a different purpose in mind, and it applied to all citizens.

The Spanish ministry had sought during the late colonial period to use state power to transform economic relationships within the American empire. By so doing, it hoped to influence the direction and capacity of trade. Gálvez, in the forefront, identified the local trade monopolies of merchant-investors and the royal district administrators as the principal obstacle. Much depended in practice, however, on the personalities entrusted with implementing Bourbon reform policies. At the root of the failure of reform at the district level was the crown's failure to provide a regular salary for the new subdelegates. The problem of the financial weakness of the central government recurred throughout the century from 1750 to 1850. The provincial elites that assumed control of political life after 1823 found themselves circumscribed by fiscal weakness and contraction of the market. The First Federal Republic had broken down over the failure to establish a financial structure capable of sustaining national government. Centralism between 1836 and 1846 similarly failed to build a lasting basis for the Mexican republic. Whichever party or faction controlled state-level institutions, Oaxaca's elite rapidly discovered that during the broader period from the 1820s to the 1880s they did not enjoy an unchallenged, hegemonic position immune to pressures from below. In consequence, they were obliged time and time again to modify their initial project in order to take account of these pressures. Although national and state institutions influenced regional society and the economy, Oaxaca's ethno-social groups largely determined the parameters of state power at least during these sixty years.

Notes

I. See H. I. Priestley, *José de Gálvez, Visitor-General of New Spain (1765–1771)* (Berkeley, 1916); Mark A. Burkholder and D. S. Chandler, *From Impotence to Authority: The Spanish Crown and the American Audiencias, 1687–1808* (St. Louis, 1977); and Colin MacLachlan, *Spain's Empire in the New World: The Role of Ideas in Institutional and Social Change* (Berkeley, 1989).

2. Brian R. Hamnett, *Politics and Trade in Southern Mexico, 1750–1821* (Cambridge, Eng., 1971), 72–94.

3. Sherburne F. Cook and Woodrow Borah, *The Population of the Mixteca Alta, 1520–1960* (Berkeley, 1968), 48–59, 78; John K. Chance, *Race and Class in Colonial Oaxaca,* (Stanford, CA, 1978), 144–85; and Marcello Carmagnani, *El regreso de los dioses: El proceso de reconstitución de la identidad étnica en Oaxaca, Siglos XVII y XVIII,* (México, 1988).

4. See Rodolfo Pastor, *Campesinos y reformas: La mixteca, 1700–1856* (México, 1987), 264–80; John K. Chance, *Conquest of the Sierra: Spaniards and Indians in Colonial Oaxaca* (Norman, OK, 1989), 102–10; Marcello Carmagnani, "Una forma mercantile coatta: Il 'repartimiento' nella regione messicana di Oaxaca nell'ultimo terzo del secolo XVIII" in *Wirtschaftskräfte und Wirtschaftswege: Festschrift für Herman Kellenbenz,* 5 vols. (Stuttgart, 1978), 4:139–46; and Horst Pietschmann, "Agricultura e industria rural indígena en el México de la segunda mitad del siglo XVIII," in Arij Ouweneel and Cristina Torales Pacheco, eds., *Empresarios, indios y estado: Pérfil de la economía mexicana (siglo XVIII)* (Amsterdam, 1988), 71–85.

5. Hamnett, *Politics and Trade,* 16–40; Pastor, *Campesinos y reformas,* 181–84, 196–98; D. Dehouve, "El pueblo de indios y el mercado: Tlapa en el siglo XVIII," in Ouweneel and Torales, *Empresarios, indios y estado,* 86–102.

6. Stephen H. Haber, *Industry and Underdevelopment: The Industrialization of Mexico, 1890–1940* (Stanford, CA, 1989), 67–83 (remarks on a similar state of affairs during the later nineteenth century).

7. María Cristina Torales Pacheco, ed., *La compañía de comercio de Francisco Ignacio de Yraeta (1767–1797): Cinco ensayos,* 2 vols. (México, 1985), 1:24–33, 62–65, 185–99.

8. Archivo General del Estado de Oaxaca (hereafter cited as AGEO), Alcaldes Mayores leg. 4, exp. 7 (1763); AGEO (LE), Aduana Box 77 (1803), 1 September 1803; Archivo Municipal de Oaxaca, Libro de Acuerdos 1820, f. 256.

9. AGEO (LE), Aduana Box 77 (1803), 17 January, 24 April, and 1 September 1803.

10. Hamnett, *Politics and Trade,* 41–71. See also Horst Pitschmann, "Revolución y contrarrevolución en el México de las reformas borbónicas: Ideas protoliberales y liberales entre los burócratas ilustrados novohispanos (1780–1794)," *Caravelle: Cahiers du monde hispanique et luso-brésilien* 54 (1990): 21–35.

11. Priestly, *José de Gálvez,* remains important.

12. Brian R. Hamnett, "Mercantile Rivalry and Peninsular Division: The Consulados of New Spain and the Impact of the Bourbon Reforms, 1789–1824," *Ibero-Amerikanisches Archiv* H. 4 (1976): 273–305.

13. Hamnett, *Politics and Trade,* 103–20, 177–82.

14. Pastor, *Campesinos y reformas,* 196; Chance, *Conquest of the Sierra,* 98. Recent studies (above, note 4) by Pietschmann and Carmagnani provide a useful contribution to this debate.

15. Archivo General de la Nación (México (hereafter cited as AGN), Historia 152, ff. 111–16v, Viceroy Apodaca to Minister of War, no. 1 (reservada), Mexico City, 31 October 1816. See also William B. Taylor, "Town and Country in the Valley of Oaxaca, 1750–1812," in Ida Altman and James Lockhart, eds., *Provinces of Early Mexico: Variants of Spanish American Regional Evolution* (Los Angeles, 1976), 63–95.

16. AGN General de Parte 67 (1785–87), ff. 113v–14v, 152–52v. AGN Minería 41, exp. 15, México, 14 April 1790. AGEO Real Intendensia II, leg. 31, exps. 16, 23, 25, 26, 29, 31, 32; leg. 32, exp. 4.

17. Brian R. Hamnett, "Oaxaca—Las primeras familias y el federalismo de 1823," in María Angeles Romero Frizzi, ed., *Lecturas históricas del estado de Oaxaca,* 4 vols. (México, 1990), 3:51–69.

18. Brian R. Hamnett, "Factores regionales en la desintegración del régimen colonial en la Nueva España," in I. Buisson, G. Kahle, and H. Pietschmann, eds., *Problemas de la formación del estado y de la nación en Hispanoamerica* (Bonn, 1984), 305–17.

19. H. G. Ward, *Mexico in 1827,* 2 vols. (London, 1828), 1:405–8, 2:289. Mr. William Glennie, director of the United Mexican Mining Company, had high hopes for the mines of Teojomulco, south of Oaxaca City.

20. AGEO Diversos Históricos (leg. 3) 1838, Prefectura de Villa Alta: Estado alfabético que manifiesta el número de extranjeros residentes en este distrito, Villa Alta, 7 December 1838; Benito Juárez, *Exposición que . . . hace el Gobernador . . . al Soberano Congreso . . . 2 julio 1848* (Oaxaca, 1848), 15. Castro was state governor three times: 3 December 1858 to 22 December 1859, 13 May to 1 December 1867, and 18 July 1872 to 4 November 1874. Francisco Meijueiro (b. Ixtlan 1833) was governor from 11 February 1876 to 1 December 1881.

21. See T. J. Cassidy, "Haciendas and Pueblos in Nineteenth Century Oaxaca" (Ph.D. diss., University of Cambridge, 1981).

22. Brian R. Hamnett, "Partidos políticos mexicanos e intervención militar, 1823–1855," in Antonio Annino et al., *America Latina: Dallo stato coloniale allo stato nazione,* 2 vols. (Milan, 1987), 2:573–91.

23. See Barbara Tenenbaum, "El poder de las finanzas y las finanzas del poder en Mexico durante el siglo XIX," *Siglo XIX* 3:5 (Jan.–June 1988): 197–221; and D. C. M. Platt, "Finanzas británicas en Mexico (1821–1867)," *Historia Mexicana* 32:2 (Oct.–Dec. 1982): 226–61.

24. Cassidy, "Haciendas and Pueblos," 109–19, 138–39; Pastor, *Campesinos y reformas,* 183–84, 229, 234–37, 263.

25. AGEO Diversos 1830B puts the value of dye production in 1844 at 627,255 pesos and silver production at 153,000 pesos. AGEO Tesorería 1846, Noticia . . . de las granas, Oaxaca, 1 July and 2 September 1846. José López Ortigoza, *Memoria de Gobierno,* (Oaxaca, 1831), no. 4, Oaxaca, 3 June 1831; Ortigoza, *Exposición que el governador constitucional del estado hizo al congreso,* (Oaxaca, 1835), no. 4, Oaxaca, 5 May 1835. Lucas Alamán, *Memoria sobre el estado de la agricultura e industria de la república* (1843), 129–206; Alamán, *Memoria* (1844), 136, 221–320; Alamán, *Memoria* (1845), 242–44; all in *Documentos Diversos,* 3 vols. (México, 1945–1946), vol. 2. David W. Walker, *Kinship, Business and Politics: The Martínez del Río Family in Mexico, 1824–1867* (Austin, 1986), 112–13, 167–68.

26. Ralph Lee Woodward, *Class Privilege and Economic Development: The Consulado de Comercio of Guatemala, 1793–1871* (Chapel Hill, 1966), 45, 48–49. Though still the country's largest export, Guatemala's cochineal fell to 688,080 pounds in 1864. Manuel Rubio Sánchez, "Apuntes para la historia de la agricultura en Guatemala," *Antropología e Historia de Guatemala* 13:1 (Jan. 1961): 15–46.

27. José Ignacio Morales, *Memoria que el Gobernador del Estado de Oaxaca presento en la apertura de las sesiones ordinarias del segundo congreso constitucional . . . 2 julio 1827* (Oaxaca, 1827), 8.

28. José de Garay, *An Account of the Isthmus of Tehuantepec* (London, 1846), 15–23, 28–29; Moisés González Navarro, *Anatomía del poder político en México, 1847–1853* (México, 1979), 216–20.

29. AGEO Diversos Históricos 1853, Luis Marguía to Director General of State Revenues, Zaachila, 3 February 1853.

30. Morales, *Memoria,* 3–5.

31. Matías Romero, *El Estado de Oaxaca* (Barcelona, 1886), 68–84; Alfonso Luis Velasco, *Geografía y estadística de la república mexicana: Geografía y estadística del Estado de Oaxaca* (México, 1895), 233; Cayetano Esteva, *Geografía histórica del Estado de Oaxaca* (Oaxaca, 1913), 25–29, 188–89. For the Guatemalan case, see David McCreery, *Development and the State in Reforma Guatemala, 1871–1885* (Athens, OH, 1983) and Julio C. Cambranes, *Coffee and Peasants in Guatemala: The Origins of the Modern Plantation Economy, 1853–1897* (Stockholm, 1985). Soconusco is dealt with in Daniela Spenser, "Soconusco: The Formation of a Coffee Economy in Chiapas," in Thomas Benjamin and William McNellie, eds., *Other Mexicos: Essays on Regional Mexican History, 1876–1911* (Albuquerque, 1984), 124–43. See also Marco Palacios, *Coffee in Colombia, 1850–1970: An Economic, Social, and Political History* (Cambridge, Eng., 1980).

32. Allen Wells, *Yucatan's Gilded Age: Haciendas, Henequen, and International Harvester, 1860–1915* (Albuquerque, 1985); Romero, *El Estado de Oaxaca,* 100–105.

33. Romero, *El Estado de Oaxaca,* 82, 109. Toward the end of the nineteenth century, coffee production developed on private estates (*fincas*) in the department of Pochutla. The rebellion there in 1892 arose from finca encroachments on village land. Small groups of merchants and landowners (several of them Spanish) dominated the coffee and cotton trades of Jamiltepec. In the Mije district of Juquila, two coffee haciendas were formed, one of them the Hacienda Cafetal Guerrero, constituted in October 1881. Manuel Martínez Gracida, *Cuadro sinóptico de los pueblos, haciendas y ranchos del estado libre y soberano de Oaxaca* (Oaxaca, 1883), a two-volume addition to the State Governor's Report, vol. 1, Juquila, n.p. Esteva, *Geografía historica del Estado de Oaxaco*, 188–89.

34. See especially Leticia Reina, ed., *Historia de la cuestión agraria mexicana: Estado de Oaxaca,* 2 vols. (México, 1988), 1:240–46.

35. For comments from differing perspectives, see T. G. Powell, *El liberalismo y el campesinado en el Centro de México (1850–1870)* (México, 1974), 12–17; François-Xavier Guerra, *Le Mexique: De l'Ancien Régime à la Révolution,* 2 vols. (Paris, 1985), 1:345, 2:74–75; John Tutino, *From Insurrection to Revolution in Mexico: Social Bases of Agrarian Violence, 1750–1940* (Princeton, 1986), 243–47.

36. AGEO Gobernación 1823, Juan Regueras to Antonio de León, Tamazola, 24 March 1823; Laureano Romero to León, no. 300, Tehuantepec, 3 May 1823; Santos de Vera to León, Miahuatlán, 6 September 1823. AGEO Gobernación 1825, Governor Morales to Comandante General de Armas, Oaxaca . . . 1825. López Ortigoza, *Memoria* (1831), 22. See Josefina Z. Vázquez, "La crísis y los partidos políticos, 1833–1846," in Annino, ed., *America Latina,* 2:557–72.

37. AGEO Fondo Especial Benito Juárez, leg. 10/13788, *Reglamento de la Guardia Nacional,* Oaxaca, 29 September 1848. See also G. P. C. Thomson, "Bulwarks of Patriotic Liberalism: The National Guard, Philanthropic Corporations and Patriotic Juntas in Mexico, 1847–188," *Journal of Latin American Studies* 22 (Feb. 1990): 31–68.

38. López Ortigoza, *Memoria,* 21.

39. In 1804, Oaxaca contributed 188,560 pesos of the total tribute revenue of New Spain, which came to 1,571,513 pesos. AGN Tributos 43, Expediente sobre la conversión de medio tributarios en enteros.

40. AGEO Gobernación 1823, Pochutla, 4 April 1823; Miahuatlán, 19 April 1823.

41. AGEO Tesorería 1844, State Secretary to Secretary of the Chamber of Deputies, Oaxaca, 9 September 1848.

42. Juárez, *Exposición* . . . 2 July 1848 (Oaxaca, 1848), 11–12, no. 6; Juárez, *Exposición* . . . 2 July 1852 (Oaxaca, 1852), 25–28; AGEO Diversos Históricos 1853, José Cristóbal Bolaños to Department Treasury, Oaxaca, 7 October 1853; *Colección de leyes y decretos del estado libre de Oaxaca* (Oaxaca, 1851), 207–18, 434–35. The law of 13 March 1825 defined the attributes of the subprefects (in succession to the alcaldes mayores and *corregidores*).

4

State Enterprise, Work, and Workers in Mexico: The Case of the Tobacco Monopoly, 1765–1850

SUSAN DEANS-SMITH

The period between 1765 and 1850 witnessed the rise and fall of the Bourbon state in Mexico, followed by the tortuous process of building Mexico's independent state. In many ways the tobacco industry, monopolized by both states, provides a fiscal mirror that reflects the fortunes and misfortunes of this state building. It is through the perspective of this state-managed industry that I will examine several issues that have relevance beyond the monopoly itself, issues regarding workers, work, and the state as entrepreneur.

By the 1790s, Mexico's royal tobacco monopoly was one of the largest organized industries in the colony (along with silver mining and textiles) and employed almost 20,000 persons. Managed by royal bureaucrats, it was vertically integrated: production and supply of tobacco leaf were regulated through contracts that determined who produced tobacco, how much was produced, the prices paid for it, and where it was to be grown. Tobacco production was restricted to one specific area in southeastern Mexico: the two small towns of Orizaba and Córdoba in what is now the state of Veracruz. Tobacco was made into cigarettes and cigars in six state-managed tobacco manufactories, the largest of which was in Mexico City, the colony's political and commercial capital.[1] Monopoly goods were marketed through government-licensed stores throughout Mexico. Private trading and manufacture of tobacco goods became illegal. Compliance was enforced by the monopoly's military corps, although contraband trade of tobacco was never eliminated. Tobacco revenues were second only to the silver tithe as a source of government income, averaging between 3 million and 4 million pesos. At their peak, they accounted for almost one-fifth of total state revenues. Despite stable demand, by 1805 problems in production and distribution of cigars and cigarettes demanded resolution. These problems were eclipsed, however, by the Hidalgo rebellion of 1810.

The tobacco monopoly survived both the formal abolition of monopolies set out in the Constitution of 1812 and the economic rhetoric of Mexican liberals, largely because of its track record as a revenue producer. Its structure and the state's role as manager of the monopoly, however, were redefined.[2] The unstable financial and political context of the 1820s and 1830s resulted in an ambivalent response to the tobacco monopoly, which was repeatedly abolished and reestablished. Ultimately, the monopoly proved to be a fiscal Humpty Dumpty, which the Mexican state never quite succeeded in putting together again. Although production of leaf for the most part remained a state monopoly nationwide, each state chose whether or not to monopolize its own manufacture of cigars and cigarettes. Thus, the manufacturing sector of the tobacco industry after 1821 consisted of a mixture of private and public manufactories.

It is not possible to examine all of the monopoly's operations in this essay. Because of the central importance of cigar and cigarette manufacture—which accounted for an average of 98 percent of total annual revenues—I have chosen the tobacco manufactories as a case study. I concentrate on the largest monopoly manufactory, located in Mexico City. The discussion that follows is organized around four questions. First, what was the state's role as entrepreneur and manager of the tobacco industry, and what were the forces that shaped the state's manufactory policies between 1765 and 1850? Because of the dominance of manual labor in the manufacture of cigars and cigarettes, one of those forces was labor. So my second question is what was the state's policy as employer of the tobacco workers? Third, how did the tobacco manufactory workers react to the work regime that the monopoly bureaucrats attempted to impose on them? Fourth, what role did the state play in shaping the strategies and actions of the manufactory workers?

I make two basic arguments. First, bureaucratic management proved responsive to problems in monopoly operations, but the contradictions inherent in Bourbon imperial policies undermined any sustained development. In the first half of the nineteenth century, the difficulties experienced by central government and the reorganization of Mexico's fiscal structure removed the possibility of direct management by the Mexican state. Fiscal conservatism rather than economic development dominated monopoly management policies after the 1790s and perhaps even those of the joint-stock companies in the 1830s and 1840s that rented the monopoly from the state. Second, as a result of the Bourbon monopolization of tobacco manufacture, workers found themselves subject to a new work regime. The state tobacco manufactory became a site of many contestations. Despite reforms the tobacco workers managed to define and defend their interests and to shape work in the manufactories to satisfy their own needs. The state-labor relations of the period support an argument recently made by Michael Seidman that "an analysis of resistance contributes to an understanding of a key function of the state in industrial societies and to the conclusion that one of the most vital functions of the state is to make workers work."[3] Based on the evidence presented in this essay, that function is not only relevant in industrial societies but in preindustrial and industrializing economies as well.

The Establishment of the State Tobacco Manufactories

The responsibility for the creation of the royal tobacco manufactories lay with the visitor-general to Mexico, José de Gálvez, who carried orders to establish them on the model of the Seville manufactory in Spain. The early economic performance of the manufactories convinced Gálvez of the wisdom of the royal mandate despite protests from the first director-general, José de Espinosa, and Viceroy Marqués de Croix, both of whom shared a mutual antipathy for Gálvez—and from the private tobacconists. The visitor-general remained firmly convinced of the social and economic utility of the manufactories for both Mexico and Spain. Located in important urban centers—Guadalajara, Mexico City, Puebla, Oaxaca, Orizaba, and Querétaro—they would provide employment for the urban poor, especially poor working women. In addition, production of cigars and cigarettes demanded high-quality paper to be supplied by paper mills in Spain, thus creating employment for Spanish workers.

The directorate-general opted for a slow phase-out of the private tobacco stores—which took almost fifteen years. Consequently, the colonial state did not fully control the tobacco industry until 1779. By that time monopoly profits stood at 2.5 million pesos, approximately 93 percent of which came from sales of cigars and cigarettes. This share increased to an average of 98 percent as the century wore on and focused considerable attention on the management of the manufactories and their work force. Between 1780 and 1821, three concerns dominated policy formation: levels of profit, worker discipline and efficiency, and supplies of paper to the manufactories.

The Question of Profitability

Given that 1779 saw the final closure of all private tobacco shops, it appears odd at first that in the very same year the director-general, Phelipe de Hierro, proposed the shutdown of the state manufactories. On closer examination, however, it is evident that he based his proposal on the perceived impact that recent price increases of leaf tobacco would have on monopoly profits. Increases were implemented in 1777 and again in 1779, on the crown's orders, largely to help pay for Spain's entry into the war of American independence. The price of leaf tobacco per pound increased from 6 and 7 reales in 1777 to eight reales in 1778 and to ten reales in 1780 (a 25 percent to 40 percent increase). The result is interesting both in its ramifications for state manufacture and as an insight into the rationale for the manufactories' existence. What the manufactory profits—as calculated by the monopoly accountants—measured was neither a rate of return nor a net profit calculation but more like an assessment of the opportunity cost of manufacture. Of the two options available to the colonial state—to monopolize sale of leaf but leave manufacture to the private sector or to monopolize both sale of leaf and manufacture—the latter proved to be the most profitable in the early experimental manufactories. When the sale price of leaf increased, however (according to royal mandate, not the market), the margin narrowed between the revenue gained through manufacture of tobacco products and that which would result from the sale of an equivalent amount of leaf tobacco used to produce a year's worth of goods. The early "profits" of the manufactories set the yardstick for continuous assessment of their economic performance by successive directors-general. Not surprisingly, as such "profits" began to show a decline, the fiscal attractiveness of manufacture decreased. For Hierro and eventually for the most ambitious of all directors-general, Silvestre Díaz de la Vega, it made sense to abandon manufacture with its attendant costs of management, production, and labor problems, and to concentrate on the monopolization of marketing raw leaf and the taxation of private cigar and cigarette manufacturers.[4]

The crown did not take Hierro's advice to abolish the manufactories, largely as the result of disagreements over what constituted "poor" profits and opposition from the accountant-general and the viceroy. As a result, the director-general instituted measures to save on the costs of production to close the perceived gap between the increasing sale value of leaf tobacco and that of manufactured cigars and cigarettes. There was a year or so of experimental production, the *nuevas labores*, which resulted in thinner cigars and cigarettes and fewer per packet. In addition, the number of workers was increased in order to expand total output as rapidly as possible.[5] Most consumers were disgusted with the new product, and the directorate-general received reports of declining consumption in some areas.[6] The nuevas labores were abandoned, although the reduction in the number of cigarettes per packet remained in force. Emphasis was placed on attempts to rationalize the work force to improve quality, reduce waste, reduce the costs of labor, and begin saving in the manufacturing process.[7]

To Work or Not to Work?

In 1792 a new administrator of the Mexico City manufactory was appointed, the reform-minded Miguel Puchet. Armed with proposals to improve worker discipline and production, Puchet argued vigorously for a reduction in the number of workers. The reduction would permit better supervision of work quality and better enforcement of rules designed to encourage regular attendance. Initially, Puchet's proposals received ambiguous support from the crown. One explanation may lie in the Bourbons' political sensitivities during the early 1790s both in Spain and in the colonies.[8] In 1792 considerable attention was paid to reports of public protests against the tobacco monopolies in the Philippines and Venezuela, and the crown considered the idea of abolishing the tobacco monopolies throughout Spanish America, although nothing came of these deliberations. It was not until 1795—a year after the Mexico City tobacco manufactory workers engaged in the Paper Riot, the largest protest against "unjust" reforms in the work place—that the directorate-general received orders from Spain to reduce the "excessive" number of workers concentrated in one place. Two years after his recommendations, Puchet received the support he had sought for policies intended to improve worker discipline and management of monopoly materials.[9]

In 1797 Puchet's plans to reduce the numbers of workers in the Mexico City manufactory, combined with the royal order to carry out such a policy, were implemented on the condition that, to avoid riots, they be carried out prudently and slowly. Vacant positions were not to be filled, and workers' relatives were no longer permitted entry to the manufactory. A further order of 17 February 1798 decreed that the most recently hired workers be dismissed. The workers who remained found themselves subject to new manufactory regulations, especially those governing worker absenteeism. Any workers absent for eight days or more without a legitimate excuse (generally defined as illness) was dismissed immediately and forbidden to work in any of the other tobacco manufactories. Puchet's reforms, particularly the reduction of worker numbers, were successful. With some pride the director-general commented that the policy of reduction had been carried out prudently, skillfully, and without the slightest sign of trouble.[10] As of 6 September 1797, the Mexico City manufactory employed 8,976 workers of both sexes (including children); by 31 October 1798, 5,007 remained employed in the manufactory. In addition, one of the proposals put forth to enforce manufactory discipline was to employ only women in the manufactories, particularly as cigarette rollers. The policy—an interesting example of ways in which states may construct gender roles—was based on the perceived docility of women and their skill at the rolling tables. It was also based on the Bourbons' encouragement of women of low status to enter the work force to become part of a "productive population." As a result, cigarette rolling became increasingly identified as a "female" occupation. In 1794 approximately 43 percent (3,055) of the Mexico City manufactory work force was women; by 1809 that percentage had increased to 71 percent (3,833).[11]

Puchet's attempted reforms built on the reorganization of the workers' confraternity, the Concordia. The reorganization was designed to prevent embezzlement of the workers' weekly contributions of half a real and to reward regular attendance. Benefits from the Concordia increasingly depended upon a specified length of service. A minimum of eight years' service in the manufactory was required before a deceased workers' family could make a claim on his or her contributions to the Concordia. Only those workers who had continual service in the manufactory for a calendar year were eligible for other benefits, such as monetary payments during times of illness and loans to cover costs of marriages and baptisms. But even after Puchet successfully engineered the reduction of the Mexico City work force between 1795 and 1798, he continued to complain about problems with discipline. In the long run, the attempts to improve worker discipline and regular attendance met with mixed results.

The Problem with Paper

Spain's incessant wars in the late eighteenth century influenced monopoly policy, not simply because the crown constantly urged the directorate-general to increase revenues to contribute to defense costs, but also because the Mexican tobacco manufactories depended upon paper supplies from

Spain and were therefore subject to breakdown during times of international conflict. Such interruptions in paper supplies threatened the level of the manufactories' output and created the possibility of their temporary closure. The supply of paper and the "efficiency" of its use by workers in the manufacturing process provide a clear example of conflicting local and imperial objectives that affected formulation of monopoly policy by the royal bureaucrats. The reform that provoked the workers' riot in 1794 aimed at more rational and careful use of paper by the workers to avoid waste. It sought to abolish the putting-out practice of manufactory production, whereby the cigarette rollers received paper each evening to prepare at home ready for the next day's production. A singular problem with this practice was that it prevented maximum control over the supply of a critical raw material. Workers routinely appropriated the cigarette paper and replaced it with inferior paper. The appropriated paper was then sold, bartered, or used to produce contraband cigarettes. More efficient use of the paper supplies and increased uniformity of the final product could only be achieved if monopoly administrators eliminated the customary practice of preparation of paper tubes in the workers' homes.

Two main considerations led to the reform's revocation. The first, the economic consideration, focused on the projected long-term effects on levels of output. The idea of employing even more workers to prepare the paper separately from the cigarette rollers was never seriously considered. The burden of reform would be borne most heavily by the cigarette rollers, who would spend part of their work day on paper preparation before they could even begin on their daily work quotas or *tareas*. The result would be fewer cigarettes produced per worker per day and a reduced daily income for the workers, especially since the manufactory administrator was not willing to approve a significantly lengthened work day. The second consideration related to the political implications of the reform and of the riot that it provoked. Both considerations combined to persuade monopoly managers to withdraw the reform measures. After 1794 no other attempts were made by the Bourbon managers to implement significant reforms in the organization of production in the manufactories.

Under the circumstances, the abolition of the reform made sense, but it was a costly decision. Supply of paper became increasingly burdensome and expensive for the monopoly. Severe shortages occurred, particularly after 1796 when shipments were temporarily suspended. After thirty-one years of reasonably stable supplies of paper at low prices, the war with England created havoc. The implications were far-reaching and left the directorate-general little choice but to buy paper wherever it could, generally at inflated prices, and to stockpile supplies. Workers experienced shortened work weeks on several occasions, cigarette output declined, and inventory stocks compensated for reduced production.

Stockpiling provided a solution to the problem of paper supplies. As a result, however, paper costs increased dramatically. Monopoly expenditure on paper ranged between 20,000 and 200,000 pesos annually between 1768 and 1796 (between 0.4 percent and 5 percent of total costs). By 1797, paper expenditure jumped to 454,601 pesos (12 percent of total costs), and by 1800 1,022,374 pesos were paid out (25 percent of total costs) to stockpile supplies. Prices paid for a ream of paper in the 1760s ranged between 3 and 5 pesos. Between 1797 and 1809, scarcity and speculation by local merchants forced prices of paper up to anywhere between 8 pesos and 20 pesos per ream.[12] Indeed, the director-general reported that merchants commissioned by the monopoly to purchase stocks of paper received orders not to reveal the true identity of the buyer (the king), arguing that if his identity were known, sellers would double the price on principle.[13]

The idea of removing the problem by establishing domestic paper mills did not escape the directorate-general. There was a brief investigation as to whether paper mills already existed and whether they could be used to provide domestic supplies of paper. None were currently in operation, and those that existed in the 1740s produced an inferior grade of paper unsuitable for cigarette production. The declaration of peace in 1802 served to forestall any further discussion of domestic production of paper. By this time, support for continued paper manufacture in Spain (Valencia and Barcelona primarily) by the treasury and the Spanish paper workers would undoubtedly have forestalled any attempts to set up paper mills in Mexico. Instead, stockpiling continued using Mexican merchants.

Another short-term adjustment made by the directorate-general focused on shifting the emphasis of production from cigarettes to cigars—the logic being, of course, that cigars needed paper only for packaging. The ratio of cigars to cigarettes sold is suggestive of this shift even as the number of cigarettes per packet in each class changed over the decades: 1773–76, 1:50; 1792–99, 1:40; 1800–1806, 1:26. A new class of cigars (No. 16s, that is, sixteen cigars per packet for half a real) was added in 1800. In contrast to cigarettes, which increased in price three times between 1778 and 1800 (due to reductions in the number of cigarettes per packet for a half real for the most popular class), the price of a packet of cigars (irrespective of class) remained the same after 1778. Even so, cigarettes constituted the most popular product and continued to provide the lion's share of tobacco revenues.[14] The supply of paper to the manufactories continued to pose a serious problem for monopoly output, one that remained unresolved even after paper mills were built in Mexico in the 1820s.

The late 1790s saw the highest revenues produced after the monopoly gained control of the domestic market in 1780. Total revenues reached 7,660,349 pesos and 8,251,574 pesos (in current pesos) in 1797 and 1798 respectively, creating the illusion that the potential of the monopoly was almost limitless. As a result of decisions taken to ensure provision of paper to the manufactories through stockpiling, and to rebuild inventories, costs rose. The effects were painfully evident in the following year, 1799, when revenues dropped from the high of 8 million to 7.5 million. Consequently, the directorate-general received new orders from Spain to prevent further reductions and to increase tobacco revenues.

Consternation caused by the protest of 1794, the discovery three years later of yet another planned uprising by some cigarette rollers to destroy tobacco stocks, further reports of falling manufactory "profits," and inadequate supplies of cigars and cigarettes all served to concentrate attention once again on the function and profitability of the manufactories.[15]

The decision on the fate of the manufactories did not lie solely with the directorate-general, very much to the chagrin of the director-general, Díaz de la Vega. Originally, one distinctive characteristic of the monopoly was its autonomy vis-à-vis the Real Hacienda and Tribunal de Cuentas. This autonomy did not survive ministerial reorganization after Gálvez's death, as the Real Tribunal y Audiencia de la Contaduría Mayor de Cuentas de México and the Tesorería General de Exército y Real Hacienda increasingly intervened in monopoly policy formation. The protracted nature of the discussions that ensued may be explained in part by the director-general's antagonism toward attacks on the independence of the monopoly's jurisdiction and decision making.[16] Eventually, the director-general recommended the elimination of all of the tobacco manufactories with the exception of the one in Mexico City. Not surprisingly, the treasury ministers, influenced by the prospect of risking 3.5 million pesos revenue (the average profit since the 1780s) disagreed with the director-general and insisted on cautious management. They discounted the argument of declining "profits" and emphasized that manufactured products were the key to monopoly revenues. More pragmatically, they argued that a return to private enterprise could not guarantee the same revenue and raised many problems.[17]

In response to the political threat posed by the large number of workers in the Mexico City manufactory—one of the arguments used to justify the closure of the manufacturing sector—the ministers of the Real Tribunal y Audiencia de la Contaduría Mayor de Cuentas de México, in viewing the workers' record of behavior until 1796, argued that the workers' motive was simply to express dissatisfaction with rulings perceived to be unfair and prejudicial to their interests. None of the outbursts was directed against the king or royal government. In a veiled attack against the director-general and an attempt to downplay the potential threat posed by the workers located in the heart of Mexico City, they shifted the focus away from the workers and onto the question of the quality of manufactory administration, arguing that with better management the workers' protests could have been avoided.[18]

By 1804, a consensus existed on the advantages of a further reduction of the work force of the Mexico City manufactory and the establishment of new, smaller manufactories. The monopoly accountant-general advised that a new state manufactory in Mexico City, which remained half-built, should be completed. Half a million pesos had already been invested in the construction, begun in 1777. In addition, the viceroy approved the establishment of four new manufactories, although only one, in the tiny, quiet villa of Guadalupe near Mexico City, was built. It opened its doors to workers in 1800. Further reorganizations of workers occurred, and the manufactories in Querétaro and Guadalupe absorbed the majority of the workers let go from the Mexico City manufactory, although Mexico City remained the largest manufactory. By 1810, the number of workers employed in the Querétaro and Mexico City manufactories totaled 3,706 and 5,437 respectively, almost three-quarters of the total manufactory work force. The newly completed state tobacco manufactory in Mexico City began operations in May 1807—an affirmation not so much of the state's commitment to manufacture and economic development as of its lack of fiscal alternatives.

Unwilling to accept the risk of reduced revenues—a real possibility if manufacture was returned to the private sector—and fearful of worker unrest in response to reorganization, the Bourbons imposed conservative policies. Despite the reformist tendencies of the monopoly bureaucrats, the manufactories' structure remained fundamentally unchanged under Bourbon management. That several experiments were made with various machines to improve the cutting of paper and shredding of tobacco and that the managers concluded they did not result in savings suggest that the relative cost of manufactory labor also acted as a deterrent to innovation in the work place.

What remained unresolved and of some concern to manufactory administrators, not just in Mexico City but in the other five manufactories as well, was the productive capacity of the manufactories and their ability to increase supplies of tobacco products. The implications of the royal order that prevented an excessive concentration of workers in one place meant in practical terms that any major increase in production could only be achieved by setting up new manufactories. Yet the treasury ministers and the *fiscal de hacienda* also argued against short-term reductions in the level of monopoly revenues until newly established manufactories could recoup their set-up costs. The directorate-general was faced with the dilemma of maintaining revenues while production costs increased.

In fiscal terms, the Bourbons took over an industry that had experienced an increase in profits from 1 million to 4 million pesos and an increase in the volume of cigarette production from 40 million to 120 million packets. The monopoly gradually abolished many of the perquisites ("bonuses" for chocolate) traditionally received by cigarette and cigar rollers during the 1780s and 1790s and, at the same time, introduced fines to penalize workers who wasted tobacco or paper. The monopoly proved to be at its least paternal in the gradual reduction of piecework rates for the cigarette rollers during the 1790s. Workers' wages remained virtually flat from the late eighteenth century to the 1840s.[19] In this respect at least, the directorate-general's behavior exhibited no marked differences from that of private entrepreneurs who sought to improve their profits.

The monopoly operations offer yet another example of an industry in late colonial Mexico that was based on extensive rather than intensive growth. The absence of any growth in productivity implied that in the long run its costs and relative prices would rise.[20] There is also evidence that costs were not the only problem: by the beginning of the nineteenth century, the capacity of the tobacco planters to grow sufficient supplies of leaf tobacco was in question, and shortages in supplies of cigars and cigarettes became more common due to distribution problems.[21] The quality of the products manufactured in the state tobacco manufactories was also still in question. In 1817 Díaz de la Vega's successor, Carlos López, lamented the low quality of manufactory cigars and cigarettes, which resulted in constant losses to the monopoly as consumers sought out contraband products.[22] Even if Mexico's transition to political independence had been relatively free of the political and financial chaos that actually ensued, it seems that the new state apparatus would still have inherited a tobacco monopoly with serious problems of manufacture, supply, and distribution. With the advantage of hindsight, the growth rates bear this out. Between 1780 and 1798 net profits grew at an annual compound rate of 2.2 percent; between 1799 and 1809, they showed very little growth (a rate of 0.4 percent). Conversely, costs of production grew at an annual compound rate of 1.7 percent between 1780 and 1798 that increased to 1.9 percent between 1799 and 1809.

The Fate of the Tobacco Manufactories, 1821–50

The raiding of the monopoly's treasury to help pay for royalist campaigns during the insurgency years of 1810–21, the instability of early republican Mexico, and the republic's politicized economy virtually destroyed any hope of managing the monopoly along the same lines as the Bourbons had done.[23] One of the most significant changes between the Bourbon and republican states lay in the fiscal relationship between central government in Mexico City and the provincial state governments. As John TePaske has pointed out, the independence movement "destroyed the network which had joined Mexico City to the rest of New Spain, fiscal ties with the periphery that had made the system work for almost three centuries."[24] The result of such a breakdown in the traditional fiscal structure manifested itself in disappointingly low monopoly revenues as individual states claimed poverty or refused to send their portion of monopoly income to Mexico City. In 1824, as part of a federalist experiment, responsibility for marketing tobacco products was divided between the states and the national government. By 1829 the project was bankrupt. Unable to administer the monopoly directly because of the lack of financial and administrative resources, the Mexican state requested the participation of private investors formerly excluded under Bourbon management. These private investors, empresarios, assumed control of the monopoly in 1830.[25] By the 1830s the state withdrew from direct management of the monopoly, probably the most obvious and significant change in organization of the enterprise between 1765 and 1850.

The Empresa del Tabaco became the largest and the best organized of a number of joint-stock companies formed by private entrepreneurs to exploit exclusive rights to control the cultivation, manufacture, and distribution of tobacco products in Mexico.[26] When the empresarios took over management of the monopoly, each state remained free to choose whether to monopolize the manufacture of cigars and cigarettes or leave it to the private sector. The major exception was in Mexico City where the state monopoly kept its manufactory in operation as the National Manufactory of Cigars and Cigarettes.[27] By 1845 monopoly manufactories also operated in Guadalajara, Guanajuato, Orizaba, Querétaro, San Luis Potosí, and

Zacatecas.[28] As a consequence of such a change, the emphasis in monopoly policy seems to have shifted to the tobacco planters in Veracruz, and the production, sale, and distribution of leaf shifted to individual states. At this stage, little information exists on levels of production, revenues, costs, and profits of the monopoly or of the manufactories as managed by the empresarios on behalf of the Mexican state, but it is possible to sketch out some of the issues that shaped policy for the tobacco manufactories.[29]

The level of influence retained by the state over manufactory policy making is unclear. The empresarios replaced the Bourbon bureaucratic directorate, but some administrators and managers were apparently recruited from the old bureaucracy.[30] Whether the state demanded the same political peace as the Bourbons had in the eighteenth century, thus restricting the policy options available to the empresarios, is also unclear. Three indications suggest, however, that it was a consideration in manufactory policy formation, regardless of where the initiative came from. The first indication is the insistence by the Mexican state that the Mexico City manufactory remain in operation so as not to spark a massive protest by its employees. Second, in 1839 new manufactory regulations designed to improve efficiency and reduce costs provoked a worker protest and were temporarily suspended.[31] Third, attempts to introduce machinery imported from England into the Mexico City manufactory in 1846 met with an immediate and hostile response from the women workers, although it is not known whether or not the machinery was installed.[32] By all accounts, it seems that manual labor dominated the manufacture of cigars and cigarettes in both monopoly manufactories and private tobacco workshops for most of the nineteenth century.[33] Although there is no direct evidence regarding problems of work discipline among the tobacco workers during the 1830s and 1840s, employers in general complained of unreliable employees who lacked work discipline, and reports of delinquent apprentices being hauled before the Tribunal de Vagos were not uncommon.[34]

Although the Mexican state pursued policies of industrialization and modernization in Mexican manufacturing between 1800 and 1850 through such institutions as the Dirección General de Industria and the Banco de Avío, political independence did little to counteract an "institutional structure that discouraged productivity, innovation and inefficiency and, instead, rewarded political prowess.[35] The stifling effects of Spanish colonialism were replaced by the continued importance of merchant capital and the external sector and by the failure of Mexico to develop a national market.[36] As a result the empresarios' policy choices were as cautious as those of the Bourbons, and given the chaotic conditions of the free market, they preferred to put their investments in a regulated market.[37] The empresarios made some attempts to modernize the tobacco manufactories in the 1840s, although their efforts seem to have been confined to streamlining the work force along the same lines as Puchet had done in the 1790s, and they experienced similar opposition. The shareholders' insistence on modernizing management practices resulted in repeated confrontations as "innovations at the workplace provoked unrelenting hostility from the traditional bureaucrats, who now fervently prayed for the dissolution of the Empresa and a return to a government-administered monopoly."[38] Although the empresarios, unlike the Bourbon bureaucrats, were not subject to the restrictions of Spanish colonialism, they were not free of other pressures—from interest groups, including the government bureaucracy; from the instability of Mexico; from the financial machinations of successive Mexican governments; and from their own interests—all of which influenced policy formation. The actors may have changed, but the monopoly remained a site of contestation that increased in intensity after 1830. As a result, the organization of the tobacco manufactories as shaped by monopoly management may have been characterized more by continuity than change during the same period.[39]

In comparison to the tobacco manufactories, the paper industry benefited from the industrializing policies of the early nineteenth-century state as domestic paper mills were constructed in the 1820s and 1830s. The old problem of paper supplies may have been solved by the establishment of a domestic paper industry. However, a clause contained in monopoly manufactory regulations for 1848 prohibiting the substitution of inferior paper for cigarette paper in the manufactories suggests that the paper problem did not disappear completely.[40]

In the long term, the importance of the manufactories to monopoly revenues and an unwillingness to risk those revenues, combined with a quest for political order, focused attention on transforming the workers into a disciplined, skilled work force.

I now turn to state policies and projects designed to "make workers work."

State Policy and Manufactory Discipline, 1765–1850

Bourbon reform measures sought to increase the strength of the state and the prosperity of its subjects and in so doing provided the framework for state-worker relations. Appalled by what it perceived as the degeneration and immorality of Mexico's lower classes, the colonial state attempted to mold "productive" citizens. Both private and public life came under the scrutiny of the Bourbon reformers as drinking and gambling were regulated, the popular expression of religious practices was attacked, the guilds were attacked and the forces of law and order were expanded.[41] Included in these reform measures were the colonial state's attempts to encourage the entry of women (of low status, of course) into the work force, engaging in occupations "suitable" to their gender.[42] The tobacco manufactories provided a miniature version of the Bourbon project to reform and control the colonial populace. Within this context the directorate-general viewed the manufactories' role as a vehicle through which to create more than discipline and order: "the perfect school to instruct all who work there not only in their tasks but in all those qualities which make a civil man. . . . because in the manufactory every person lives subject to the voice which commands."[43] In the minds of the bureaucrats, then, good workers and obedient servants of the state were synonymous. Whether monopoly management succeeded in molding obedient employees is in question, but it is clear that the relations established between administrators and workers, for the most part, functioned quite well, especially when the absence of serious conflict between the bureaucratic managers and the tobacco workers is taken into account. Before the disruption of manufactory production because of the independence wars, there was not a single year in which cigars and cigarettes were not produced.

The tobacco manufactories were organized along capitalist lines, which created a division of labor based predominantly on free-wage labor. The system incorporated a combination of fixed daily wages for supervisory employees and piecework rates for the majority of the tobacco workers, most notably the cigarette and cigar rollers. Although the manufactories themselves were a response not to changing technologies or industrialization (indeed, manual labor dominated the work process), but to fiscal pressure, their organization and management created a series of problems typical of many early industrial establishments. Attempts at internal regulations and their daily enforcement depended upon the much wider problem of maintaining a regular, disciplined work force—no easy feat if one considers that at its peak almost 9,000 workers were employed in the Mexico City manufactory. It is a commonplace now that the concentration of large numbers of workers and their subjection to work discipline "was one of the most difficult problems encountered by early factory masters."[44] The Mexico City tobacco workers proved to be no exception despite manufactory regulations that were intended to inculcate habits of regular, diligent work, sobriety, and obedience, and despite attempts to construct paternalist foundations for management-worker relations. Three broad groups of rules which the administration imposed to improve organization and discipline may be identified as follows: those that related to achieving a reliable, organized work environment by penalizing late arrival, failure to register with the guards, theft of monopoly goods, and inefficient use of raw materials; those that mandated obedience and regulated worker-supervisor relations; those that encouraged good morals and civil behavior by punishing drunken or offensive behavior, gambling, card playing, and other "scandalous" behavior. All of these infractions carried gradations of punishment which ranged from a stint in the manufactory stocks, payment for materials wasted, and suspension from work to permanent prohibition from employment in any of the state tobacco manufactories.[45]

It may be argued that the agenda for molding productive citizens set out by the Bourbons was taken up by the Mexican state, particularly Mexican liberals, with the establishment of institutions such as the *Dirección General de Instrucción Pública*. The goals remained the same for the most part; if anything was different, it was the scope of the reforming projects. This modernizing project of the state included a technological education of the populace through the Lancasterian system (the monitorial system) to instill habits of disciplined work that would sustain the first stages of industrial development.[46] There was certainly continuity in the monopoly manufactory regulations issued in the 1840s, which constantly reiterated the need for *moralidad y buen orden* and were closely modeled on those compiled by the Bourbons.[47] Changes may have occurred in areas related to the state's attitudes towards women's participation in the work force. It is known that private opinion regarding the employment and training of women remained cautious at best, hostile at worst, and that the "goal of expanding women's work was not adopted as readily as the goal of educating them," partly because of widespread male unemployment. As the economic situation deteriorated, appeals for women to enter the work force diminished."[48] The rhetoric of the early republican state on the role of the working woman and how that role affected the composition of the work force and the construction of work identities has yet to be analyzed.

In summary, manufactory regulations transcended the limits of the work place and demanded reform of workers' morals and social mores, a reform that impinged upon the workers' wider culture and independence.[49] We may understand something of the state's attitudes and attempts to mold disciplined workers, but how successful was it in practice and how did the workers respond to such measures?

The Tobacco Manufactory Workers—Compromise and Conflict

The abolition of the tobacco shops took almost fifteen years to complete, giving the workers time to adjust to the reorganization. Those individuals affected were assured of alternative employment in the manufactories. As a result, workers were incorporated as collaborators in the establishment of the manufactories and acquired a vested interest in the monopoly's existence. There was, then, a mutuality of interest, but a mutuality that was constantly challenged and renegotiated with costs to both sides. Richard Price argues: "Men and women finding themselves in certain social relationships which involve authority and obedience are constantly struggling over the limits, the frontiers at which obedience begins and ends. It is in the continual search from both sides for a better bargain that the dynamic of the labour process in labour's history can be seen to lie."[50] The search for the "better bargain" brings me now to a consideration of the workers' concerns and actions, how they set about defending them, and with what success.[51]

In the long term, the Bourbon bureaucrats' attempts to discipline the manufactory workers met with mixed results. The manufactory work rooms became a battleground between two opposing sets of ideals—one that demanded efficient work habits, the other predicated on self-preservation and control over disposal of time and materials. The objectives of the tobacco workers' actions, however, were not to challenge the monopoly or the state—the source of their security—but to defend what they perceived to be their rights, which included a particular way of life, the very one the colonial state attempted to extinguish. In the analysis that follows, most of the evidence is drawn from the late eighteenth century, and my argument is more speculative for the period 1821 to 1850.

The tobacco workers used three main methods to exert pressure and present their demands: petition to manufactory authorities, manipulation and disobedience, and "bargaining by riot." The most common method used by workers to defend their interests was the one established by the state: the submission of petitions, a procedure that promoted negotiation. Complaints came from individuals and specific *cuerpos* of workers, such as cigarette rollers, packers, and box sealers. More rarely they came as a generalized response that cut across cuerpos, gender, and the supervisor-worker dichotomy. Worker petitions reveal five broad categories that brought the workers into conflict with the monopoly: management of time and work discipline; fraud and abuse of power by supervisory staff (including intimidation and physical abuse); wage levels; violation of customary practices (such as nonmonetary perquisites and access to raw materials); and hiring practices (including both unfair dismissal and securing positions for relatives).[52] Indeed, the Mexico City manufactory administrator complained of the pressure brought about by the daily flood of complaints and petitions. The workers' grievances concentrated on "maligning others of better merit or me . . . because I refuse to accede to their requests."[53] In general, the concerns of the tobacco workers in the late eighteenth century focused on control of time and on the number of new workers hired; wages and wage levels did not stand out as an excessive problem. There is insufficient evidence to argue how this changed in the 1830s and 1840s, but my impression is that the emphasis shifted to wage levels and protection of jobs. I cannot illustrate each type of grievance or action here, but the example that follows demonstrates workers' actions and engagement with monopoly management.

The imposition of work discipline based on manufactory regulations proved difficult to enforce, as previously argued. Manufactory regulations give the impression of an ordered and uniform work day, yet practice suggests something rather different. The time constraints on workers remained remarkably flexible, largely because piecework was easily manipulated by some of the workers. The manufactory administrator commented on the problems of enforcing regular work habits "since the workers have always been able to come and go from their work as they please."[54] The problem was not that workers did not go to work each day but that they often worked only for half a day and left at noon having completed only a proportion of their *tareas.* The manufactory administrator reported that on one day about 4,900 tareas were distributed based on the number of workers listed. But no more than 3,600 were completed, leaving 1,300 unfinished due to "the continuous and voluntary lack of attendance by workers on a regular basis."[55] By the beginning of the nineteenth century the director-general still complained that levels of production remained uncertain because of discretionary attendance by some of the workers.[56] One must bear in mind, however, that these are simply observations that say nothing about the frequency of worker absenteeism, which was undoubtedly less than bureaucratic reports would indicate, given the volume of cigarette production annually.[57]

Discretionary movement in and out of the work place, made possible by piecework, was undoubtedly a response to the changing needs of household economies and individual workers alike. Despite the general regularity of manufactory work, declining wages and the potential for layoffs exacerbated uncertainty about daily survival and created imperatives that conflicted with those of the monopoly, which demanded regular attendance and careful work habits. As Richard Whipp has argued, in constructions of time and work "the emphasis is on uncertain outcomes. Timing becomes crucial in the experience of work. . . . The points of intersection between an individual's or family's life cycle with wider economic movements become vital in understanding how people experience work in a total sense."[58]

That resolutions made by the monopoly were not always in favor of the workers' petitions and that the workers did not perpetually take to the streets suggest a general acceptance of the authority that made these decisions and its legitimate right to do so. There were limits to compromise, however, that resulted in collective protest by the tobacco workers, called "bargaining by riot."[59]

Between 1765 and 1850 collective protest (defined as walkouts and mass marches into the streets) by the tobacco manufactory workers occurred in 1780, 1782, 1794, 1839, and 1842. All were provoked by acts that were deemed to be arbitrary, threatened the workers' standard of living and income, or violated customary practices, such as the preparation of paper at home. As far as I know, all were shortlived—action and resolution occurring within a few hours—although previous planning was evident in at least one of the protests, that of the 1794 Paper Riot, which contained elements of strike action. In the case of the 1794 riot, workers submitted petitions in the days following the announcement of the reform, but to no avail. The result: an estimated 1,400 men and women workers from the Mexico City tobacco manufactory marched on the viceregal palace to protest. The workers were eventually pacified by troops and local priests and returned to their work at the tobacco-rolling tables. Preparation of paper at home permitted workers time to produce their quotas on a daily basis and earn the daily rate, and it provided them with a nonmonetary item that could be used to supplement their income when necessary, rather like the *partido* system among silver miners. The collective action taken suggests the workers' assessment that the reform would have a disastrous impact upon their income.

It would be a crude oversimplification, indeed misrepresentation, to argue that the tobacco workers' protest of 1794 prevented a change in the organization of production that might have improved the use of paper in the production process. In all likelihood, after a few months of the new system, with or without worker protest, the old method of paper preparation would have been reestablished to avoid a fall in cigarette production. There are three important considerations here. First, the resolution was ostensibly in the workers' favor—affirming the justice of the investigation and resolving the uncertainties created by the intended reforms. Second, the colonial state remained unwilling to undertake economic innovations at the price of social peace. Third, the 1794 protest illustrates quite clearly the interrelationship between production and politics as shortages of paper (a consequence of Spanish colonial policy) were transformed into a problem on the workshop floor to which workers reacted with violence.

Worker protests did not stop with the changing of the political regime. Indeed, there appears to be considerable continuity in issues and strategies. In 1839, 5,000 workers employed in the Mexico City manufactory rioted over rumors that José Azcúnaga, a new administrator hired by the Empresa del Tabaco, intended to fire half the labor force. The empresa had to rehire José Mariano Campos, the manager of the Mexico City manufactory, recruited from the state-managed monopoly. Campos had resigned in protest over the empresa's intention to reduce manufactory production from sixteen classes of cigarettes and cigars to three. To avoid continued conflict and work stoppages, Campos was restored to his position. Shortly after, however, the new work regulations were implemented. Campos thereupon resigned permanently.[60] The workers' reactions and fate are not known. In 1842 women tobacco workers protested against their payment of wages in copper and demanded either to be paid double or to be paid their usual wages in silver. The government ordered the riot to be repressed but—to show justice and to avoid a demonstration of violence against women—also ordered that force was not to be used. The following day the women received their wages in silver.[61]

Worker response to the manufactory regulations and policies ran the gamut from covert individual action to overt, collective action and protest in the face of orders or regulations perceived to be unjust. Operating within the framework of a moral economy, the workers made their petitions according to certain rights they claimed for themselves: to receive respect, not to be abused, to retain control over time and materials. In short they claimed the right to justice and, if necessary, the right to ensure that justice was administered. I commented earlier on the relative absence of overt, collective conflict between the monopoly and the tobacco workers between 1765 and 1850. The significance of such an absence is not that the tobacco workers were so hopelessly exploited or submissive, but that they found ways to accommodate their needs by manipulating the work regime without taking to the streets.[62]

The methods and strategies used by the tobacco workers raise the issue of "how the political contexts created by state authorities established the vocabularies and institutional forms that workers would develop to shape and represent their demands directed both to employers and to the state in the early industrial period."[63] I cannot speak to the question of vocabularies, an important consideration for future research, but I can make a few general points about how the wider political and specific work contexts shaped the workers' strategies and expectations.

The political sensitivities of the Bourbon and Mexican states provided a context that favored small compromises over large confrontations. The workers' penchant for complaint brings to mind a point made by E. P. Thompson in his discussion of the moral economy of the English crowd. Thompson argued that "this moral economy impinged very generally upon eighteenth century government and thought and did not only intrude at moments of disturbance."[64] In their management of the workers, the directorate-general and manufactory administrators constantly cast a wary eye over proposed new policies or regulations that could elicit protests, and they tried to gauge their responses to balance economic reform in the work place with its political fallout. Perhaps this is best illustrated through two examples. The first concerns the investigation of the misuse of Concordia funds in 1781. The beginning of the investigation coincided with Holy Week. The directorate-general argued that normally loans were advanced to the workers during the feast but that with the investigation in process, no advances should be made. The administrator countered this suggestion: "Knowing the character and way of thinking of these people . . . we will have a riot aimed at the directorate-general or the Royal Palace to request the loan."[65] For the administrator, the issue was not whether the action suggested was justified but how to avoid conflict. The loans were paid. The second example relates to one of the arguments made to keep the Mexico City tobacco manufactory open in the 1820s, the reasoning being that it was politically inadvisable to fire such a large number of workers. The English consul general Charles O'Gorman reported that all tobacco manufactories were closed down in 1821 but that "the immense Manufactory in this Capital is however to subsist, and no doubt will be maintained. . . . It would indeed, in a political, as well as financial point of view, have been highly injurious to have suddenly deprived about 4,000 men, women, and children of the subsistence they derived from the employment given in various ways by that Establishment."[66]

Potential conflict was also minimized through the deliberate emphasis on submission of petitions to the manufactory administration. The state thereby encouraged negotiation and compromise guided by its "unwritten constitution."[67] By recognizing workers' petitions the directorate-general legitimized them and thereby encouraged (not necessarily intentionally) the creation of a work order that sanctioned the declaration of grievances on both an individual and collective level. That the workers appeared to accept the denial of some of their petitions suggests they acknowledged the legitimacy and justice of the process.

Political relations between the manufactory administration and the tobacco workers were also shaped by the paternalist ethos the state attempted to create, at least under the Bourbons. This paternalism helped to channel and diffuse conflict on a daily basis. It was conveyed in the informal name given to the manufactory, the Casa del Rey (House of the King) and further supported by the workers' use of the term El Rey Padre (the Father-King) and their belief in the king as a just and merciful arbitrator.[68] Work conditions and organization reflected monopoly paternalism in several ways. During periods of reduced production of cigars and cigarettes, instead of laying off workers, the monopoly divided production quotas on a pro rata basis so that everyone could earn something. When it was necessary to close the manufactory for several days or weeks (which was very rare), the monopoly advanced loans to the workers.[69]

One of the major changes in the workers' lives was the ability to form associations on a scale impossible in their previous situations dispersed throughout Mexico City. At the local level, the lives of the tobacco workers were shaped through a variety of institutions and social relations that incorporated both work and home, through the occupational cuerpos within the manufactory, and through the Concordia. There is no evidence that the tobacco workers were organized within a guild before creation of the monopoly. The workers, on their own initiative, requested permission to organize a confraternity, the Concordia, which provided rudimentary social insurance against illness and death. The colonial state agreed to its establishment and approved its regulations. In so doing, it increased the dependence of workers upon the monopoly if they were to benefit from their weekly monetary contributions. However, the Concordia simultaneously became the workers' symbol of independence and security, an unanticipated outcome. Although the Concordia represented the potential for collective action by the workers and a wider class identity, the structure and composition of the work force within the manufactory counteracted such potential. The tobacco workers remained divided according to their respective task-related cuerpos and by status, family, ethnicity, income, and gender. Such a grid of associations enabled the workers to act collectively yet contributed to social cleavages among them. Historians who have argued that the reorganization of the private tobacco shops transformed the tobacco shop owners and their workers into a homogeneous work force of wage earners have overstated the case.[70] Their actions resemble the phenomenon Alf Lüdtke has identified as *eigensinn* (observed in German factory workers) in which the work experience and domestic situation promote a sense of collective identity and a corresponding sense of individualism.[71]

How the change in manufactory management and a kingless polity influenced workers' strategies and organizations in the 1830s and 1840s is open to question. There is no evidence, for example, that the Concordia survived the change of regime.[72] One may speculate that the courts began to play an increasing role in workers' lives through the Ministry of Justice and Ecclesiastical Affairs as the dominant locus of justice transmigrated from the king to the courts. As Frederick Shaw has argued regarding labor relations in general, although appeal to the courts came from both employer and employee, the courts did not sanction physical abuse of workers or the withholding of wages. Workers were not slow to seek legal protection from such abuses, and the very fact that "these cases appeared before the courts at all is proof that the aggrieved employees expected a fair hearing."[73] In 1841, encouraged by the government, Mexico City's wealthiest artisans formed the Junta de Fomento de Artesanos. The junta's objectives concerned educating workers, raising the moral level of the artisans through religion, and creating charitable institutions to protect artisans from need. Where the tobacco workers, as semiskilled workers, fit into this organization is not clear, and it may be that the junta acted as a cooptive organization in much the same way as the Concordia. Other institutions formed by the workers included the Junta Protectora de las Clases Menesterosas. According to one scholar it was the workers' initiative and their conflicts with the authorities, and not a benign, paternalist attitude of the authorities, that resulted in the formation of such organizations.[74]

A new forum through which workers presented their grievances was the press. The Junta de Fomento de Artesanos even published a weekly newspaper, the Seminario Artístico, although its contents stressed morality and education rather than incendiary denunciations of employers. In contrast: On 24 April 1846, the women workers of the Mexico City tobacco manufactory signed a protest against the proposed mechanization of the manufacture of cigarettes. They argued that it was unfair to benefit the few at the expense of the many, and that the cigars and cigarettes currently made by hand helped to support more than 30,000 needy families. If they were made redundant they would be unable to find other employment. What was different about this particular petition was that it was printed in a newspaper, *El Monitor,* for everyone to read.[75]

In a study of French workers Michael Sonenscher argued, "What changed in France between 1748 and 1848 was not so much the relationship between workers and employers, or the immediate circumstances in which production was carried out, as the identity of the public to which actors in conflicts appealed and the manner in which those appeals were couched. Instead of lawyers and magistrates, nineteenth-century workers and employers addressed other workers or employers and, increasingly, their own political intermediaries or representatives."[76] In the Mexican case for the same period, the workers appeared to place increasing emphasis upon the courts. What is comparable to the French case, however, is the new use of the press as a public forum in which workers articulated their demands to their employers and to other workers.

The state was confronted by a paradox: associations created to maintain loyalty to and dependence upon the monopoly could be used to challenge the state's mandates. To reestablish peace, the state acted in a concessionary manner but attempted, at the same time, to turn its concessions to the monopoly's advantage. Both actions resulted in compromise solutions that may have increased the state's control over the workers but also satisfied to some degree the demands made by the workers. What remains to be studied is how the manufactory workers' bargaining power was affected by the high levels of unemployment during the 1830s and 1840s; how the deteriorating situation of workers in general affected their relationship to the state, to employers, and to other workers; and how it influenced workers' strategies and the construction of class identities.

Conclusion

One distinguishing characteristic of state-owned or state-managed enterprises is that their policy choices often reflect priorities different from those of a private enterprise. Decisions normally made by the market for private enterprises are more often the result of a combination of political as well as economic decisions in the case of state-owned enterprises.[77] It is evident that the monopoly bureaucracy proved quite adept at the identification of problems and attempts to solve them and that it proved to be more efficient and perceptive at entrepreneurial management than has previously been acknowledged. But in the case of the state tobacco manufactories, it is equally evident that political priorities as well as the fiscal demands of Spanish colonialism restricted the choices available to bureaucratic managers who sought to increase monopoly revenues by modifying the original organization in any way. Although the evidence is fragmentary, I would also argue that political as well as fiscal concerns continued to influence policies formulated by the Mexican state and the empresarios between 1824 and 1850. During that period, the importance of the tobacco manufactories in the monopoly's operations declined as the decision whether to monopolize the manufacture of tobacco products was left up to the individual Mexican states. In the long run, however, the manufacturing sector faced what Ravi Ramamurti has termed a "bureaucratic" mode of behavior, characterized by a limited capacity to respond to changes and a high exit barrier.[78] Cautious management, not risk taking, characterized manufactory management under the Bourbons and, as far as I can tell, the management policies of the empresarios in the 1840s. Thus between 1765 and 1850, the organization of the manufacturing sector of the monopoly was characterized more by continuity than by change. (No major technical innovations were introduced during this period.)

Labor constituted a major element in policy decision making. It contributed to conservative management in the case of the Bourbons and probably in the Mexican state as well. The role of the state is clear in its attempts to create paternalist and cooptive relations with the tobacco workers and to provide institutions that channeled grievance and conflict. While measures to streamline production in the manufactories and to make "workers work" were partially successful, the tobacco workers managed to maintain some control over the conditions in the workplace and to negotiate for that "better bargain." Their ability to do so derived from their own initiatives as well as government sanction of organizations such as the Concordia and encouragement of the workers to present their grievances. The workers refashioned those institutions and used them to carry out actions often unintended by the government. Evidence for the workers' actions during the building of the Mexican state and the reorganization of the monopoly is sketchy. The few existing descriptions, however, suggest that the tobacco workers continued to use similar and different strategies to press for their interests and to protest unacceptable reforms. In the 1830s and 1840s, although the figure of the king as a just and merciful arbiter disappeared, the focus on justice and the right to justice remained as a framework that shaped the manufactory workers' actions, as did the workers' insistence that the state ought to act as a just arbiter between employers and workers.[78]

I have traced here some continuities in the state's projects to mold disciplined workers, whether the shaping of the "new man" of the Bourbons or of the Mexican liberals.[80] Much more research is required, however, to fully understand how "transformations of state structures, changes in economic structure and political discourse, new or preexisting networks of social relations" shape workers' actions, demands, organizations, and methods of representation.[81] One theme that has remained implicit in this essay is the question of gender in the work place and in relation to the state, and the most I can do is to point to its importance. Clearly, the Bourbons actively encouraged women to enter the work force, and such encouragement went beyond mere rhetoric. What is not clear is how the state's rhetoric and practice were affected by deteriorating conditions for workers in the face of high unemployment in the 1830s and 1840s. Finally, and related to the previous question, is the question of the construction of workers' identities and their conception of themselves and the work place, and how gender and state policies influenced this construction. Only when we have insight into such constructions will we have a better understanding of the daily lives and actions of the Mexican workers and their responses to the state and to one another.

Notes

Support for this research was provided by the Institute of Latin American Studies at the University of Texas at Austin from funds granted to the institute by the Andrew W. Mellon Foundation and by the National Endowment for the Humanities. This essay is a modified version of my article that appeared in *The Journal of Policy History,* 2, 1 (1990). Portions of the article are reprinted here by kind permission of the Pennsylvania State University Press.

1. Mexico did not export tobacco except in very small quantities, and only erratically, to Peru and Chile.

2. See John H. Hann, "The Role of the Mexican Deputies in the Proposal and Enactment of Measures of Economic Reform Applicable to Mexico," in *Mexico and the Spanish Cortes 1810–1822,* ed. Nettie Lee Benson (Austin: University of Texas Press, 1966).

3. Michael Seidman, *Workers Against Work—Labor in Paris and Barcelona During the Popular Fronts* (Berkeley and Los Angeles: University of California Press, 1991), p. 315.

4. See, for example, Archivo General de la Nación (hereafter cited as AGN), Tabaco 495, report of accountant-general, 3 August 1795.

5. AGN, Tabaco 495, report of Díaz de la Vega, 10 July 1795.

6. AGN, Renta del Tabaco 67, administrator to directors-general, 12 June 1786.

7. As Stephen Marglin has observed, "the discipline and supervision afforded by the manufactory had nothing to do with efficiency, at least as this term is used by economists. Disciplining the workforce meant a larger output in return for a greater input of labour, not more output for the same input." See Stephen A. Marglin, "What Do Bosses Do? The Origins and Functions of Hierarchy in Capitalist

Production," in *The Division of Labour: The Labour Process and Class-Struggle in Modern Capitalism,* ed. André Gorz (of Indiana Univ. Press, Bloomington, Ind. Harvester Press, 1976), p. 36.

8. The conde de Campomanes had argued as early as 1788 that the tobacco monopoly in Spain ought to be abolished. See his "Carta Tercera," 26 August 1788, in *Cartas político-económicas escritas por el Conde de Campomanes, primero de este título, al Conde de Lerena,* with an introduction by Antonio Rodríguez Villa (Madrid: Librería de M. Murillo, 1878), pp. 139–41. Jacques Barbier argues that by 1795 problems reached "crisis proportions" as insurrectionary publications circulated in various cities and towns, including Mexico City, Caracas, and Quito. See Jacques A. Barbier, "The Culmination of the Bourbon Reforms, 1787–1792," *Hispanic American Historical Review* (hereafter cited as HAHR), 57 (1977), p. 67.

9. AGN, Tabaco 149, Royal Order, 8 January 1795.

10. AGN, Tabaco 241, director-general to viceroy, 31 March 1799.

11. These figures are based on a variety of reports taken from the Ramo de Tabaco, Ramo de la Renta de Tabaco, Indiferente General in the AGN; from the Archivo Histórico de Hacienda, and from the Audiencia de Mexico in the Archivo General de Indias (hereafter AGI). For a further discussion of sources and interpretation, see Susan Deans-Smith, "The Tobacco Manufactories: Rationale, Organization, and Production," in *Bureaucrats, Planters, and Workers: The Making of the Tobacco Monopoly in Bourbon Mexico* (Austin: University of Texas Press, 1992).

12. See AGI, Mexico 2259, report of directors-general, 10 October 1776; AGN, Tabaco 241, report of accountant-general, 7 October 1795; AGI, Mexico 2268, Maniau y Torquemada, Tomás Murphy to director-general, 11 January 1799; AGI, Mexico 2269, report of accountant-general, 11 December 1809.

13. AGI, Mexico 2302, report of viceroy, 29 February 1820.

14. For a more detailed discussion of cigar and cigarette production, see Deans-Smith, *Bureaucrats, Planters and Workers,* chap. 5.

15. AGN, Tabaco 358, José Luis Rodríguez to Puchet, 8 September 1797.

16. See D. A. Brading, *Miners and Merchants in Bourbon Mexico* (Cambridge: Cambridge University Press, 1971), pp. 56–81. For the reorganizations following Gálvez's demise and the rule of Charles IV, see Jacques Barbier, "The Culmination of the Bourbon Reforms," and Allan Kuethe, "Towards a Periodization of the Reforms of Charles III," both in *Iberian Colonies, New World Societies: Essays in Memory of Charles Gibson,* ed. R. L. Garner and W. B. Taylor (State College, PA: privately published, 1986).

17. AGN, Tabaco 241, report of the ministers of the Tesorería General de Exército y Real Hacienda, 23 November 1795.

18. AGN, Tabaco 241, report of ministers of Real Tribunal y Audiencia de la Contaduría Mayor de Cuentas de México, 9 March 1796.

19. There were a few increases registered at the supervisory levels, and the practice of individual petition permitted some workers to increase their daily wages. Newly employed pieceworkers, however, suffered an absolute decrease when by the late 1790s they were hired at a rate that began at 1.5 reales per tarea and climbed to 3.5 reales. The rate that prevailed when the manufactories opened was between 2 and 4 reales. As such the manufactory workers fared no better than other urban workers between 1750 and 1850. AGI, Mexico 2281, Relación de los empleados

que havia en el año de 1775; AGN, Tabaco 241, report of accountant-general, 20 July 1795; reports from various volumes of AGN, Tabaco, Renta de Tabaco.

20. On the limited productive capacity of the colonial economy, see Richard L. Garner, "Further Considerations of 'Facts and Figments' in Bourbon Mexico," *Bulletin of Latin American Research,* 6 (1987), pp. 55–63. See also the discussion on obstacles to growth in the textile industry in colonial Mexico by Richard J. Salvucci, *Textiles and Capitalism in Mexico—An Economic History of the Obrajes, 1539–1840* (Princeton: Princeton University Press, 1987).

21. For a discussion of this point, see Deans-Smith, *Bureaucrats, Planters, and Workers,* chaps. 3, 5.

22. AGI, Mexico 2302, report of López, 10 November 1817.

23. David W. Walker, *Kinship, Business, and Politics: The Martínez del Río Family in Mexico, 1824–1867* (Austin: University of Texas Press, 1986).

24. John J. TePaske, "The Financial Disintegration of the Royal Government of Mexico during the Epoch of Independence," in *The Independence of Mexico and the Creation of the New Nation,* ed. Jaime E. Rodríguez O. (Los Angeles: UCLA Latin American Center Publications, 1990), p. 73. On the instability of Mexico in the immediate postindependence decades, see Donald Fithian Stevens, *Origins of Instability in Early Republican Mexico* (Durham, NC, and London: Duke University Press, 1991).

25. David W. Walker, "Business As Usual: The Empresa del Tabaco in Mexico," *HAHR,* 64, 4 (November 1984), p. 677.

26. *Ibid.,* p. 676.

27. Biblioteca Nacional, Caja Fuerte, Guía de hacienda de la republicana mexicana, Parte legislativa, Secretaría de ministerio de hacienda, México, 30 April 1825, pp. 118–19. See also Baker Business Library, Harvard University, M-1, mss. relating to the tobacco monopoly, 1821–50.

28. AGN, Tabaco 14, Administración general de la Renta, 7 October 1845.

29. There is impressionistic evidence that the monopoly under private management proved quite lucrative, but there is no quantitative basis for such an assessment. See, for example, Rosa María Meyer, "Los Béistegui, especuladores y mineros, 1830–1869" in *Formación y desarrollo de la burguesía en México, siglo XIX,* ed. Ciro F. S. Cardoso (México: Siglo XXI, 1978); also Walker, *Kinship, Business, and Politics.*

30. Walker, "Business As Usual," pp. 683–84.

31. Ibid., pp. 684–85.

32. Luisa Ahumada, "Representación que las maestras, oficialas y demás empleadas de la fábrica de tabacos dirigen al supremo gobierno," *El Monitor,* 24 April 1846.

33. It was not until 1910 that the Decouflé crimping process was introduced to improve manufacture of cigarettes. See Rodney D. Anderson, *Outcasts in Their Own Land—Mexican Industrial Workers, 1906–1911* (DeKalb: Northern Illinois University Press, 1976), p. 225.

34. Frederick Shaw, "The Artisan in Mexico City (1824–1853)," in *El trabajo y los trabajadores en la historia de México,* ed. Elsa Cecilia Frost, Michael C. Meyer, and Josefina Zoraida Vázquez (México: El Colegio de México and University of Arizona Press, Tucson), pp. 411–12.

35. David Walker, *Kinship, Business and Politics,* p. 24.

36. Guy P. D. Thompson, "Traditional and Modern Manufacturing in Mexico, 1821–1850," in *América Latina e la época de Simón Bolívar: La formación de las economías europeos 1800–1850,* ed. Reinhard Liehr (Berlin: Bibliotheca Ibero-Americana, 1989), p. 84.

37. Ibid.

38. Walker, "Business as Usual," p. 684.

39. Thompson, "Traditional and Modern Manufacturing in Mexico," p. 84.

40. See the manufactory regulations for Guanajuato, AGN, Tabaco 238, Article 33 of the "Reglamento . . .," 27 April 1848.

41. See Gabriel Haslip Viera, "The Underclass," in *Cities and Society in Colonial Latin America,* ed. Louisa Schell Hoberman and Susan Migden Socolow (Albuquerque: University of New Mexico Press, 1986); Michael Scardaville, "Alcohol Abuse and Tavern Reform in Late Colonial Mexico," *HAHR,* 60, 4 (November 1980) pp. 643–671; D. A. Brading, "Tridentine Catholicism and Enlightened Despotism in Bourbon Mexico," *Journal of Latin American Studies,* 15 (1983). pp. 1–22.

42. See Sylvia M. Arrom, *The Women of Mexico City 1790–1857* (Stanford: Stanford University Press, 1985), pp. 28–29.

43. AGN, Renta del Tabaco 49, Manifiesto que se hace en defensa de las fábricas de cuenta de S.M. en su Real Renta del Tabaco de Nueva España . . . (1795?).

44. Joel Mokyr, "The Industrial Revolution and the New Economic History," in *The Economics of the Industrial Revolution,* ed. Joel Mokyr (New Jersey: Roman & Allanheld, 1985), p. 30.

45. AGN, Tabaco 146, Ordenanzas de la Real Fabrica de Puros y Cigarros, 15 June 1770; AGN, Renta del Tabaco 67, Prevenciones de la dirección general, que deben observarse exactamente en la fabrica de puros y cigarros de esta capital . . ., 20 March 1792. The literature on early factory organization demonstrates similarities in terms of structures and the content of rules imposed on workers. See Reinhard Bendix, *Work and Authority in Industry—Ideologies of Management in the Course of Industrialization* (New York: John Wiley & Sons, 1956).

46. Alejandra Moreno Toscano, "Los trabajadores y el proyecto de industrialización, 1810–1867," in *La clase obrera in la historia de México: De la colonia al imperio,* ed. Enrique Florescano (México: Siglo XXI, 1980), pp. 338–42.

47. See above, note 40.

48. The only reformer after independence to raise the issue was Esteban de Antuñano, who in 1837 published an essay titled *Political, Civil, Manufacturing, and Domestic Advantages of Employing Women also in the Modern Mechanized Factories Beginning to Be Erected in Mexico,* in which he discussed the economic and moral advantages of employing women. See Arrom, *The Women of Mexico City,* pp. 30–31.

49. As has been argued for economic reforms directed against journeymen in eighteenth- and nineteenth-century Europe, they were "not only against a specific form of economy but also against a specific form of popular culture" (Hans-Ulrich Thamer, "Journeyman Culture and Enlightened Public Opinion," in *Understanding Popular Culture—Europe from the Middle Ages to the Nineteenth Century,* ed. Steven L. Kaplan [Berlin and New York: Mouton, 1984], p. 227).

50. Richard Price, "The Labour Process and Labour History," *Social History* 8, 1 (January 1983), p. 62.

51. My approach to the consideration of state-worker relations is very much influenced by the works of labor historians Richard Price and Michael Sonenscher. Price argues that to understand working-class formation, labor movements, and the role of the state, scholars should avoid "the teleology of writing labour history as either conforming to or deviating from a certain trajectory." Doing so shifts one's perspective to examine the workers on their own terms and according to their own logic. It takes into account the constraints under which they operated. See Richard Price, *Labour in British Society* (London: Croom Helm, 1986), pp. 7–12. See also Michael Sonenscher, *Work & Wages—Natural Law, Politics & the Eighteenth Century French Trades* (Cambridge: Cambridge University Press, 1989).

52. The letters and petitions are scattered throughout the volumes of Tabaco, Renta de Tabaco, and Indiferente General in the AGN, and in Audiencia de México—Tabaco, AGI.

53. AGN, Tabaco 482, Puchet to director-general, 12 August 1794.

54. AGN, Tabaco 241, Díaz de la Vega to viceroy, 31 March 1799.

55. Ibid.

56. Ibid.

57. AGI, Mexico 2264, Díaz de la Vega to Ex. Sr., 22 January 1789.

58. Richard Whipp, "A Time to Every Purpose: An Essay on Time and Work" in *The Historical Meanings of Work,* ed. Patrick Joyce (Cambridge: Cambridge University Press, 1987), p. 222.

59. See Catharina Lis and Hugo Soly, "Policing the Early Modern Proletariat, 1450–1850," in *Proletarianization and Family History,* ed. David Levine (New York: Academic Press, 1984), p. 212.

60. Walker, "Business as Usual," pp. 684–85.

61. Carlos María de Bustamente, "Historia de la moneda de cobre y motín de las estanqueras del tobaco," reprinted in *Guía de Forasteros, Estanquillo Literario para el año de 1842,* (México: Instituto de Bellas Artes, 1971) 5 vols., 5:7, p. 5.

62. See Michael Sonenscher's discussion on this point, *Work & Wages,* p. 367.

63. Ira Katznelson, "Working-Class Formation and the State: Nineteenth-Century England in American Perspective," in *Bringing the State Back In,* ed. Peter Evans, Dietrick Rueschemeyer, and Theda Skocpol (Cambridge: Cambridge University Press, 1985), p. 260.

64. E. P. Thompson, "The Moral Economy of the English Crowd in the Eighteenth Century," *Past and Present,* 50 (February 1971), p. 79.

65. AGI, Mexico 2313, Isidro Romaña, Perez de Acali to director-general Hierro, 9 April 1781.

66. "Report on Tobacco," Charles O'Gorman, consul general, 12 February 1825, Mexico, ff. 165–81v. FRO Parliamentary Papers, Group 203, vol. 4, microfilm Benson Latin American Collection, f. 169.

67. John Leddy Phelan, "Authority and Flexibility in the Spanish Imperial Bureaucracy," *Administrative Science Quarterly,* 5, 1 (June 1960), pp 47–65.

68. For further discussion of this point, see Deans-Smith, *Bureaucrats, Planters, and Workers,* chap. 7.

69. AGN, Tabaco 356, Razon de las tareas . . ., accountant-general, 23 July 1781.

70. See María Amparo Ros T., *La producción cigarrera a finales de la colonia: La fábrica en México* (México: Instituto Nacional de Antropología e Historia, 1984), p. 44.

71. Alf Lüdtke, "Cash, Coffee-Breaks, Horseplay: Eigensinn and Politics Among Factory Workers in Germany circa 1900," in *Confrontation, Class Consciousness, and the Labor Process—Studies in Proletarian Class Formation,* ed. Michael Hannagan and Charles Stephenson (New York: Greenwood Press, 1986), pp. 65–96.

72. It is known that by 1887, after the monopoly was abolished, the women cigarette workers in Mexico City founded the Sociedad Mutualista Hijas de Trabajo del Ramo de Obreras de Cigarrería with legal consultants. See Carmen Ramos Escandón, "Mujeres trabajadoras en el México Porfiriano: Género e ideología del trabajo femenino, 1876–1911" (forthcoming), pp. 38–40.

73. Shaw, "The Artisan in Mexico City," pp. 410–11.

74. Moreno Toscano, "Los trabajadores," pp. 345–46.

75. Luisa Ahumada, "Representación . . . ," *El Monitor,* 24 April 1846.

76. Sonenscher, *Work & Wages,* p. 375.

77. For a good introduction to the political economy of state-owned enterprises, see Ravi Ramamurti, *State Owned Enterprises in High Technology Industries* (New York: Praeger, 1987).

78. Ramamurti, *State Owned Enterprises,* pp. 281–82.

79. For an example of the expectations of the workers in the 1840s, see Luisa Ahumada, "Representación . . . ," *El Monitor,* 24 April 1846.

80. For later examples of the Mexican state's attempts to mold citizens and workers, see Adrian Bantjes, "Politics, Class, and Culture in Post-Revolutionary Mexico, Cardenismo and Sonora, 1929–1940" (Ph.D. University of Texas at Austin, 1991); and William French, "Peaceful and Working People: The Inculcation of the Capitalist Work Ethic in a Mexican Mining District (Hidalgo District, Chihuahua, 1880–1920)" (Ph.D. diss., University of Texas at Austin, 1990).

81. William H. Sewell, Jr., "Uneven Development, the Autonomy of Politics, and the Dockworkers of Nineteenth-Century Marseille," *American Historical Review,* 93, 3 (June 1988), p. 637.

5

The Politics of Protection: Interpreting Commercial Policy in Late Bourbon and Early National Mexico

RICHARD J. SALVUCCI, LINDA K. SALVUCCI, AND ASLÁN COHEN

The breadth, depth, and persistence of political instability in independent Mexico have long been the object of historians' attention. "Mexico," writes one, "experimented with monarchy, moderate constitutional republic, radical populist regime, conservative government, and liberal government; each in turn failed to produce stability."[1] From 1824 through 1853, Mexico experienced the "institutionalized disorder" of "manifold pronunciamientos . . . endless cabinet changes, and several lurches to the political left or right."[2] Repeatedly invaded, blockaded, partitioned, and plunged into civil war between 1835 and 1867, Mexico was for most of its early history more a geographical expression than a political one. "The present state of anarchy [has] lasted for a quarter of a century," editorialized *The Economist* in 1861. "There is no power in Mexico. . . . It is not a nation. It is not a state. It is not a government at all."[3] This was not an isolated opinion.

Endless turmoil—the absence of an effective, legitimate, and enduring center of power—gives rise to no end of explanations. Lucas Alamán (1792–1853)—historian, statesman, political economist, and above all no liberal—blamed skepticism, the Enlightenment, and the collapse of the Spanish Empire for Mexico's difficulties. The fall of the Bourbon monarchy in 1808 revealed deep divisions whose legacy Mexico had never quite overcome. Catholicism and colonialism were the elements that had bound the nation, but they did so no longer.[4] In a different vein, Thomas Jefferson spoke for republicans who found Spanish America's "regal Catholicism" abhorrent. By 1817 Jefferson was predicting a future of Bonapartes, if not Bonapartism, for the insurgent colonies.[5] And, indeed, by the Mexican War (if not before), most observers in the United States thought that Mexico was hopelessly corrupt, ill-governed, and deficient in republican civic consciousness: a priest-ridden nation to which progress came slowly, if at all.[6]

Economic explanations of Mexican instability focus on the trade cycle. In the long run, the volume and value of trade linked public finance to the tariff. The ebb and flow of trade made recurrent revenue crises inevitable, and shortfalls were "militarized" by the large share of the military in national spending. As Anthony Butler, the American chargé d'affaires in Mexico in 1830, put it, "The praetorian bands of Mexico, like those of ancient Rome, must have money and indulgences, and those who promise fairest secure their aid, until one promise fails or a better one is made."[7]

Yet the story was rather more complex. Mexico now confronted something other than a world of recurring, but essentially predictable, trade cycles. For the independence of Mexico coincided with a profound change in the dimensions and pattern of international trade.[8] By the 1830s, the volume and value of this trade were expanding rapidly, and the terms of trade—the relative prices of exports and imports—were in a state of flux as well.[9]

Moreover, nations such as Mexico and Peru were more than passive bystanders in the international arena. Each reacted to the changing circumstances of international trade in ways that reflected their own domestic political interests and economic endowments. In this context, the shaping of commercial policy—the making of the tariff—was a critical and widespread concern of early national political economy in Spanish America. There were perfectly logical reasons for this pervasive concern. Only trade restrictions in some form could "moderate" the disruptive effects of the new trade in wage goods, such as inexpensive cottons. Trade adjustment in early national Spanish America was a prolonged, painful, and costly process. As patterns of comparative advantage shifted, protection offered relief, if not salvation, to producers whose very existence was threatened. In independent Mexico, then, political economy was essentially the political economy of the tariff. The economics of the tariff was the economics that really mattered. Hence the focus of this essay.[10]

History and Theory

The story begins with the commercial history of the Spanish Empire under the Hapsburgs and the Bourbons. In broad outline, the tale is well known.[11] Here we need only repeat that trade between the Indies and Spain was in theory governed by a detailed and closely regulated regime. For fiscal and military reasons, formal access to the trade was restricted to licensed groups of merchants in Mexico City, Lima, Seville, and, later, Cádiz. Of course, the reality was far different. English, French, Dutch, and

Portuguese smugglers had made significant inroads into legal trade by the late seventeenth century, and crises, such as the War of Spanish Succession (1700–1713), were marked by pervasive contraband.[12]

Nevertheless, it was not until the eighteenth century that formal, systematic changes in the trading system were undertaken. Until the 1780s, consumer demand in the Indies (with the exception of small, peripheral economies such as Chile, Venezuela, and to a lesser degree Peru) was far from integrated into the international economy. Historically, Spanish fleets carried textiles that cost far too much to be consumed by any but a small segment of the colonial elite. In Mexico perhaps one in six people could afford imported textiles at the end of the eighteenth century, and some contemporaries judged the market even smaller.[13]

Yet by the middle of the eighteenth century, significant changes in this well-established regime were clearly visible. Because of the growth of mining, Mexico's capacity to import expanded, and its demand for imports increased. Contraband grew to perhaps half of all international trade, and the colony's older artisan textile industry was placed at risk.[14]

In other words, the extension of "free trade" to Mexico after 1789 revealed the nature of its comparative advantage. With the advent of this looser system, the famous if misnamed *comercio libre,* Mexico received larger quantities of European (and English) textiles than before. As the supply of shipping to the Indies grew, the cost of transportation fell (abetted by technological improvements), and cheaper goods, such as English cottons, could be imported. The new system may not have been revolutionary, but the traditional import-export merchants, who hated competition, protested vigorously.[15] By the 1810s some of them alleged that the old woolen manufactories of Querétaro, Mexico City, and Guadalajara—holdovers from an age when the colony of necessity produced much of its own textiles—faced a cost disadvantage of as much as 50 percent in dealing with imported British cottons. The artisan communities of Mexico City, where thousands went unemployed, and those in Puebla, Querétaro, Oaxaca, and San Miguel demanded protection from imports. These complaints continued well into the 1820s and 1830s.[16]

In the century after 1750, in short, the Mexican economy entered a new international environment. The growing productivity of British textile manufacturing and shipping led to a sharp fall in import prices, particularly after the transient inflation of the Napoleonic Wars (1793–1815) had passed. The volume of international trade then expanded dramatically after 1815, and the terms of trade slowly improved.[17]

Still, old patterns of production in Mexico died hard, and painful adjustments were necessary. The manufacture of colonial woolens, for example, was nearly as old as the Spanish presence in Mexico and supplied everyday fabrics for a variety of uses. It could not withstand the "new international order" of the nineteenth century. By the late 1810s, the price of imports into Mexico had fallen sharply. By the 1820s, it was reportedly a half or a third of what it had been under the old Hapsburg fleet system.[18]

Nevertheless, as David Brading pointed out nearly two decades ago, the impact of comercio libre was by no means uniform. As new merchants in Veracruz, for example, competed away the profits of a formerly restricted trade, alternative investments became more attractive. Indeed, Brading ascribes the late colonial mining boom in part to a flow of resources from other sectors of the economy.[19] In this he was undoubtedly correct, as the following example suggests.

Consider the case of textiles. A fall in the international price of textiles implied a rise in the price of Mexican silver in terms of textiles—change in relative prices, in other words.[20] A given quantity of Mexican silver could now purchase more cloth. The profitability of mining would rise, and in relation to it the profitability of domestic textile production would fall. If possible, and over time, Mexican investors would shift from manufacturing textiles to mining more silver; if possible, labor would move as well. As a result, the patterns of trade and domestic production would change. Mexico would manufacture fewer textiles and mine more silver in order to import cloth. And in fact this is more or less what happened.[21]

This example suggests the possibilities inherent in a systematic analysis of responses to commercial change in early nineteenth-century Mexico. And indeed, models of trade adjustment provide one avenue of study. They explain the shape and substance of commercial policy in an economy confronted by profound changes in the international arena. But just as important, they illustrate Mexico's ability—or inability—to adapt to changes that coincided with the early years of independence. In so doing, they shed more than a little light on the dynamics of the economic crisis that confronted Mexico after separation from Spain.

A Specific-Factors Model of Trade

Let us examine a simple model of the Mexican economy at the end of the colonial period, a so-called specific-factors or short-run model.[22] It assumes that the economy has only two sectors, textiles (T) and mining

(M), and that only capital (K) and labor (L) are employed in producing cloth or silver. The level of capital is specific to each industry. That is, specific machines can be used only for a specific purpose. Looms have no use in mining, nor picks and shovels in weaving. On the other hand, labor is mobile and can move between textiles and mining. Supplies of labor and capital are assumed to be stable and fully employed. Finally, the economy is a small one; its actions have no effect on the world price of silver or cloth. Of course, it is possible to relax or change the assumptions of the model and obtain different results.

But even modeling Mexico as a small economy whose actions cannot affect the price of cloth or silver is not unrealistic. At the peak of the Mexican silver bonanza of the late eighteenth century, the price of silver on the London market fell by less than 4 percent, even as production rose by more than 50 percent.[23] In other words, an elastic demand for specie and bullion worldwide boosted real revenues from silver production in Mexico almost as rapidly as silver could be mined. Small wonder that many Mexicans believed the road to wealth was paved with silver.

This model has several implications. Given its assumptions, Mexican (domestic) prices are given by

$$P_t = P_t^{\,*} (1 + z_t)$$

$$P_m = P_m^{\,*} (1 + z_m)$$

where P_t and P_m are the domestic prices of textiles (T) and silver (M) respectively; an asterisk denotes foreign prices, which are assumed to be given to the country; and z is the import tax rate levied on any of the commodities. Consequently, even if the country is small and cannot affect world prices, a change in the import tax rate will have a direct effect on the level of domestic prices.

Consider what occurs when the relative price of Mexican silver (M) increases. (This, we recall, is what happened as English industrialization, changes in the supply and productivity of shipping, and modifications in Spanish commercial policy combined to drive down the world price of textiles [T] even as the price of Mexican silver remained stable.) Producing silver rather than textiles becomes more attractive to Mexicans, since the purchasing power of a unit of silver increases. As a result, resources should flow from domestic textile production to silver mining. But, by assumption, capital is fixed in each sector so that labor alone can move. As a result, capital in mining becomes more productive. If payments to labor and capital reflect their relative productivity, the owners of mining capital will receive a higher return. Indeed, the rental rate of mining capital will increase by a larger margin than any of the prices of final goods (that is, textiles and silver). By the same token, the productivity of capital in domestic textiles would fall, and its owners would receive a lower return.

What happens to labor? As workers move toward mining, their productivity in mining must fall, thus reducing the real wage.[24] However, and for similar reasons, the productivity of the remaining textile workers must rise, as does their real wage. Since, by assumption, labor is free to move between sectors, wage rates must ultimately equalize, and labor will migrate until that result is achieved. But it is impossible to say whether or not the overall real wage has risen or fallen. This depends on the basket of goods consumed by labor and, in particular, on the proportion of their income (π) given over to textiles. The real wage will increase only if the percentage increase in the money wage exceeds the increase in $\{\pi P_t + (1 - \pi) P_m\}$.

If we let ∂ denote percentage change, R the rate of payment to owners of capital, and W the wage rate, the results can be summarized in the following simple expression:

$$\partial R_m > \partial P_m > \partial W > \partial P_t > \partial R_t$$

The inequalities would, of course, be reversed if the original (exogenous) increase had been in the relative price of textiles.

In simple terms, the results mean that the beneficiaries of the rising relative price of silver (or falling relative price of textiles) are the owners of mining capital. The owners of capital in textiles are the clear losers. The position of the workers is indeterminate and lies somewhere between mining and textiles. As a consequence, it is easy to see that the owners of capital will favor protection (an increase in the rate of the import tax) of the goods in their own industry and will oppose protection of the other. The workers' position on questions of trade protection is necessarily ambiguous, but some tentative observations may be made.

Back to the Past

The historian's road to heaven is paved with evidence. As G. K. Chesterton once remarked, to enter the world of facts is to enter a world of limits. Did Mexicans behave in ways that accord more or less with the predictions of the model? If not, then why not? And what can we say about agriculture, a sector that has gone unmentioned until now?

We have already mentioned the complaints of the great import-export merchants about the extension of comercio libre in 1789. As Brading suggests, the new system altered their investment incentives and channeled more capital into silver mining.[25] Yet merchant capital had also migrated into woolen production in Querétaro and Acámbaro.[26] By definition, this investment became less attractive, hastening the reallocation that Brading observed. There were also merchants and merchant houses that owned textile manufactories, of which the firm of Vértiz and Oteyza in Mexico City was the most important.[27] Nevertheless, there were few other instances of direct ownership. The network of merchants who distributed domestic cloth, financed its production, and supplied raw materials was more important than the ownership of the manufactories themselves. These merchants handled cottons and woolens and could be found in Mexico City, Puebla, Guadalajara, Tlaxcala, San Miguel el Grande, Oaxaca, and indeed throughout the colony.[28] Consequently, important segments of the colonial merchant community opposed free trade. Merchants who had gotten rich under the old fleet system hated comercio libre. Those who furnished and financed colonial textile production were no more sympathetic. In Guadalajara, for instance, where commercial capital had underwritten cotton production, the merchant guild argued that imports from Manila would ruin local industry.[29] On the basis of naked self-interest, only the parvenu merchants of Veracruz, tied to foreign suppliers and schooled in the virtues of expansive demand, generally leaned toward free-trade liberalism.[30] And even they regarded "free" trade as *their* exclusive preserve. The participation of Havana merchants in the trade, for instance, was not welcome.[31]

If merchants who supplied, produced, and marketed domestic textiles were opposed to freer trade, the position of urban artisans and industrialists was similar. As far as artisans were concerned, there was a sensible economic rationale for their belief. Many urban artisans owned the looms they used, in effect tying their capital to the textile industry. As a result, it was difficult for them to move to other activities; this made trade protection an attractive, even vital, policy.[32]

A vigorous defense of the artisans' position was written in 1811 by Juan López Cancelada, a Spaniard for whom mercantilist principles were less pressing than imperialist xenophobia.[33] He warned his Mexican compatriots against trading with foreigners: "The cloth and serges of Querétaro, Acámbaro, Cholula, Aguascalientes, La Quemada, Potosí and other places are what men and women wear. . . . I don't know if you could think of a worse fate than taking their money and making them wear foreign fashions. . . . Mexicans *are capable of making anything made anywhere else in the world*" (italics in original).[34] The merchant guild of Mexico City went further. Writing in the wake of the Hidalgo rebellion, the merchants sounded an old theme: "If direct trade with foreigners destroys our industry and factories, and reduces thousands of workers in both Americas to poverty, who can deny that this trade will extinguish the fire of patriotism and loyalty that still exists in their hearts?"[35] Defenders of restricted trade had long argued that commercial liberalism and Spanish hegemony were mutually exclusive. As it happens, they may have been right.[36]

Independence from Spain changed the context and possibilities of the debate, but not its substance. Both the Junta Nacional Instituyente (1823) and the Congreso Constituyente (1823–24) witnessed heated clashes over commercial policy. In both, spokesmen for artisan and industrial interests demanded outright prohibition of certain cottons or substantially increased levels of protection. And in both forums, their opponents argued that protection distorted incentives and risked alienating Great Britain, which had yet to formally recognize independent Mexico. Most important, the latter said, protection taxed the mass of consumers for the benefit of a smaller number of artisan textile producers. Some opponents of protection virtually asserted this: "Our confederation is not composed of manufacturers, but of landowners, farmers, and miners, the true basis of our wealth."[37] In other words, everyone understood that commercial policy affected the distribution of wealth. As the tariff commission of 1824 wrote, "The great conflict [we] face has been to reconcile the interests of producers of raw materials and [those] of artisans with the least prejudice to the consumer."[38]

The statistics available indicate that these pressures did not go unheeded, at least from the standpoint of artisans and industrialists. One very crude way of judging the strength of pressures for protection is by computing the implicit tariff index, or the ratio of "external" taxes (taxes on trade) to the current value of imports. This procedure, of course, does not produce a wholly satisfactory index of protection. As Robert Lipsey observes, "The level of the tariff rate on a commodity influences the weight of the commodity in the index. A sufficiently high tariff could conceivably remove itself from the index by eliminating the import."[39] Indeed, the Tariff of 1837 legislated the outright prohibition of most inexpensive cottons. As a result, the statistics that appear in table 1, especially in the 1840s, are conservative measures of the level of protection.

Table 1 Implicit Index of Tariff Protection: Trade Taxes as a Percentage of Current Peso Import Values

Year	Percentage
1821	25
1825	32
1825–26	46
1826–27	47
1827–28	30
1840	36
1841	42
1842	44
1843	55
1844	56
1845	35

Sources and Computation: 1821 assumed as a maximum from the ad valorem rate. Trade tax figures from *Estadísticas históricas de México,* 2:629, cuadro 18.3. Peso imports from 1840 through 1845 estimated as the sum of France, United States, and Great Britain, drawn from Inés Herrera Canales, *El comercio exterior de México* (México, 1977), 82. Trade taxes include relatively small figures for export duties. See Miguel Lerdo de Tejada, *Comercio exterior de México* (1853; México, 1967), Table 43. There are discrepancies between the totals reported by Lerdo de Tejada and by the *Estadísticas históricas,* which draw on data supplied by Matías Romero.

At no time in the mid to late 1820s did the ratio of external taxes to the current value of imports fall to anything approaching its low level in 1821, and by the early 1840s, it was nearly twice as high. In its movements, the statistic confirms what historians now know. After an early flirtation with low tariffs, Mexican politicians opted for significantly higher levels of protection. We have thus far suggested why there was significant protectionist pressure, but we have not explained why there was significant tariff *protection.* To make sense of what happened, we need to return to the model, to consider the role of agriculture, and to assess the relative strength of groups that could benefit from commercial liberalization.

From the standpoint of the model, miners were most favored by low taxes on trade. But there were not that many miners or mine owners. Brading gives a rough estimate of "three thousand odd mines found in New Spain by the last decades of the colonial period."[40] Even considering the complex connections among suppliers, financiers, investors, merchants, silver bankers, and mine owners, it is hard to imagine that more than 150,000 persons (3,000 mines × 50 per mine) had a direct claim on mining profits, and that figure may be exaggerated in view of the tendency toward concentration in ownership and supply. Moreover, the abortive revolution that shook the colony in the 1810s wrecked parts of the industry, especially in the Bajío. Silver coined at the Mexico City mint fell from a yearly average of 21.5 million pesos (1800–1809) to 8.9 million (1810–19), while the price of silver on the London market during the 1810s jumped 10 percent.[41] Clearly shaken by the conflict, the cadre of silver miners that had constituted one of the backbones of Bourbon society existed in diminished form in the 1820s and exercised less influence. Its only clear objective was, perhaps, to maintain the unrestricted export of specie and bullion, a position justified by the Hume specie-flow mechanism of trade adjustment.[42]

Phantom Farmers

It is useful to look at the situation in agriculture in concrete historical terms. After all, there were some who saw Mexico as the potential granary for a Spanish Caribbean basin whose specialization in sugar, tobacco, and coffee was rapidly emerging. The famous secretary of the consulado of Veracruz, José María Quirós, said just this in 1808: "In times of peace, the island of Cuba can be completely supplied with necessary foodstuffs by this Kingdom [Mexico] and by the other Spanish colonies. Its ports should be closed to foreigners."[43] Yet in 1793 Revillagigedo the Younger, New Spain's brilliant viceroy, had predicted that "wheat flour from this kingdom, the most important branch of the export trade, will never be able to compete with that from the United States."[44] In this case, an argument to authority settles nothing. Both men knew the colony well, although Quirós was not above stretching the truth to bring Veracruz a little business or investment.

In fact, the historical evidence favors Revillagigedo. Even conservative calculations suggest that it would have been necessary to divert at least the entire supply of Mexico City's wheat flour to feed the city of Havana alone, and this by estimating Havana's needs most modestly. Mexico could not possibly have served as a granary for Cuba, let alone the entire Caribbean, whatever its own production may have been.[45] Yet this same evidence implies that there was a potentially large Caribbean market for agricultural exports in the early nineteenth century. Why were Mexicans unable to tap it?

In the late 1770s, wheat flour exports through Veracruz averaged roughly 20,000 *tercios* per year, or some 18,000 North American barrels. The merchant guild of Veracruz estimated in 1809 that public and private shipments of flour to Havana regularly reached 30,000 tercios, or 26,700 barrels. But Mexican shipments were trivial in comparison with North American ones. Even small Mexican exports varied inversely with North American shipments, as the negative correlation (–.45) between the two series in table 2 suggests. As North Americans sent more, the market for Mexican flour shrank. Mexico simply could not compete with the bread-basket of the middle states.

To illustrate this further, let us examine one analysis of the situation in 1808 by the Cuban political economist Francisco de Arango.[46] According to Arango, the purchase price in Puebla of 100 tercios (17,500 pounds or 89 barrels) of flour was 700 pesos. To ship the flour to the Gulf Coast of Mexico a substantial 400 pesos. Once in Veracruz, the cargo was liable for three separate municipal taxes, as well as for dockage and brokerage fees. Combined, these added another 126 pesos to the 1,100 already spent on purchase and transportation. It cost another 200 pesos to ship the flour,

Table 2 Mexican Wheat Flour Exports to Spanish America Versus U.S. Wheat Flour Exports to the Spanish West Indies, 1802–12

Year	United States (Barrels)	Mexico (Tercios) Converted to U.S. Barrels
1802	70,238	20,343
1803	36,314	17,351
1804	93,071	23,470
1805	131,026	2,642
1806	113,178	2,375
1807	166,170	4,960
1808	44,778	18,755
1809	143,857	23,784
1810	138,892	14,269
1811	124,735	8,634
1812	119,440	1,387

Sources: Mexican exports are drawn from Lerdo de Tejada, *Comercio exterior,* throughout and converted to U.S. barrels by multiplying by .89; U.S. exports from Linda K. Salvucci, "Development and Decline: The Port of Philadelphia and Spanish Imperial Markets, 1783–1823" (Ph.D. diss., Princeton University, 1985), p. 136.

presumably uninsured, from Veracruz to Havana. At this last destination, there were three more local levies plus brokerage and commission fees, as well as charges for delivery to the warehouse. In sum, the outlay after leaving Veracruz fixed another 384 pesos to the total. The overall figure for Mexican flour delivered to Havana thus came to 1,610 pesos, or about 16 pesos per tercio.

By contrast, 100 barrels of Philadelphia flour cost at most 650 pesos and weighed 2,100 pounds more than 100 tercios, so that tercio-barrel comparisons are somewhat biased against the North American measure. Once purchased, the Philadelphia flour was subject to 62 pesos in costs for cooperage, commissions, and insurance at 2.5 percent. To transport the American cargo to Havana cost 200 pesos, or exactly the same as to carry flour from Veracruz to the Cuban port. Upon arriving in Havana, the Philadelphia barrels paid municipal taxes, as well as brokerage, commission, and delivery fees; these came to about 15 pesos more than those paid by Mexican grain. Still, total expenditure on flour from Philadelphia amounted to 1,121 pesos, or 11 pesos per barrel. A barrel of Philadelphia flour delivered to Havana thus cost 5 pesos less than a Mexican tercio, even though it weighed 21 pounds more and was generally regarded as far superior in quality to the Mexican product.

If we look at these figures from a different perspective, the significance of transportation costs emerges. Assume, for the moment, that Mexican and Pennsylvania flour were available at equal cost, and that neither was subject to any charge other than transportation. In that case, the difference in cost between a Mexican and a Philadelphian shipment was 450 pesos [(700 + 400 + 200) – (650 + 250)], or somewhat more than the cost (400 pesos) of transporting flour from Puebla to Veracruz. Under conditions of competitive free trade, then, these figures indicate that Mexican flour could not compete with flour from Pennsylvania even if the cost of transportation were subsidized by the Spanish crown or extracted involuntarily from Cuban planters. Of course, by taxing the Mexican flour both in Veracruz and in Havana, Spanish policymakers only made a difficult situation impossible. Mexico had no comparative advantage in agriculture.

There are some interesting implications. Had Spain not lost Mexico in 1821, Mexico could have sold agricultural surpluses to Cuba and Puerto Rico. But the Cubans would have paid more for less, since colonial priorities inevitably take precedence over allocative efficiency. The island would have grown more slowly, since Cuban growth during the first sugar boom was tied to staples, such as wheat flour from the United States. Trade, as always, facilitated specialization. In such a world, Mexicans would have had more agricultural employment, and Cuban planters would have possessed fewer slaves. For once, it is hard to make an issue of efficiency. An empire in which Cuban sugar planters played second fiddle to Mexican *labradores* requires imagination enough.

However provocative this analysis may be, it can do no more than suggest why there was no agricultural export interest in Mexico. It cannot explain why farmers and landowners who faced deteriorating internal terms of trade because of protection did not protest much. Colonial interest groups were never reticent in their opposition to new taxes and other such "novelties." Why should they have been so in this case?

There are a few possible explanations. David Brading noted the ostensible weakness of the landed classes in his analysis of Mexico's late colonial elite: "Ownership of a great estate brought more prestige than legal status. In general, the Mexican *hacendado* lacked the privileges, the fiscal exemptions and the command of political office that was associated with gentry status in Europe."[47] Or consider Guy Thomson's characterization of farmers in the Puebla district: "Landowners remained a shadowy and unassertive political force in the thirty years following Independence, in contrast to the more articulate merchants, artisans and manufacturers who devised Puebla's protectionist political economy [and] organized the protectionist lobby."[48] The formation of commercial policy in early national Mexico clearly supports these observations.

Mexico's class structure mattered as well. In the early nineteenth century, an agrarian "bourgeoisie" that lived exclusively on land rents existed only in embryo.[49] To be sure, there were small farmers—the labradores of Atlixco, for example—who specialized in growing cereals for the domestic market. For most large landowners, however, land was just another investment. Examples of merchant-landlords or industrialist-landlords (owners of *obrajes* who were hacendados as well) abound. To judge their attitudes toward commercial policy by separate economic criteria is akin to asking which part of their portfolios did the thinking. Moreover, historians know that the great estates changed hands frequently. An entrenched landowning class could scarcely have maintained itself. This, too, arrested the formation of a stable, coherent, and politically powerful landed elite.

Moreover, Mexico's landowners were a disparate lot, with diffuse interests and incentives. Maize farmers, sheep and cattle ranchers, and tobacco planters were a heterogeneous group. They differed in commercial orientation, capitalization, and sensitivity to novel patterns (and price levels) in foreign trade. Even if their aggregate losses from commercial policies were large, the landowners could be mobilized only with great difficulty. It took a major threat, such as the *consolidación de vales reales* in 1804, to weld together a powerful agrarian coalition. And then, survival rather than mere discomfort was at issue.[50]

Desperate Diseases, Desperate Remedies

For various reasons, neither miners nor landowners formed parts of a viable coalition of free traders. Yet protection was scarcely the product of default. Even Mexican textile entrepreneurs experienced persistent instability in their ranks.[51] Nevertheless, the demands of these entrepreneurs and their allies were coherent enough to shape a protectionist policy. Why?

In part, the channels of influence through which entrepreneurs and merchant capitalists could operate were well defined, well known, and well used. Industrialists could modify policy under the aegis of the Banco de Avío (1830–42) or, beginning in 1843, the Dirección de la Industria Nacional. In these years, textile manufacturers enjoyed considerable support. Perhaps the comment of the merchant Pedro Ansoategui says it best: "There are at present [1841] many enterprises and projected factories for making yarn in various parts of the republic and associated with these can be found persons of consequence for their wealth and connections."[52] Wealth, connections, and access to power always help in making policy. So, too, does the use of special pleading, and in the case of textile manufacturers and workers, the pleading was special indeed.

The influence of urban artisans, laborers, and their employers is easy to comprehend. As an organized—or even disorganized—political force, these groups were powerful. During the late eighteenth century, Spanish officials were obsessed with avoiding urban violence of any sort and took steps to prevent it, including the requisition of vital food supplies.[53] This concern translated into a distinctly ambivalent attitude toward industrialization. The creation of an urbanized factory labor force with its concentration of potentially seditious and unruly individuals was not especially desirable.[54] Such fears were seemingly vindicated in 1810 by the bloody Hidalgo rebellion, a movement allegedly nourished by the adherence of textile workers from the city of Querétaro.[55] The disruptive potential of the urban underclass was again emphasized in late 1828 by the sack of the Parián in Mexico City.[56] As a result, the specter of unemployed artisans and urban textile workers was worrisome to governments of all stripes. In the principal cities of the country—Mexico City, Puebla, Querétaro,

Oaxaca, Guadalajara, and Valladolid—textile workers were found in significant numbers. To throw them out of work was to invite disaster in an already tense political environment. Weak regimes bent on self-preservation could not afford to have large concentrations of urban artisans and workers put out of work by foreign competition. Support for protection thus was based on painful experience as well as on political expediency. Desperate diseases call for desperate remedies.

Conclusions: Beyond the Bourbon Reconquest

Applying insights from the simple model of trade adjustment to the history of early national Mexico suggests several conclusions. Perhaps most important, divisions over commercial policy per se contributed little to political instability in the first decades of Mexican independence. This is not as counterintuitive as it might seem. There could be no real conflict over a matter about which, in practical terms, there was no real disagreement. Of course, there was a theoretical and ideologically sophisticated free-trade interest in Mexico. But it represented cosmopolitan and eclectic thinkers familiar with Adam Smith and David Ricardo rather than any concrete socioeconomic interest group. The debate spilled much ink, but it could not have spilled much blood. We may eliminate commercial policy as a source of political contention. Mexico's protectionist consensus was based on utter realism. Protection was viewed as a matter of political or material survival by many, and there was little organized opposition to it.

As things stood at the turn of the nineteenth century, Mexico could not compete with the United States in the growing agricultural markets of the Spanish Caribbean. Costs of transportation prevented it. Absent imperial subsidies, there could be no Cuban or Puerto Rican market for Mexican wheat flour. There were no Mexican estate owners bent on preserving free trade, for few could have seen any prospect of substantial export.

Mutatis mutandis, there were no miners who said or cared much about commercial liberalism. This had nothing to do with incentives or self-interest. The industry was badly damaged during the 1810s, and it took until the 1840s before the mines were again capable of generating the same kind of growth that had occurred between 1760 and 1800. As a result, the economic contraction that Mexico faced in the early nineteenth century was a painful one. In the short run, at least, growth required the export of silver, but that possibility was largely foreclosed. Labor from the declining colonial textile industry could not find employment in any growing export sector. Plagued by persistent underemployment, agriculture could never compete with silver as a source of exports. Lucas Alamán, a stateman of considerable brilliance, knew what he was doing in advocating both the rehabilitation of mining and the creation of a mechanized textile industry.

At the same time, allegiance to established ways of doing things on the one hand and the changing international economic regime on the other created powerful constituencies. The old colonial woolen industry and an artisan cotton industry of more recent vintage depended on merchants for finance and distribution. Such merchants could not look favorably on free trade in English cottons, nor could the import-export merchants of Mexico City, who had been raised on the rents of the fleet system. Aside from Quirós and the Veracruz merchant guild, there were few who supported free trade. If merchants did not preach the gospel of expanding demand, then who would?

The real losers in the process of trade adjustment that began under the Bourbons were naturally opposed to it. Owners of obrajes and their spokesmen sensibly resisted freer trade in textiles. Artisans in the major cities who had their accumulated capital at risk were similarly opposed. Their stance is no mystery. And by the same token, the very strength of the urban artisan class—its concentrated numbers—made insecure regimes loath to provoke it. Experience and an obsessive concern with urban violence made protection politically expedient, for tariffs protected the income of people and resources wedded to the industry. The political benefits of supporting this group were manifest, and the economic costs, diffused. The political costs of opposing protection, on the other hand, must have been all too obvious to precarious governments.

Our final point concerns the necessary restructuring of the Mexican economy after 1750. For a generation, historians have recognized the agricultural adjustment required by Indian depopulation over the course of the sixteenth century. Obscured, perhaps, by terms such as *depression* and *crisis,* this change has been rebaptized as a "primitive emancipation" by John Lynch and accorded a positive interpretation in terms of investment in agriculture and industry, creole political hegemony, and more. Yet the Bourbon Reforms themselves served to accelerate an equally profound economic adjustment. They represented considerably more than a bureaucratic "reconquest": they actually speeded the integration of the Mexican economy into a growing international market for raw materials and cheaper wage goods. Indeed, their lowering of transportation and transaction costs in international trade was tantamount to reducing effective levels of protection. Of all the "novelties" of which the

Bourbons were accused, this may well have been the most novel, and, to date, the least appreciated.[57]

In this sense, later protectionist policies of the early republican and *santanista* regimes were counterrevolutionary. They sought to undo what the Bourbon reforms had wrought. As the first president to don the tricolor sash, Santa Anna undertook more than a Mexican emulation of the July Monarchy in France. The champion of stringent tariff protection and prohibitions was now the nation's advocate as well. Nationalism and protection were thereby united in Mexican political culture. In the final analysis, the victor at Tampico was truly the scourge of the Bourbons.

Notes

We are grateful to Ken Andrien, Woodrow Borah, Pedro Freile, Alan Knight, Pedro Pérez Herrero, Enrique Semo, Gabriel Tortella, and Jan de Vries for helpful comments on earlier versions of this essay.

1. Jan Bazant, *A Concise History of Mexico from Hidalgo to Cárdenas, 1805–1940* (New York, 1977), 61.

2. David Brading, *The Origins of Mexican Nationalism* (Cambridge, Eng., 1985), 68.

3. *The Economist* (London), 19 October 1861.

4. Lucas Alamán, *Historia de México desde los primeros movimientos que preparon su independencia en el año 1808 hasta la época presente,* 5 vols. (México, 1850–52; rpt., 1985), 5:918–31.

5. Anthony Pagden, *Spanish Imperialism and the Political Imagination* (New Haven, 1990), 140.

6. Robert Johannsen, *To the Halls of the Montezumas: The Mexican War in the American Imagination* (New York, 1985), 293–96. The Constitution of 1824 also elicited unfavorable comment in the United States because of its failure to disestablish the Catholic Church.

7. Anthony Butler to the Secretary of State, Mexico City, 5 January 1830, in Carlos Bosch García, ed., *Documentos de la relación de México con los Estados Unidos*, 4 vols. (México, 1983–85), 2:180.

8. Donald F. Stevens, "Economic Fluctuations and Political Instability in Early Republican Mexico," *Journal of Interdisciplinary History,* 4 (1986): 645–65.

9. Arthur Leewis, "The Rate of Growth of World Trade, 1830–1973," in Sven Grassman and Erik Lundberg, eds., *The World Economic Order: Past and Prospects* (New York, 1981), 12.

10. For example, see Paul Gootenberg, *Between Silver and Guano: Commercial Policy and the State in Postindependence Peru* (Princeton, 1989); or more generally, Joseph L. Love and Nils Jacobsen, eds., *Guiding the Invisible Hand: Economic Liberalism and the State in Latin American History* (New York, 1988). Ronald Rogowski, *Commerce and Coalitions: How Trade Affects Domestic Political Align-*

ments (Princeton, 1989), came too late to be incorporated into this paper but offers a related approach to the political economy of changing trade regimes, namely the two-good, two-factor Stolper-Samuelson model. The model we employ, a specific factors model, is simply a variant of the Stolper-Samuelson approach.

11. See John Lynch, *Spain under the Habsburgs,* 2 vols. (New York, 1981), 1:155–75, 2:174–211, for the earlier period. Antonio García-Baquero, *Cádiz y el Atlántico (1717–1778)* 2 vols. (Seville, 1976), provides a good sketch of Bourbon policy.

12. Carlos Daniel Malamud Rikles, *Cádiz y Saint Malo en el comercio colonial peruano (1698–1725)* (Cádiz, 1986).

13. Luis Chávez Orozco, *La libertad del comercio en la Nueva España en la segunda década del siglo XIX* (México, 1943), 103; Javier Ortiz de la Tabla, *Memorias políticas del consulado de Veracruz, 1796–1822* (Sevilla, 1985), 221.

14. Richard J. Salvucci, *Textiles and Capitalism in Mexico: An Economic History of the Obrajes, 1539–1840* (Princeton, 1987), 135–69. For contraband, see A. M. Bernal, "Libre comercio (1778): Un primer ensayo de modelo general," in Antonio Miguel Bernal, ed., *El comercio libre entre España y América Latina, 1765–1824* (Madrid, 1987), 21.

15. Bernal, "Libre comercio (1778)," 20–21. One point on the economics of contraband: Carlos Malamud terms contraband "direct trade," implying that the term can be substituted for fair trade. But although contraband evaded trade taxes, its cost to the consumer necessarily reflected the risk of seizure. That premium disappeared when trade was legalized. Even if comercio libre did no more than rechannel hitherto smuggled goods, it necessarily provided a greater stimulus to growth by removing the smuggling premium. Thus "direct" trade and "legal" trade are not economically interchangeable.

16. Chávez Orozco, *La libertad del comercio,* 147, 152, 178; Salvucci, *Textiles and Capitalism,* 160, 163. Others have discerned sharply falling prices for imported goods (especially cloth) in Chile, Arequipa, Potosí, and Charcas as well. See the essays by Kendall Brown (183–84), José Larraín (123), and Enrique Tandeter and Nathan Wachtel (202–12) in Lyman L. Johnson and Enrique Tandeter, eds., *Essays on the Price History of Eighteenth-Century Latin America* (Albuquerque, 1990).

17. Simon Kuznets, *Modern Economic Growth: Rate, Structure, and Spread* (New Haven, 1966), 305.

18. Luis Chávez Orozco, *El comercio exterior y el artesano mexicano* (México, 1965), 150.

19. David Brading, *Miners and Merchants in Bourbon Mexico, 1763–1810* (Cambridge, Eng., 1971), 114–15, 152.

20. As we indicate below, the price of silver on the London market scarcely varied at all between 1760 and 1800.

21. Salvucci, *Textiles and Capitalism,* 135–69.

22. A basic discussion of this model appears in Richard E. Caves and Ronald W. Jones, *World Trade and Payments: An Introduction* (New York, 1985), 95–101.

23. Our calculation is based on decade averages between 1760 and 1800. See U.S. Congress, Senate, *Report from the Secretary of the Treasury . . . Respecting the Relative Value of Gold and Silver,* 21st Cong., 1st sess., 4 May 1830, 93, Table EE.

For silver output, see *Estadísticas históricas de México,* 2 vols. (México, 1985), 2:437–subperiods 1761–80 and 1781–1800.

24. Readers may recall the troubles at the Real del Monte mine over Regla's less than coincidental attempt to reduce the mining wage. See Brading, *Miners and Merchants,* 148.

25. Ibid., 152.

26. Salvucci, *Textiles and Capitalism,* 89, 91–93.

27. Cristiana Borchardt de Moreno, *Los mercaderes y el capitalismo en México (1759–1778)* (México, 1984), 158–59.

28. Brian Hamnett, *Politics and Trade in Southern Mexico, 1750–1821* (Cambridge, Eng., 1971), 118–19; Salvucci, *Textiles and Capitalism,* 59–60; Guy Thomson, "The Cotton Industry in Puebla During the Eighteenth and Early Nineteenth Centuries," in Nils Jacobsen and Hans-Jürgen Puhle, eds., *The Economies of Mexico and Peru During the Late Colonial Period, 1760–1810* (Berlin, 1986), 179–80.

29. Chávez Orozco, *La libertad del comercio,* 146.

30. Hamnett, *Politics and Trade,* 154–55.

31. Javier Ortiz de la Tabla, *Memorias políticas y económicas del consulado de Veracruz, 1796–1822* (Sevilla, 1985), 205–26.

32. Salvucci, *Textiles and Capitalism,* chap. 1.

33. Michael P. Costeloe, *Response to Revolution: Imperial Spain and the Spanish American Revolutions, 1810–1840* (New York, 1986), 24, 33–34, 57–58, 130–31.

34. Enrique Florescano and Fernando Castillo, *Controversia sobre la libertad de comercio en Nueva España, 1776–1818,* 2 vols. (México, 1975), 2:101–2, 109.

35. Chávez Orozco, *La libertad del comercio,* 153.

36. Costeloe, *Response to Revolution,* 130–31; Humberto Tandrón, *El comercio de Nueva España y la controversia sobre la libertad de comercio, 1796–1821* (México, 1976), 35–41.

37. *Actas constitucionales mexicanas,* 10 vols. (México, 1980), 7:255–75, 9:543–65.

38. Chávez Orozco, *El comercio exterior,* 156.

39. Robert E. Lipsey, *Price and Quantity Trends in the Foreign Trade of the United States* (Princeton, NJ, 1963), 5.

40. Brading, *Miners and Merchants,* 132.

41. Our calculations. For coinage, see Alamán, *Historia de México,* 1:4. For silver prices, see U.S. Congress, Senate, *Relative Value of Gold and Silver,* table EE.

42. México, Congreso Constituyente, Comisiones de sistema de hacienda y minería, *Dictamen presentado al soberano congreso general constituyente . . . sobre que no se aumenten los derechos de extracción del oro y la plata* (México, 1823), 5, 9–10. In essence, the specie-flow mechanism "ensures" that trade deficits will be self-limiting. The drain of specie needed to finance an excess of imports brings down the domestic price level and in so doing promotes exports.

43. Ortiz de la Tabla, *Memorias políticas,* 175.

44. Florescano and Castillo, *Controversia sobre la libertad de comercio,* 2:40.

45. Juan Carlos Garavaglia and Juan Carlos Grosso, "La región de Puebla-Tlaxcala y la economía novohispana (1670–1821)," *Historia mexicana,* 35 (1986):

549–99; Clara Elena Suárez Arguello, *La política cerealera en la economía novohispana: El caso de trigo* (México, 1985), 58–70.

46. For a discussion of North American competition in the Spanish Caribbean, see Linda K. Salvucci, "Development and Decline: The Port of Philadelphia and Spanish Imperial Markets, 1783–1823" (Ph.D. diss., Princeton University, 1985), 74–79. Arango's analysis appears in "Expediente instruido por el Consulado de la Habana sobre los medios que convenga proponer para sacar la agricultura y comercio de esta isla del apuro en que se hallan" (Havana: Oficina del Gobierno y Capitanía General, 1808), nos. 7–8, Archivo General de Indias, Santo Domingo, leg. 1157. See also Alamán, *Historia de México,* 1:109–10.

47. David Brading, "Government and Elite in Late Colonial Mexico," *Hispanic American Historical Review,* 53 (1973): 389–414.

48. Guy P. C. Thomson, *Puebla de los Angeles: Industry and Society in a Mexican City, 1700–1850* (Boulder, CO, 1989), 55.

49. Enrique Semo, *Siete ensayos sobre la hacienda mexicana, 1780–1880* (México, 1977), 13.

50. See the useful collection of protests against the consolidación in Masae Sugawara H., *La deuda pública de España y la economía novohispana, 1804–1809* (México, 1976).

51. Salvucci, *Textiles and Capitalism,* chap. 3.

52. David Walker, *Business, Kinship and Politics: The Martínez del Rio Family in Mexico, 1823–1867* (Austin, TX, 1986), 151.

53. Gabriel Haslip Viera, "Crime and the Administration of Justice in Colonial Mexico City, 1696–1810" (Ph.D. diss., Columbia University, 1980), 75–104, 265–78; Gloria Artis Espriu, *Regatonas y maquileros: El mercado de trigo en la ciudad de México (siglo XVIII)* (México, 1986), 67–68.

54. Susan Deans-Smith, "The Gentle and Easy Tax: The Bourbons and the Royal Tobacco Monopoly of New Spain, 1765–1821," (Ph.D. diss., University of Cambridge, 1984), 292–303.

55. Torcuato di Tella, "The Dangerous Classes of Early Nineteenth-Century Mexico," *Journal of Latin American Studies,* 5 (1973): 79–105.

56. Michael P. Costeloe, *La primera república federal de México (1824–1835)* México, 1975), 214–15; Harold Sims, *Descolonización en México: El conflicto entre mexicanos y españoles (1821–1831)* (México, 1982), 74–89.

57. The nature and consequences of the Bourbon reforms are questioned in Linda K. Salvucci, "'Costumbres viejas, hombres nuevos': José de Gálvez y la burocracia fiscal novohispana, 1754–1800," *Historia mexicana,* 33 (1983): 224–64.

6

Mexican Merchants and Their Links to Spain, 1750–1850

JOHN E. KICZA

Many of the leading merchants of late colonial Mexico City were natives of Spain who had come to New Spain as youths to make their fortunes. Despite their origins and abiding identification with Spain, they responded rapidly and effectively to the shifting economic currents of the eighteenth century, although most of these changes increasingly disadvantaged the long-suffering economy of their mother country. As a consequence of this responsiveness, Mexico City's wholesalers remained preeminent within the colony and regularly carried out profitable trade with ports throughout the empire and at times with non-Spanish destinations in both the Americas and Europe. Colonial traders did not hesitate to circumvent government initiatives intended to bring their trade, income, and unrivaled control over Mexico's silver production under tighter regulation by the state.[1] This is not to deny that the colonial government played a significant role in the economy by virtue of the size of its bureaucracy, its taxation and regulatory systems (which, even if evaded, helped to frame economic options), and certain official monopolies.

By and large, the governments of late colonial and early independent Mexico were equally ineffectual in imposing themselves in the affairs of the large trading firms, though the national government was in a far greater state of disrepair than its predecessor. Much more devastating to these international merchants were the collapse of the country's credit and marketing systems during the disruption of the wars for independence and the accompanying collapse of the silver-mining industry. The latter is illustrated in table 1. However, they shifted their investments and business practices accordingly, with the result that many of these families would retain their wealth and social prominence throughout the nineteenth century.

Despite their economic alienation from Spain and their presence during Mexico's long and bitter struggle for independence, these merchant fami-

Table 1 Mexican Precious Metal Exports, Annual Average per Quinquennium, 1781–85 to 1846–50

Period	Annual Average Export (Pesos)
1781–85	20,249,114
1786–90	18,541,482
1791–95	23,246,841
1796–1800	23,093,611
1801–5	22,559,967
1806–10	22,771,278
1811–15	7,093,371
1816–20	11,189,772
1821–25	4,827,821
1826–30	2,111,193
1831–35	1,071,887
1836–40	1,243,094
1841–45	1,950,320
1846–50	1,951,807

Source: Miguel Lerdo de Tejada, *Comercio exterior de México* (México, 1853), app. 54.

lies retained close emotional ties to Spain throughout the nineteenth century, even though many came under creole leadership during its initial decades. In their deep devotion to the Catholic Church, their loyalty to strong central governments—and sometimes to monarchical schemes—and their belief in the superiority of traditional Spanish cultural norms and practices, these families were instrumental in shaping the conservative movement that would emerge in the 1840s to become a powerful force in the 1850s and 1860s. They provided Mexico with political and cultural continuity from the late colonial period until at least the Porfiriato, though it was a viewpoint often at odds with the liberalism that dominated the country during much of this time. Some members become targets of strident Mexican nationalists, first in the late 1820s and then again with the collapse of Maximilian's empire in the second half of the 1860s. In general, however, they were able to ride out these waves of resentment, benefiting at least somewhat from their close personal and business ties with leaders from the other side of the political spectrum. By at least 1750 the international wholesalers clustered in the prosperous colonial capital of Mexico City had typically developed diversified commercial networks that were little dependent on Spain as a producer of goods or on its merchant houses as suppliers of manufactured items from elsewhere. As earlier, most of the colonial merchants were immigrants from Spain itself, but commonly they were affiliated with already established local elite families who sponsored and financed them. Ultimately, their success would be affirmed and their loyalty sealed through marriage into their sponsoring families, often to their cousins.[2]

Spain's growing economic weakness was matched by its government's diplomatic and military ineptitude, which placed yet greater strain on overseas business operations. Nonetheless, despite the obvious and painful decrepitude of the mother country and their own predictable absorption into the creole elite of Mexico City, the international traders of that city consistently defended Mexico's colonial status against the rising current of patriotic sentiment during the first two decades of the nineteenth century. Their notorious political leanings threatened their standing in Mexico once independence was attained. Despite this, even Mexican-born members of these mercantile families—whose numerous business interests were no longer directed toward or dependent on Spain—would retain close cultural and family identification with that country. Strong attachments to religious and ethnic organizations, alienation from the anticlerical liberalism that characterized Mexico's political leadership in the nineteenth century, and continued contact with blood relatives in Spain through both correspondence and travel fostered such attitudes.

Overall, these families prospered at least to the extent necessary to remain within the Mexican elite in this period, and their members held positions in both local and national governments increasingly as the century passed. Though sometimes required to participate in the new political system to protect their particular interests, these families did not view themselves as "part of the system" in early national Mexico, and most of their prominent members gave strong support to the empire of Maximilian in the 1860s. But even after the Liberal defeat of the French intervention, these families remained in Mexico and, unlike some others, were not dispossessed by the victorious political faction. They passed into the Porfiriato still wealthy, prominent, and entrenched, and their members thrived as businessmen, professionals, and financiers up until at least the Revolution.

The primary family traced in this study is the Iturbe e Iraeta. It initially rose into prominence in the second half of the eighteenth century and intermarried or entered into long-term business arrangements with other families that also achieved elite standing through commerce at this time. These include most prominently the Icaza and also the Echave and the Alvarez Arizpe. By early in the nineteenth century, marriage had brought the Iturbe e Iraeta into close alliance with a more established, but still commercially oriented, creole family, the González Garay. The routes these families followed, first to commercial success and then to long-term elite status reflect well the changed business world of the late eighteenth century and the peripheral role that Spanish interests already played, at least in some sectors.[3]

Nothing distinguished Francisco Ignacio de Iraeta from scores of other Basque immigrants to Mexico in the 1740s. He was only twelve years old and without any prospect of a secure profession or a significant inheritance in his home town of Anzuola in the interior of Guipúzcoa Province. He had distant relatives in Mexico City, but they did not afford him such assistance as to make his career, and after four years he embarked for Manila. Based there over the next decade, he made a comfortable living and, more important, a reputation as a knowledgeable and upright young merchant. When he returned to Mexico City in 1758, he was able immediately to enter into a partnership to import goods from Manila. Within five years he had married the sole daughter of an established international trader, Pedro de Ganuza, and went into business with him. In 1769, upon Ganuza's death, Iraeta, still only thirty-seven years of age, assumed sole control over the family commercial house, with the widow turning her inheritance over for him to manage.[4]

Iraeta and the later directors of the merchant house during the remainder of the colonial period regularly traded with Spanish firms, but they never subordinated themselves to any European-based business. In fact, they commonly dealt with a half-dozen Spanish merchant houses, most of them in Cádiz, but also a couple in Bilbao, and they knew traders located in other Spanish ports. However, in their letters from the 1790s and 1800s, Iraeta and his successors frequently complained about the difficulty of selling goods imported from Spain.[5] There was little residual demand for them, and they could command only low prices. But this persistent problem did not significantly handicap the family trading firm, for it had long ago shifted the emphasis of its trade to other parts.

For at least a half-century, and even for some years after independence, Iraeta and his successors traded extensively with the Pacific ports of Spanish South America—particularly Guayaquil and Lima—with Manila, and with the circum-Caribbean region, particularly Guatemala City, Havana, and New Orleans. Cacao from Guayaquil and Chinese-produced goods brought through Manila enjoyed great demand in Mexico. Cochineal and indigo were brought from Oaxaca and Guatemala, along with Indian-manufactured mantas and other items. Apparently, they also sought to sell manufactured goods throughout the Caribbean. In addition, there are some hints that this merchant house had at least irregular trade with Jamaica.

All of these trading routes without links to Spain could be maintained because of the economic growth these regions experienced over the course of the eighteenth century and their continued prosperity as that century neared its end. The Mexican market economy, spurred by the resurgence of silver mining, the rise of dye production, and a vast increase in commercial agriculture, had expanded to the point—extending even into Guatemala—that the larger colony approximated a single integrated zone of exchange.[6] The Iturbe e Iraeta trading firm ensured that it had continual access to silver specie, for previous metals gave it a favorable purchasing posture and also the ability to expand that access to ready cash into far more extensive lines of credit. Depending on the specific transaction, the trading house could extend credit, make loans to obtain an account, or seek favorable terms of repayment from a supplier.

The tremendous resurgence of silver production after 1750 extended over roughly a sixty-year period until gravely damaged by the wars for independence. In an influential article, John Coatsworth has demonstrated that use of a reasonable deflation index suggests that the value of Mexican silver production actually stagnated from the 1790s on.[7] Nonetheless, his own figure displaying this trend shows that even this deflated mining output by quinquennium did not notably decrease between the 1750–54 period and 1810, except for the years of 1785–89.[8] Thus Mexican merchants, whose mechanisms for guaranteed access to silver specie have been the subject of several works, enjoyed a very strong international commercial position until 1810. Table 1 displays the level of Mexican precious-metal exports from 1781–85 to 1846–50. The high value and stability of these exports are obvious.

Although powerful and usually autonomous in their own right, the merchant princes of Mexico City appreciated the advantages gained from coordinating the activities of several of their firms. The closest enduring alliances were characteristically sealed through marriage between the families of the directors. In 1782 Iraeta's eldest daughter married Isidro Antonio de Icaza, an international trader from Mexico City who was about twenty years her senior and a close business associate of her father.

Isidro Antonio and his four brothers had prospered by taking to a greater extreme the commercial disassociation from Spain evinced by Iraeta. Also of Basque descent, they were natives of Santiago Veragua in the province of Panama. The five men distributed themselves along the Pacific Coast of Spanish America, functioning as a profitable commercial network, dealing especially in cacao out of the port of Guayaquil, where one of Isidro's brothers was stationed. Another brother eventually migrated to Mexico, becoming a trusted manager for both Isidro Antonio and the Iturbe e Iraeta family. The other two brothers situated themselves in Lima and Tierra Firme. Soon after establishing himself in Mexico City, Isidro Antonio de Icaza took into his business a relative of Iraeta through the maternal line, José María de Echave, who had likewise come over from the Basque country. A much younger man, he rose through partnerships with Icaza to become a major merchant and member of the consulado and married a daughter of another Icaza brother.[9]

Early in the last decade of the eighteenth century, Iraeta and Icaza gained the opportunity to espouse their distinctive trading philosophy against fellow members of the traders' guild and to make common cause with the powerful viceroy Revillagigedo, who remained their advocate even after his return to Spain.[10] After the extension of formal free trade to Mexico in the late 1780s, the consulado issued a series of statements denouncing the new policy as pernicious to the orderly supply and distribution of goods to the colony. The colonial government sought out dissenters among the wholesale merchants who would support the new policy. In 1791 it found only three: Tomás Murphy, closely affiliated with the Gálvez faction that designed so many of the new colonial commercial regulations, Iraeta, and Icaza. As noted, Iraeta remained a close friend of Revillagigedo for the rest of his life, writing the former viceroy after his return to Spain and even shipping money across the ocean on his behalf.

Once having assumed the directorship of a major Mexico City trading house, Francisco Ignacio quickly transformed himself into the family patriarch, favoring the relatives he brought over to Mexico and those who remained in his home town. After only a few years, Iraeta was surrounded by trusted kinsmen, some of whom eventually established businesses under their direction, although they were typically affiliated with the businesses of Francisco Ignacio. A cousin, José de Iraeta, became a primary assistant, serving as Francisco Ignacio's manager in both commercial and agricultural enterprises. A nephew, Gabriel de Iturbe e Iraeta—one of four brothers who all answered their uncle's summons to the colony—served a commercial apprenticeship under Iraeta, married his daughter, and on Iraeta's death in 1797, assumed control over the trading house and the larger sphere of family affairs and kept it until his own death in 1812.

But Iraeta did not recruit relatives to Mexico just to serve as trading associates. Another cousin, Pablo Antonio de Iraeta, was brought to Mexico to be trained as a cleric, not as a merchant. Francisco Ignacio financed the education of his cousin, and Pablo Antonio remained in Mexico for a couple of decades after ordination, enjoying revenue from several chaplaincies and the curacy of San Cristóbal Ecátepec. Around the time of Mexican independence he returned to the Basque provinces, though he retained his income from these clerical endowments. In 1843 he dispatched a power of attorney to Mexico to ensure collection of the funds still owed him from these posts.[11]

Two of the four Iturbe e Iraeta brothers whom in Francisco Ignacio brought to Mexico were also educated as priests under his aegis. One lived out his life as the curate of Tenancingo, but the other, José Ignacio, returned to his Basque hometown some years after his ordination. There he became responsible for the general well-being of the many family members living in the area—at least in the eyes of his uncle in Mexico. Francisco Ignacio continually sent him advice, orders, funds, and reminders to write to him about the Spanish branch of the family more often and to do still more on its behalf. Iraeta's heavy-handed domination over family affairs in Spain is evident in letters to this nephew, in which he stated that female relatives who did not follow his recommendations regarding marriage partners could expect no money toward their dowries.[12]

The fourth Iturbe e Iraeta brother, Manuel, came to Mexico only after failing to get a post as a commercial clerk in Cádiz despite efforts by his uncle. Once in Mexico he dedicated himself to a military rather than a commercial career. This soon required his return to Spain, but sometime in the early 1790s he was rotated back to Mexico as a junior officer in one of the Spanish units permanently stationed there. In 1795 his uncle intervened in his career, writing to an acquaintance in Madrid to request his assistance in getting Manuel promoted to captain.[13] He soon received the promotion. While stationed in Guanajuato, Manuel wed María de la Luz Alamán, a member of the mining elite of that society and the sister of the famous conservative politician and financier of early independent Mexico, Lucas Alamán, a figure with whom the family had recurring business dealings. In 1804 Manuel became military commander of a northern province in New Spain. In 1811 a widespread insurrection inspired by the Hidalgo Revolt forced his unit to retreat south under great duress; Manuel himself barely survived. Ultimately, Manuel did not live to see Mexican independence. The conditions of his death—including whether he died on active duty—remain unknown.

The relative of Iraeta who received the greatest and most consistent aid in the advancement of his military career was yet another nephew, Gabriel María de Mendizábal, who never departed from Spain. In letters to business and political associates in Spain, Iraeta made it very plain that they were to spare no expense or effort in furthering Mendizábal's career. Iraeta may have expended around 100,000 pesos in this regard, including 30,000 pesos to finance Mendizábal's successful candidacy to become a Gentleman of the Order of Calatrava. Iraeta's death did not end activities by the Mexican branch of the family to assist Mendizábal's military undertakings. In 1811 Gabriel de Iturbe e Iraeta, himself Mendizábal's cousin and of course Iraeta's successor as head of the merchant house, joined with several other Spanish-born Mexico City merchants to promote a patriotic subscription there for the aid of the Seventh Army under the command of General Mendizábal fighting against the Napoleonic invasion.[15] Mendizábal's career continued on the ascent: he held high-ranking posts in the military and the government of Spain after the expulsion of the French until his death in 1833.

Francisco Ignacio de Iraeta's continuing devotion to his home town and province was shown through his absentee officeholding and funding of local improvements. In 1765 Iraeta actually held the post of *alcalde proprietario* in the *cabildo* of Anzuola, even though he was in residence in Mexico. His father and brother also occupied posts in the town government that year. Iraeta was preoccupied with reestablishing and maintaining the preeminence of his lineage in Spain. To that end he repeatedly transmitted large sums of money to improve his family's residence there, to enlarge the roads and the lands around it, to build an addition to the local parish church, and to have an elaborate altarpiece constructed for the church.[16]

The French invasion of the Basque provinces in 1794 and 1795 caused Iraeta great travail and his family a considerable loss. Anzuola was overrun, but Iraeta initially expressed great relief, for all of his relatives escaped safely. Acting as the patriarch of the Spanish branch of the family, he directed the refugees in their behavior toward each other and in sharing the properties and funds they now had available. In another letter of May 1795 after Iraeta had been informed that his eldest brother had fled Anzuola without first burying the family silver, he excoriated him for failing to take even the most basic precautions.[17]

Iraeta and his successors as head of the Mexican branch of the family celebrated their profound pride in their Basque heritage primarily through membership in the Cofradía de Nuestra Señora de Aránzazu, the patron saint of the Basque territories. Family leaders characteristically joined the

Cofradía del Santisimo Sacramento, perhaps the most prestigious and best funded confraternity in Mexico City up to the Reform, and they occasionally acknowledged in letters to each other that they used leadership positions in confraternities to further family interests through the naming of chaplains, the granting of dowries, and the making of loans from organizational funds. But their deep devotion to the Aránzazu confraternity cannot be doubted. Iraeta held the post of treasurer in 1767 when the confraternity inaugurated Las Vizcaínas, its famous school for girls of Basque descent, in Mexico City. He rose to become rector in 1794–95. His son-in-law, Isidro Antonio de Icaza, served as rector in 1806–7, and José María de Echave, related through blood or marriage to both of them, was rector three times: 1814–15, 1822–23, and 1829–30. In fact, relatives held the rectorship from 1829 through 1835. Nine separate members of the family were represented on the confraternity's board of directors between 1822 and 1873, and a family member was on the board for all but two years (during the late 1840s) over this entire fifty-two-year period.[18]

During his sixteen-year term as head of the family after Iraeta's death in 1797, Gabriel de Iturbe e Iraeta followed most of the policies and practices of his predecessor. Himself a native of Anzuola, despite having emigrated to Mexico at about the age of sixteen, Iturbe e Iraeta maintained close contact with his relatives back home, and it is clear that he felt warmly toward them. However, unlike Iraeta, he was not a demanding patriarch. He did not recruit large numbers of junior relatives to train under him in Mexico, and he was not fervently committed to embellishing the family name in its ancestral home, perhaps because Iraeta had already done that so well. His patterns of commerce closely approximated those of his predecessor, with emphasis on trade with other American colonies and the Philippines and on the shipment of highly valued commodities, such as cacao, cochineal, and indigo. His business manager, who was always subordinate to him even when in partnership, was a Basque, Leonardo Alvarez, who had married in Arizpe. Yet another Basque lineage, the Arizpe family had intermarried with the Iturbe e Iraeta family back in Spain. In the 1811 census of Mexico City, Iturbe e Iraeta had two peninsular-born merchant apprentices living with him.[19] Both were trained in commerce along with his own son, Gabriel Manuel de Iturbe e Iraeta, and became his son's business associates in the years after independence.

In 1809, responding to the crisis in Spain brought about by the Napoleonic invasion, Lieutenant Colonel Gabriel de Iturbe e Iraeta of the Mexico City militia company of merchants loaned 100,000 pesos to the mother country to fund its defense.[20] He remained a firm loyalist until his death in 1812.

Despite these activites, Mexican-born family members seemingly never visited Spain, and this preeminent branch was entrenching itself ever more deeply in the Mexican social and business elite. The family in Mexico City had less immediate and compelling associations with Spain and their many relatives still living there. Whereas Francisco Ignacio de Iraeta had married his three daughters to two Spanish-born merchants and one Spanish-born colonial judge, Gabriel married most of his children to locally born individuals. The one exception, the marriage of a daughter with a government official, had a disastrous result, as the husband proved to be quite inept and a bit disreputable. The marriages of two other daughters to sons of Isidro Antonio de Icaza, who had themselves become merchants, strengthened a vital business relationship. And the son of Gabriel who succeeded him as head of family affairs, Gabriel Manuel (the only other son was simpleminded and was always cared for by family members), married a member of the González Garay, an elite creole family that had remained very active in overseas trade. The González Garay were leaders of the Montañés party, the Basque party's rival in the merchants guild. So by the early nineteenth century, the Iturbe e Iraeta were not such ardent Basque loyalists as to let that identity interfere with an advantageous marriage.

When Gabriel Manuel inherited the family's trading firm in 1812, it became the second of the three major commercial operations within the larger family group to come under creole direction. In 1808 upon the death of Isidro Antonio de Icaza, two of his locally born sons assumed control of that family's business operations. Only José María de Echave would continue to head his own firm well past independence. But in time his creole sons likewise became merchants with diversified interests.

Their Mexican birthplace and their negligible economic links to Spain notwithstanding, Gabriel Manuel and his siblings never wavered from their loyalty to Spain at least up to the Iturbide revolt. Like his father, Gabriel Manuel became a lieutenant colonel in the merchants' militia of Mexico City and also served on the city council, becoming a *regidor* as an archroyalist in 1818.[21] With so many family members being of Mexican birth and with all their holdings and valuable business networks rooted in Mexico, the extended Iturbe e Iraeta lineage never considered relocating in Spain during the independence struggle. In fact, a couple of young Spaniards, at least one of whom was a relative, immigrated to Mexico around the time of the insurgencies, affiliated themselves with family businesses, eventually married into the kin group, and became prominent actors in the business of the new nation.[22]

The documentation examined to date does not reveal the relationship of the Iturbe e Iraeta family with Agustín de Iturbide, but so far the indications are that the kin group made its peace with his successful independence movement, and at least a couple of members became caught up in it. Isidro Ignacio de Icaza, a cleric and member of the university faculty, was a signer of the Act of Independence. His brother, Juan de Icaza, loaned Iturbide 40,000 pesos to help stabilize his government and was promoted to colonel of the army during the regency.[23] Also, a couple of family members were named to the Order of Guadalupe, the unsuccessful attempt by Iturbide to attract support from prominent families by creating an officially recognized elite.

The devastation caused by the wars for independence and the collapse of the credit and marketing systems that had previously prevailed crippled the economy of early national Mexico.[24] Table 1 shows the rapid and enormous falloff of precious-metal exports that befell the country after independence. This development gravely damaged Mexican merchants' ability to operate successfully against foreign competitors, who now had unprecedented access to the national market. Table 2 shows the contraction of exports after independence, while imports remained reasonably high.

The Iturbe e Iraeta wholesale house sought to maintain its established trading networks despite the great political changes and economic upheaval that were occurring. It imported goods from Manila on a large scale at least through 1826 and brought in cacao from Guayaquil well into the 1830s. Of course, its small amount of direct commerce with Spain ceased after 1821, but this was replaced by greater trade with England.[25] The firm dealt directly with London trading firms through the late 1820s and seemingly into the 1830s, when the international aspects of the family's business activities declined notably.[26] The family continued to organize its commercial operations into partnerships, just as it had in earlier generations. Gabriel Manuel maintained three successive commercial partnerships after independence. Each ended with the death of his partner, until the third, which ended with his own demise in the late 1830s.

Although the collapse of silver production had gravely handicapped the Iturbe e Iraetas' foreign trade, they benefited after independence from the diversity of markets and products that they had developed late in the eighteenth century. They were heavily involved in the shipment of cochineal dye from southern Mexico, and the export of this commodity remained substantial at least into the 1830s. Table 3 shows the value of

Table 2 Import and Export Figures for the Ports of Veracruz and Alvarado Combined, 1802–28

	Exports (Pesos)	Imports (Pesos)	Exports Minus Imports (Pesos)
1802	38,400,000	22,000,000	16,400,000
1803	14,500,000	19,900,000	−7,400,000
1804	21,500,000	16,500,000	5,000,000
1805	900,000	3,400,000	−2,500,000
1806	4,100,000	7,100,000	−3,000,000
1807	22,500,000	16,700,000	5,800,000
1808	14,600,000	10,400,000	4,200,000
1809	28,300,000	20,400,000	7,900,000
1810	15,900,000	20,400,000	−4,500,000
1811	9,900,000	11,300,000	−1,400,000
1812	5,100,000	5,200,000	−100,000
1813			
1814	N.A.	N.A.	N.A.
1815			
1816	7,700,000	10,000,000	−2,300,000
1817	8,500,000	8,800,000	−300,000
1818	4,700,000	5,800,000	−1,100,000
1819	8,700,000	10,100,000	−1,400,000
1820			
1821	N.A.	N.A.	N.A.
1822			
1823	2,300,000	4,400,000	−2,100,000
1824	4,500,000	11,800,000	−7,300,000
1825	7,600,000	15,500,000	−7,900,000
1826	7,600,000	15,500,000	−7,900,000
1827	12,200,000	14,900,000	−2,700,000
1828	14,500,000	10,000,000	4,500,000

Source: Lerdo de Tejada, *Comercio exterior,* app. 15–35.

cochineal exports and their share of total exports in the 1820s. The stability of their total value on an annual basis was a special asset in a time of sudden fluctuations.

The other commodity that favored the Iturbe e Iraeta in this era was cacao, which remained in considerable demand in Mexico. The family had imported this product in a major way since at least the 1790s, as it exploited its ties to the branch of the Icaza family based in Guayaquil. Table 4 records the continuing preeminence of cacao from this source in the late 1820s.

Table 3 Major Export Products of Mexico, 1821 and 1823–28

Year	Total Value (Pesos)	Minerals	Dyes	Dyes as Percentage of Total
1821	9,969,517	8,423,966	1,395,053	14.0
1822	NA	NA	NA	NA
1823	2,346,137	1,324,970	923,867	39.4
1824	4,490,515	2,836,132	1,568,987	34.9
1825	5,082,240	3,704,123	1,113,116	21.9
1826	7,648,137	5,854,160	1,504,824	19.7
1827	12,171,780	9,670,358	1,207,508	9.9
1828	14,488,793	12,391,467	1,812,561	12.5

Source: Inés Herrera Canales, *El comercio exterior de México, 1821–1875* (Mexico, 1977), 60, table 21.

The close ties that had developed among these families in the decades before the outbreak of the independence movement were reinforced in the early national period. The social and economic imperatives that had fostered such affiliations throughout the colonial period remained just as strong—perhaps stronger—in the distressed political and economic climate after independence. At least eight cross-cousin marriages took place within this group of families in the generation that entered young adulthood around the time of independence, and at least as many took place in the next generation. In several cases, when a spouse died, the survivor married yet another relative, perhaps a younger sister of the late wife. Many members of these families never married, but few entered the church.

Table 4 Cacao Imports from Guayaquil and Mexico, 1825–28

Year	Mexico Total (Pesos)	Guayaquil (Pesos)	Guayaquil as Percentage of Total
1825	463,641	358,464	77.3
1826	481,570	424,969	88.2
1827	523,505	386,379	71.8
1828	369,547	254,440	68.9

Source: Herrera Canales, *El comercio exterior,* 44, table 16.

Marriage outside of the group usually occurred with offspring of other prominent local business families. There were some matches, though, with wealthy or prestigious immigrants, including an Englishman and a German as well as several Spaniards. Two Alvarez Arizpe daughters who married Spaniards moved with them to Spain. After one of the husbands died, his children eventually immigrated to Mexico City but retained claims to funds and properties in Spain. In 1855, fully twenty years after their father's demise, some of these children were still dispatching powers of attorney—sometimes with Mexican relatives who were going to Spain on business—to try to gain their shares of their paternal grandparent's and their father's estates.[27] The Arizpes had always been among the most dispersed of the several families intermarried with the Iturbe e Iraeta, with some continually present in Seville, others in Mexico, and some regularly moving back and forth.[28]

Donato Manterola left Guipúzcoa for Mexico despite the ongoing insurrections there that culminated in independence. He prospered as an international merchant and married a daughter of José María de Echave in the 1830s. By that time he had become a close business associate of the interrelated families, serving as a bondsman for some of the members who assumed posts of public trust and investing in businesses with the Iturbe, Icaza, and Echave.[29] He continued to be deeply engaged in overseas commerce until his premature death in 1848 and served as rector of the Cofradía de Nuestra Señora de Aránzazu shortly before his passing. As was the pattern with so many others, he, and later his parents, left behind them properties and businesses in the Basque country that were inherited in part by his two surviving children and his wife.[30]

The debilitated governments of early national Mexico could do little in a positive way to shape the business and investment preferences of wealthy families.[31] Further, the Liberals, whose factions controlled the government most of the first several decades of independence, believed that the economy would benefit most if the state did not try to affect its direction. The liberals were also reluctant to interrupt any flow of revenue to the chronically bankrupt government, and most of the government's income flowed from excise taxes on imports. The collapse of the national economy, as partly evidenced in tables 1–4, did far more to influence family economic decisions, though some prominent investors came to depend heavily on financing the chronically bankrupt federal government.[32] Others prevailed upon the government for franchises to build roads and railroads or to operate the official tobacco monopoly, but such activity was never of the scale necessary to undergird a family's long-term prosperity.

The nationalist sentiment that developed in Mexico in the late 1820s did threaten some family members who were well known for their pro-Spanish sentiments.[33] At least one had his business attacked. Francisco Antonio de Iturbe, a native of Vergara, a neighboring town of Anzuola in Guipúzcoa Province, and a relative of the Iturbe e Iraeta family, lived most of his adult life as a storekeeper in Pátzcuaro, Michoacán, successively marrying three women there.[34] In 1827, as reported by Lucas Alamán, a force of perhaps thirty men attacked his establishment. Not much more than a year later, he and his family had relocated to Mexico City, where at least some of them lived in the Iturbe e Iraeta family mansion and business headquarters on Calle de la Palma. Francisco María de Iturbe, the son of Francisco Antonio, became Gabriel Manuel de Iturbe e Iraeta's business associate, and after the latter's death he became head of the extended family until his own death in 1861. Along the way Francisco María became one of the most notorious *agiotistas* of his time, a major investor in mines, textile mills, and road construction, and even briefly minister of the treasury.[35]

In late 1828 José María de Echave was so convinced that he would soon be expelled from the country under anti-Spanish legislation that he issued a power of attorney to his wife and two of his sons enabling them to manage his enterprises in his absence and answer for him to the Public Treasury.[36] But not four months later he was one of three family members on the list of government-approved exceptions to the Expulsion Law of 20 March 1829, the others being Francisco Antonio de Iturbe and Pedro Lascuraín, Gabriel Manuel de Iturbe e Iraeta's junior business partner, who was married to one of the daughters of Isidro Antonio de Icaza.[37]

The extended Iturbe e Iraeta family was in no way exceptional in the early national period in having Spanish-born members, remaining active in the business world of the new nation, and retaining strong attachments to Spain—either as homeland, refuge, or the source of an admired cultural tradition. Other families that became centered in Mexico City had similar characteristics and provided some of the core members of a politically and culturally conservative group of prominent businessmen. For example, the Alonso de Terán family of merchants brought over a nephew in 1818. Upon inheriting his uncle's estates in 1835, he emerged as one of the most powerful businessmen and financiers of mid-nineteenth-century Mexico.[38]

Other Spaniards who had migrated to the provinces of Mexico in the late colonial period moved to the capital after independence, recognizing the business opportunities available in Mexico City that no longer prevailed in the deteriorated economic setting of their former bases. Juan Antonio de Béistegui stands in sharp contrast to the Iturbe e Iraeta family's pattern of maintaining its already well-established wealth and social position. He was one of the many poor immigrants to move to Mexico from the north of Spain in the late colonial period. He first based himself in Guanajuato, where he enjoyed only moderate success as a storeowner and married a local woman of modest circumstances. It was not until 1830 that he and his family moved to Mexico City. There Béistegui set up a merchant house with initial capital of 16,000 pesos, a modest sum (international and provincial wholesalers of the city commonly funded their operations in the hundreds of thousands of pesos). But he enjoyed immediate and dramatic success in his business, and by 1838 he declared that his commercial firm was worth 250,000 pesos. Like its counterparts in the colonial period, the business loaned money in addition to selling goods and also took in deposits to expand the scale of its commercial operations.[39]

Béistegui trained his sons in the business and eventually drew them into partnerships. Like some other merchant-bankers of his era, he typically insisted on real estate as collateral from borrowers. As a consequence of the default of such debts, Béistegui became a major proprietor of urban properties. With the Liberal Party victory in the War of the Reform, he invested heavily in the acquisition of Mexico City buildings alienated from the church.[40]

By the late 1830s Béistegui had established himself as a successful agiotista. In 1848 he expanded this type of endeavor by participating with other prominent financiers in renting the tobacco monopoly from the government. The following year, this same consortium bought out the Real de Monte mining company from its British owners. Just three years later the mines hit a bonanza.[41] The Béistegui family also invested in textile mills, but, significantly, it never considered rural estates to be an attractive option. In this it differed from the investment choices of many wealthy businessmen. At his death in 1865, Juan Antonio left an estate valued at over 7.6 million pesos. Given his unimpressive career, scant wealth, and deficient web of connections until he made his mid-career move to Mexico City, his subsequent achievements may constitute the most remarkable success story in Mexico over at least the first two-thirds of the nineteenth century.

Even some of the individuals who had fled to Spain during the insurgency returned eventually and became wealthy businessmen. Born in Veracruz, the creole son of a peninsular merchant, Isidoro de la Torre migrated with his family to Spain near the end of the wars for independence. But he returned sometime in the 1830s and soon set himself up as a merchant-financier with a nephew and the noted Swiss investor Juan B. Jecker. This import-export house dealt heavily in cotton and war matériel, the latter making it a business favored by the various Mexican governments of the time. By the mid-1850s, De la Torre had founded yet another commercial firm with Jecker, this one operating out of Mazatlán and oriented toward trade with the United States. It also made loans to miners, exported silver to the Orient, took over operation of Mexican government mints in the north, and finally invested directly in mining and in ironworks.[42] During all of its involvement in these manifold undertakings, the company also functioned as a banker to both private businessmen and the government. In 1853 it even invested in a planned railway across Tehuantepec, but construction never began. De la Torre dissolved his company with Jecker after a couple of years, but not in order to leave commerce. Rather, he founded a commercial house of his own. Like Béistegui, he invested heavily in urban real estate with the disamortization of church properties.

Then in the 1860s De la Torre moved substantially into commercial agriculture, acquiring sugar estates in the present state of Morelos. Despite this shift, he never abandoned his mercantile firm. Operating in a manner that would have been familiar in eighteenth-century Mexico, De la Torre coupled diversification of his investments with vertical integration, seeking to control production, processing, and marketing. He owned a flour mill and a sugar mill near Mexico City in which he refined the output from his own estates. In the 1870s, De la Torre's interest in railroads was revived. He placed some funds in rail lines to the sugar-growing country where his own estates were located.[43]

Already established in 1857 as a major actor in the Mexico City business world, De la Torre married advantageously. He wed the daughter of Gregorio de Mier de Terán—the Spanish-born nephew of the merchant Alonso de Terán—who was notably successful as a merchant-financier and large-scale agriculturalist in nineteenth-century Mexico.

Francisco Somera was born in Jalapa, Veracruz, to a Spanish immigrant who became a wine merchant. He traveled to Spain to study as a civil engineer before returning to Mexico in 1842. Somera made himself indispensable to the city council of Mexico City, serving as its engineer. After some years he himself became a city councilman. By 1856 he had bought twenty houses through disamortization, and his urban real estate investments grew dramatically over the next decade, as he undertook to develop neighborhoods in outlying areas. But Somera became an ardent backer of Maximilian and fled to Paris for three years upon the defeat of the French intervention. After his return to Mexico City in 1870, he resumed acquiring large tracts of suburban property to build residential developments. He also served as a lender to private businessmen, generally demanding real estate as collateral. At the time of his death, he was worth 2.25 million pesos, 57 percent of it in the form of urban and suburban real estate, with only an insignificant amount composed of rural properties.[44]

As these examples demonstrate, the Iturbe e Iraeta family and its close associates were not exceptional in resisting total withdrawal from foreign and domestic commerce in the years between independence and the Porfiriato. Over time the Iturbe e Iraeta certainly diminished the share of their business undertakings that involved international trade, but they never sought to retreat into estate ownership—even in combination with loans to the government—though probably every branch of the family held agricultural properties of some sort by the 1840s. Instead they were active investors in silver mines, processing plants, and textile mills, both as sole proprietors and as members of large investing groups, and in commercial undertakings of every variety. An 1842 census of Mexico City merchants conducted by the municipal government located at least six different commercial establishments owned by this intermarried set of families.[45] These kinsmen and their close associates regularly invested in combinations and turned to each other for loans and other forms of business assistance when needed. When a couple of members faced bankruptcy, they were bailed out by consortia of kinsmen and in-laws. In the 1840s the Iturbe, Icaza, and Echave branches all loaned large sums to the government and functioned as financiers to private business concerns.[46] In 1846 four members of the lineage bought shares of a 800,000-peso loan the government demanded from the archbishopric of Mexico.[47]

Intermarriage, business partnerships, deep Catholic religiosity and membership in confraternities, a shared and meaningful ethnic identity, and conservative political values bonded these separate households and families into a remarkably cohesive and powerful group in the middle years of the nineteenth century. This political conservatism is evinced by the solid support that the families gave to the imperial government of Maximilian during the French intervention of the 1860s. A couple of Icazas received medals for their support of the emperor, and yet others served in his government. At least four family members entered the Assembly of Notables. Others who participated include a Supreme Court judge, the director of the imperial archive, a chief of section of the treasury, and the president of the merchants' exchange. Three were identified in 1864 as wholesale merchants and two others as storeowners. Five had become lawyers, and other family members held academic posts as a professor of classics, a theologian, and a philosopher. Several family members were attached to the diplomatic service.[48]

As the empire collapsed before Liberal political and military offensives led by Benito Juárez, some family members prepared themselves for exile, with Spain as their choice of destination. Ultimately, however, few if any seem to have had to leave the country or to have been punished severely for their support for the conservative cause. In this good fortune they were unlike most other prominent families who had supported the losing side, some members of which were stripped of their properties and businesses. What saved the extended Iturbe e Iraeta group remains unknown. Certainly, though, they were a Mexico City–based family network deeply entrenched in the capital's society. Since before independence its members had been notable for their political and business activities involving, almost inevitably, dealings with powerful political actors, some of whom were ardent Liberals. Also, some Liberals were distinguished members of the Cofradía de Nuestra Señora de Aránzazu and so had close contact with this Basque lineage.

Whatever the explanation, these families remained prominent and prosperous into the Porfiriato. They continued to intermarry frequently but also wed with important immigrants, especially financiers. Some family members themselves became successful bankers both in Mexico City and in the provinces during the spate of bank openings that occurred in this era.[49] Their profound Catholicism, pride in their Basque heritage, enduring if diminished contact with their transatlantic relatives, and cultural identification with Spain continued unabated as distinguishing characteristics, even generations after their economic and political links to the mother country had dissolved.

Notes

1. The most powerful, concerted argument favoring the assertion that the merchants of Mexico City successfully evaded late colonial government initiatives that attacked them is expressed in Pedro Pérez Herrero, *Plata y libranzas: La articulación comercial del México borbónico* (México, 1988). See also D. A. Brading, *Miners and Merchants in Bourbon Mexico, 1763–1810* (Cambridge, Eng., 1971), parts 1 and 2.

2. Works of importance on the commercial and social world of late colonial Mexico City include Brading, *Miners and Merchants in Bourbon Mexico, 1763–1810;* Doris M. Ladd, *The Mexican Nobility at Independence, 1780–1826* (Austin,

1976); John M. Tutino, "Creole Mexico: Spanish Elites, Haciendas, and Indian Towns, 1750–1810," (Ph.D. diss., University of Texas at Austin, 1976); John E. Kicza, *Colonial Entrepreneurs: Families and Business in Bourbon Mexico City* (Albuquerque, 1983); Christiana R. Borchart de Moreno, *Los mercaderes y el capitalismo en México (1759–1778)* (México, 1984); and María Cristina Torales Pacheco et al., *La compañía de comercio de Francisco Ignacio de Yraeta (1767–1797): Cinco ensayos,* 2 vols. (México, 1985).

3. A perspective on the nature and volume of trade between Spain and its American colonies, and more particularly Mexico, can be gained from Antonio García-Baquero González, *Comercio colonial y guerras revolucionarias: La decadencia económica de Cádiz a raíz de la emancipación americana* (Sevilla, 1972); and Javier Ortiz de la Tabla, *Comercio exterior de Veracruz, 1778–1821: Crisis de dependencia* (Sevilla, 1978).

4. Torales Pacheco, *La compañía de comercio,* vol. 1, 25–28.

5. Iturbe e Iraeta Papers, Princeton University, Box 2, Letterbooks for 1781–1782, 1791, 1795–1798, 1798–1801.

6. Besides the works cited above, note 1, writings on the character of the late colonial Mexican economy include Charles H. Harris III, *A Mexican Family Empire: The Latifundio of the Sánchez Navarro Family, 1765–1867* (Austin, 1975); Eric Van Young, *Hacienda and Market in Eighteenth-Century Mexico: The Rural Economy of the Guadalajara Region, 1675–1820* (Berkeley, 1981); John H. Coatsworth, "The Limits of Colonial Absolutism: The State in Eighteenth Century Mexico," in Karen Spalding, ed., *Essays in the Political, Economic and Social History of Colonial Latin America* (Newark, DE, 1982), 25–51; and the essays by John H. Coatsworth, Eric Van Young, Guy Thomson, Nils Jacobsen, and John J. TePaske in Nils Jacobsen and Hans-Jürgen Puhe, eds., *The Economies of Mexico and Peru During the Late Colonial Period, 1760–1810* (Berlin, 1986).

7. Coatsworth, "The Limits of Colonial Absolution."

8. Ibid., Fig. 3.

9. Archivo de Notarías del Departamento del Distrito Federal (hereafter cited as AN), Juan Manuel Pozo, 17 May 1802 and 14 January 1805; Francisco de Madariaga, 24 July 1821.

10. The 1791 statements by Iraeta and Icaza are in the appendices, which make up vol. 2 of Torales Pacheco, *La compañía de comercio.*

11. AN, Ramón de la Cueva, 6 April 1843.

12. Torales Pacheco, *La compañía de comercio,* vol. 1, 38–39.

13. Iturbe e Iraeta Papers, Princeton University, 1795–1798 Letterbook, 4 September 1795.

14. Archivo General de la Nación, México (hereafter cited as AGN), Historia, Tomo 104, Exp. 2, 9, 10, and 35, reports from Manuel de Iturbe e Iraeta to Viceroy Venegas dated Feb.–Apr. 1811.

15. *Gazeta del Gobierno del México,* 3 December 1811, 1125–27.

16. Iturbe e Iraeta Papers, Princeton University, Box 3, Letters from José Ignacio de Iturbe to Gabriel de Iturbe e Iraeta, 1783–87; Archivo del Antiguo Ayuntamiento de la Ciudad de México (hereafter cited as AAM), Libro Nobiliario, n. 4, 1769–72, Executoria de Hidalguía de Francisco Ignacio de Iraeta.

17. Iturbe e Iraeta Papers, Princeton University, Box 2, 1795–1798 Letterbook, 27 February 1795 and 3 May 1795.

18. Enrique de Olavarría y Ferrari, *El Real Colegio de San Ignacio de Loyola* (México, 1889), app. 49, doc. 2, 119–25.

19. AGN, Padrones, vol. 54, 11, 1811.

20. Lucas Alamán, *Historia de Méjico desde los primeros movimientos que prepararon su independencia en el año de 1808 hasta la época presente,* vol. 1 (México, 1849), 305.

21. AAM, Ayuntamiento, leg. 395, exp. 155, 1818.

22. These two arrivals seem to have been just part of a larger migration of both new and already established merchants from abroad who came to Mexico to make their business careers during and immediately after the independence struggle. See Richard B. Lindley, *Haciendas and Economic Development: Guadalajara, Mexico, at Independence* (Austin, 1983), 95–99; Barbara A. Tenenbaum, *The Politics of Penury: Debts and Taxes in Mexico, 1821–1856* (Albuquerque, 1986), 73; and David W. Walker, *Kinship, Business, and Politics: The Martínez del Río Family in Mexico, 1823–1867,* (Austin, 1986), 29–30.

23. AGN, Colegios, vol. 4, exp. 15, 181; Félix Osores, *Noticias bio-bibliográficas de alumnos distinguidos del Colegio de San Pedro, San Pablo y San Ildefonso de Mexico, Tomo II,* in Genaro García, ed., *Documentos inéditos o muy raros para la historia de México* (México, 1975), 770; Romeo Flores Caballero, *Counterrevolution: The Role of the Spaniards in the Independence of Mexico, 1804–1838* (Lincoln, Neb., 1974), 64.

24. The fullest treatments of the postindependence collapse are Ladd, *The Mexican Nobility,* chap. 7; and John H. Coatsworth, "Obstacles to Economic Growth in Nineteenth-Century Mexico," *American Historical Review,* 83:1 (1978): 80–100.

25. Two excellent books have recently appeared on Spain's policies toward its insurgent colonies and the subsequent independent nations: Timothy E. Anna, *Spain and the Loss of America* (Lincoln, Neb., 1983); and Michael P. Costeloe, *Response to Revolution: Imperial Spain and the Spanish American Revolutions, 1810–1840* (Cambridge, Eng., 1986).

26. Iturbe e Iraeta Papers, Princeton University, Box 3, Letter from Juan de Marticorena to Gabriel Manuel de Iturbe e Iraeta, 17 August 1827; AN, Francisco de Madariaga, 30 January 1827.

27. AN, Francisco Calapiz y Aguilar, 25 April 1825; Francisco de Madariaga, 1 March 1855.

28. AN, Francisco de Madariaga, 6 October 1839.

29. Ibid., 19 July 1848.

30. Ibid., 19 June 1850.

31. For the weakness of the national government in the decades following independence, see Michael P. Costeloe, *La Primera República Federal de México (1824–1835)* (México, 1975); Jaime E. Rodríguez O., *Down from Colonialism: Mexico's Nineteenth-Century Crisis* (Los Angeles, 1983); and Donald Fithian Stevens, *Origins of Instability in Early Republican Mexico* (Durham, N.C., 1991). The Mexican government's primary economic initiative in the early independence era is treated in Robert A. Potash, *The Mexican Government and Industrial Development in the Early Republic* (Amherst, MA, 1983).

32. See Tenenbaum, *The Politics of Penury.*

33. The most systematic treatment of this anti-Spanish campaign is Harold Dana Sims, *The Expulsion of Mexico's Spaniards, 1821–1836* (Pittsburgh, 1990).

34. AN, Francisco de Madariaga, 10 December 1841.

35. A perspective on some of his activities may be gained from Tenenbaum, *The Politics of Penury.*

36. AN, Francisco de Madariaga, 29 December 1828.

37. Bancroft Library, "Lista general de los españoles a quienes el Supremo Gobierno ha expedido el correspondiente documento de escepción de la ley de 20 de marzo último, por haber acreditado previo díctamen de facultativos, que tienen impedimento físico temporal para salir de la república," 20 April 1829.

38. Tenenbaum, *The Politics of Penury,* 31.

39. Rosa María Meyer C., "Los Béistegui, especuladores y mineros, 1830–1869," in Ciro F. S. Cardoso, ed., *Formación y desarrollo de la burguesía en México, siglo XIX* (México, 1978), 109–15.

40. Jan Bazant, *Los bienes de la Iglesia en Mexico (1856–1875)* (México, 1971), 94–96.

41. Tenenbaum, *The Politics of Penury,* 109–10.

42. María Teresa Huerta, "Isidoro de la Torre: El caso de un empresario azucarero, 1844–1881," in Cardoso, ed., *Formación y desarrollo de la burguesía en México, siglo XIX,* 164–74.

43. Ibid., 181–85.

44. María Dolores Morales, "El comportamiento empresarial de dos pioneros de fraccionamientos en la Ciudad de México," in Enrique Florescano, ed., *Orígenes y desarrollo de la burguesía en América Latina, 1700–1955* (México, 1985), 124–34.

45. Biblioteca Nacional, México, "Lista de los individuos del comercio de esta capital que deben contribuir con las cuotas que se espresan para el sosten de la fuerza de seguridad pública, conforme al superior decreto publicado en 20 de Diciembre del año anterior," 1842.

46. Tenenbaum, *The Politics of Penury,* 74.

47. Ibid., 81, table 10.

48. Juan N. del Valle, *El Viajero en México: Completa guía de forasteros para 1864* (México, 1864).

49. Ricardo Ortega y Pérez Gallardo, *Historia genealógica de las familias mas antiguas de México,* vol. 2 (México, 1908), "Icaza"; Leonor Ludlow, "La construcción de un banco: El Banco Nacional de México (1881–1884)," in Leonor Ludlow and Carlos Marichal, eds., *Banca y poder en México (1800–1925)* (México, 1986), 333, 342–44. Overall, the findings of this essay are congruent with the patterns of family organization and conduct described in Diana Balmori et al., *Notable Family Networks in Latin America* (Chicago, 1984), and contradict the behavior described in Eugene W. Ridings, "Foreign Predominance among Overseas Traders in Nineteenth-Century Latin America," *Latin American Research Review,* 20:2 (1985): 3–27.

7

The Spanish Imperial Mercury Trade and the American Mining Expansion under the Bourbon Monarchy

KENDALL W. BROWN

Research over the past two decades has succeeded in establishing the dimensions of mining in Spanish America during the eighteenth century.[1] Although silver production had fallen off significantly in Mexico and Peru from heights reached during the seventeenth century, it not only recovered during the 1700s but even surpassed its previous levels.[2] This was particularly true of Mexico. In that viceroyalty silver production had not exceeded 60 million *pesos de ocho* in any decade before 1700. The closest it came was 1681–90, when output reached 58.5 million pesos. But during the second decade of the eighteenth century, it surpassed 61 million and then rose steadily until it reached 201 million for 1801–10. Peru likewise recovered, although less spectacularly. After a high point of 82.7 million for 1631–40, a long decline beset Peruvian output until 1720. Thereafter, Peruvian output began a modest rise, showing its most dramatic spurt from 1791–1800, when it finally generated 86.8 million pesos, its all-time record for a single decade.[3]

Many components affected mining output and therefore played a role in the resurgence. These included availability and cost of capital, labor, and other industrial inputs, royal fiscal and administrative policies; technological innovations; ore quality; and discovery of new mining districts. Critical to the recovery was mercury, an essential element in refining silver ores through amalgamation, the most common form of processing used in Spanish America. Mexican operators had begun to use amalgamation in the 1550s, and the technique had spread to Peru within twenty years. Peruvian refiners became almost entirely dependent upon it, and the Mexicans used it to process probably two-thirds to three-fourths of their silver.[4]

This meant that for an expansion in silver output to occur, mercury had to be available. Yet making mercury available was no easy task. Within the

Spanish empire, the only significant mercury mines exploited in early modern times were Almadén in Spain and Huancavelica in Peru. By 1700 both belonged to the crown, which operated the Almadén mines directly while it contracted with a guild of Peruvians to exploit Huancavelica. In both cases, however, the government monopolized the sale and distribution of quicksilver. This made the crown responsible for providing the American refiners with sufficient mercury at prices low enough to stimulate silver mining.

Most of the recent studies on colonial Spanish American mining deal to some extent with mercury's role in the industry. In this chapter I will attempt to demonstrate its significance quantitatively. In so doing, I will present data on the amount of mercury used by Mexican and Peruvian miners over the eighteenth century during the expansion in silver output.[5] I will trace the relationship between mercury usage and fluctuations in the amount of silver produced. Still, it is important to recognize that mercury was only one of many factors influencing the colonial mining industry.

Mexico

According to John TePaske's figures, Mexican silver production languished in the mid-seventeenth century, averaging about 3.4 million pesos per year.[6] This average may have been an underestimation, however, because neither Guanajuato nor Pachuca had royal treasuries, and Peter Bakewell suspects that substantial amounts of their silver escaped registration. When the crown established treasuries in those districts—in 1665 at Guanajuato and in 1667 at Pachuca—silver smuggling declined markedly. At the same time, the discovery of rich ores at Sombrerete and the subsequent installation of a treasury there added to the total Mexican output, which reached 58.5 million pesos during the 1680s.[7] This output was greater than ever before, although without knowing the extent of smuggling at Guanajuato and Pachuca before the establishment of the *cajas,* it is difficult to gauge the extent of the boom.

More significant for the purposes of this chapter, however, the late seventeenth-century expansion occurred without a simultaneous increase in mercury supply. Instead, it resulted primarily from an increase in smelting, the discovery of Sombrerete, and perhaps greater activity at Guanajuato and Pachuca. During the mid-1600s, because the crown gave preference to Peru over Mexico in the mercury it supplied from Europe,

Table 1 Mercury Received by Mexico and Silver Officially Produced, 1681–1810

Decade	Mercury[a] (in Quintales)	Percent Change	Silver (in millions of Pesos)	Percentage Change
1681–1690	28,327		58.5	
1691–1700	26,942	−5	49.1	−16
1701–1710	(30,000)	11	47.1	−4
1711–1720	37,274	24	61.4	30
1721–1730	36,860	−1	75.4	23
1731–1740	50,072	36	83.5	11
1741–1750	59,727	19	92.9	11
1751–1760	81,055	36	107.5	16
1761–1770	94,498	17	97.2	−10
1771–1780	104,319	10	132.7	37
1781–1790	132,105	27	157.8	19
1791–1800	119,790	−9	192.4	22
1801–1810	(108,966)	?	201.2	5

Sources: For the mercury totals, see table 1; Peter Bakewell, *Silver Mining and Society in Colonial Mexico: Zacatecas 1546–1700* (New York, 1971), 254; Mervyn F. Lang, "Las exportaciones de azogue peruano en la época colonial," *Scientia et praxis,* 7 (1972): 119. For the amount of silver officially registered, refer to John J. TePaske, "Bullion Production in Mexico and Peru, 1581–1810" (unpub. paper, 1987), which should be compared with Alexander von Humboldt, *Political Essay on the Kingdom of New Spain,* 4 vols. (New York, 1966), 3:292.

[a]I have used Bakewell's figures for 1681–1700, although they are for the two decades 1680–89 and 1690–99, and have increased them according to the shipments of mercury from Peru mentioned by Lang, estimating those shipments to have averaged 2,500 quantales each. The quantity for 1701–10 is little more than an informed guess. As for the last decade shown, the quantity indicated includes only mercury that received for 1801–5, when the series of accounts contained in AGI ends. But shipments continued from Almadén for several more years until interrupted by the French occupation of the mines, and consequently the total received from 1801–10 was undoubtedly the largest amount ever sent to Mexico.

the northern viceroyalty suffered a shortage, and many Mexican operators consequently turned at least partially to smelting to extract the silver from their ore. According to Peter Bakewell, the revival of smelting around 1660 stopped the decline in Mexican silver output, and smelting remained significant after 1700.[8]

Despite Mexico's problems, however, TePaske's treasury data show Mexican silver output rising earlier than the booms studied by either David Brading or Richard Garner (Table 1). Brading emphasized the huge upsurge in silver output in the 1770s and attributed it especially to the government-sponsored mining reforms, particularly the easier availability of mercury that resulted from both larger supplies and lower prices.[9] Writing a decade later, Garner focused upon the early 1700s, arguing that "the silver boom had its roots in the first half of the 18th century when production rose between two and three hundred percent." He thereby accorded less importance than Brading to "the *visita* of José de Gálvez and the mining reforms which followed."[10]

Although mercury had played almost no role in the late seventeenth-century mining revival, it proved vital in the periods analyzed by Garner and Brading. Garner's early upsurge would have been impossible without the resurrection of the Almadén mines. Plagued by crisis during the final third of the seventeenth century, Almadén's mercury output lagged and its shipments to Mexico were curtailed. In the 1690s Almadén averaged little more than 1,000 *quintales* of mercury per year.[11] Huancavelica meanwhile was able to do little more than provide occasional shipments to the northern viceroyalty. But then in 1699 a new, rich mine, El Castillo, was discovered at Almadén, and it was in full production by 1702.[12] Deeply concerned about the colonial mines, Philip V created the Junta de Azogues on 15 October 1708, charging it to run Almadén, provide 5,000 quintales of mercury per year for Mexico, and pay Almadén's operating expenses through the sale of mercury in the New World.[13]

Shortly thereafter, the Junta established the office of general superintendent of mercury for Mexico and appointed Juan José de Veitia Linage to the post, giving him private jurisdiction over the distribution and sale of mercury within the viceroyalty.[14] From their office in Puebla until 1740 and thereafter from Mexico City, Veitia and the succeeding superintendents provided efficient and honest management. Yearly accounts attested to the amount of mercury received, the amount distributed, the money resulting from the sales, and the quantity of silver refined (Table 2). In 1751 the crown again brought the administration of mercury under the control of the Mexican viceroy, eliminating the private jurisdiction of the superintendency. Nevertheless the administration continued to be extremely effective in distributing the mercury and accounting for it.[15]

The new Almadén mine and more effective administration reaped quick profits. Almadén's annual output exceeded 4,000 quintales during the first decade of the century (table 3) and neared 6,000 during the following decade. Since none of this mercury was sent to Peru, it far surpassed the normal amounts being consumed in Mexico around 1700, when the crown was typically able to make only 2,500 to 3,000 quintales available each

Table 2 Mercury Received by Mexico, from Almadén, Idria, and Peru, 1710–1805, in Quintales

Year	Almadén	Idria	Peru	Total
1710	6,948	0	0	6,948
1711	4,000	0	0	4,000
1712	4,000	0	0	4,000
1713	0	0	0	0
1714	0	0	0	0
1715	0	0	0	0
1716	10,997	0	0	10,997
1717	7,999	0	0	7,999
1718	0	0	0	0
1719	10,278	0	0	10,278
1720	0	0	0	0
1721	4,000	0	0	4,000
1722	7,996	0	0	7,996
1723	0	0	0	0
1724	5,997	0	0	5,997
1725	0	0	0	0
1726	3,000	0	0	3,000
1727	0	0	0	0
1728	7,994	0	0	7,994
1729	5,073	0	0	5,073
1730	2,800	0	0	2,800
1731	7,836	0	0	7,836
1732	7,846	0	0	7,846
1733	7,995	0	0	7,995
1734	5,862	0	0	5,862
1735	0	0	0	0
1736	4,916	0	0	4,916
1737	6,745	0	0	6,745
1738	5,992	0	0	5,992
1739	0	0	0	0
1740	2,880	0	0	2,880
1741	4,065	0	3,127	7,192
1742	3,834	0	0	3,834
1743	4,371	0	0	4,371
1744	4,740	0	0	4,740
1745	11,677	0	0	11,677
1746	3,472	0	0	3,472
1747	5,755	0	0	5,755
1748	13,062	0	0	13,062
1749	3,634	0	0	3,634
1750	1,990	0	0	1,990
1751	10,428	0	0	10,428
1752	3,816	0	0	3,816
1753	6,729	0	0	6,729
1754	10,015	0	4,838	14,853
1755	17,778	0	4,975	22,753

Table 2 *Continued*

Year	Almadén	Idria	Peru	Total
1756	0	0	0	0
1757	4,070	0	0	4,070
1758	1,688	0	0	1,688
1759	3,729	0	0	3,729
1760	10,993	0	1,996	12,989
1761	11,900	0	0	11,900
1762	5,649	0	0	5,649
1763	12,323	0	0	12,323
1764	4,046	0	0	4,046
1765	12,924	0	0	12,924
1766	18,213	0	0	18,213
1767	5,651	0	0	5,651
1768	2,345	0	0	2,345
1769	9,657	0	0	9,657
1770	11,790	0	0	11,790
1771	6,785	0	0	6,785
1772	6,773	0	0	6,773
1773	7,328	0	0	7,328
1774	7,505	0	0	7,505
1775	8,079	0	0	8,079
1776	6,486	0	0	6,486
1777	22,030	0	0	22,030
1778	17,324	0	0	17,324
1779	7,163	0	0	7,163
1780	14,846	0	0	14,846
1781	0	0	0	0
1782	26,500	0	3,480	29,980
1783	12,943	0	0	12,943
1784	12,002	0	0	12,002
1785	6,501	0	0	6,501
1786	11,009	3,500	0	14,509
1787	5,708	6,956	0	12,664
1788	3,906	12,200	0	16,106
1789	9,008	7,501	0	16,509
1790	8,796	2,095	0	10,891
1791	12,911	11,768	0	24,679
1792	15,373	9,391	0	24,764
1793	9,269	0	0	9,269
1794	16,660	0	0	16,660
1795	3,501	12,219	0	15,720
1796	12,060	0	0	12,060
1797	0	0	0	0
1798	0	0	0	0
1799	9,522	2,851	0	12,373
1800	4,265	0	0	4,265
1801	1,450	0	0	1,450
1802	19,314	0	0	19,314
1803	38,900	0	0	38,900

Table 2 *Continued*

Year	Almadén	Idria	Peru	Total
1804	28,318	0	0	28,318
1805	20,984	0	0	20,984

Source: Antonia Heredia Herrera, *La renta del azogue en Nueva España: 1709–1751* (Seville, 1978), 234–36; Archivo General de Indias (hereafter AGI), Contaduría 1043–1048B; AGI, Mexico 2174–2184.

year. By 1717 the central storehouse in Puebla had a reserve of more than 10,000 quintales, which reached 13,000 in 1722.[16] Obviously, these surpluses signalled that shipments from Almadén initially outstripped the Mexican refiners' demand, partly because of the widespread use of smelting and partly due to the lack of mining activity.

Table 3 Average Annual Mercury Production and Expenses of Almadén by Decade, 1701–1839

Decade	Mercury (quintales)	Expenses (reales)
1701–9	4,109	742,404
1710–19	5,737	774,945
1720–29	2,281	545,940
1730–39	6,151	586,694
1740–49	7,580	1,109,335
1750–59	5,606	2,546,921
1760–69	11,637	3,267,259
1770–79	13,900	4,442,808
1780–89	13,586	6,279,007
1790–99	18,970	6,292,121
1800–1809	20,040	6,239,709
1810–1819	12,815	?
1820–1829	19,399	?
1830–39	21,150	6,021,333

Source: Rafael Dobado González, "Salarios y condiciones de trabajo en las minas de Almadén, 1758–1839," in Pedro Tedde, ed., *La economía española al final del antiguo régimen,* vol. 2: Manufacturas (Madrid, 1982): 385, 387.
Note: There are no expense figures recorded for the years 1810–1839.

Stimulated to some extent by easier access to mercury, the Mexicans expanded their operations. When Almadén's production collapsed to slightly more than 2,000 quintales per year during the 1720s (because of drainage problems and the government's failure to provide adequate operating capital), the reserves helped tide Mexico over the crisis. Almadén's new governor and administrator, Joseph Cornejo y Ibarra, appointed in 1729, succeeded in expanding output to more than 6,000 quintales per year during the 1730s.[17] By this time, however, demand for mercury in Mexico had risen so high that it was impossible to rebuild the reserves (table 4).

Whereas silver production grew rapidly from 1711 to 1730 (note the percentage change for those decades in table 2), growth slowed considerably during the next thirty years, despite the fact that the viceroyalty received larger shipments of mercury each decade, reaching an average of more than 8,100 quintales per year during the 1750s. In short, increasingly abundant, if occasionally irregular, mercury supplies between 1710 and 1730 helped cause Garner's boom, and Almadén managed to produce enough mercury during the following three decades to keep silver output rising, albeit at a lower rate.

According to Brading, a major cause of the explosion in silver production in the 1770s was the crown's decision to lower the price of mercury from 82 to 41 pesos per quintal in two stages between 1767 and 1778. He suggests that Gálvez was able to reduce the price because of a decline in mercury production costs at Almadén.[18] But production costs had fallen precipitously at the beginning of the century. By 1710 because of the rich ores of the new Castillo mine, the cost per quintal had dropped to 3.5 pesos, compared to 31 around 1700.[19] Transportation to Veracruz probably did not bring the total cost to more than 30 pesos.[20] This compared with 58 pesos at Huancavelica until 1760 when it rose to 73 pesos.[21]

The crown did not reduce the cost of mercury to the Mexican refiners before 1767 for two reasons. First, Peruvian operators, dependent on Huancavelica, had to pay much more for mercury than their Mexican counterparts, and it seemed unjust to create a great disparity in the price level between the two viceroyalties. Second and most important, the crown made a sizable profit off the sale of cheap Almadén mercury to the Mexicans. Although the idea that the crown could more than offset lost profits on the sale of mercury by lowering the price and stimulating greater silver production was not original with Gálvez, he deserves credit for implementing the decision to cut the price.

Table 4 Mercury Distributed and Held in Reserve at End of Year by General Administration of Mexico and Marks of Silver Produced, 1714–1800

	Mercury (Quintales)		
Year	Dist.	Reserve	Silver (Marks)
1714	2,072	2,410	731,861
1715	1,906	9,511	749,284
1716	6,030	5,481	767,969
1717	3,250	10,230	794,204
1718	1,676	8,554	843,951
1719	6,077	12,757	853,963
1720	3,491	9,267	926,390
1721	2,112	11,165	1,113,027
1722	5,988	13,174	1,038,109
1723	6,001	8,381	953,805
1724	2,102	12,276	926,214
1725	5,238	7,041	867,037
1726	5,798	4,240	966,017
1727	3,021	1,222	956,833
1728	4,823	4,493	1,085,711
1729	4,547	5,015	1,037,055
1730	6,441	1,412	1,146,573
1731	6,827	2,421	992,926
1732	7,554	2,712	1,026,642
1733	6,294	4,413	1,177,623
1734	7,618	2,657	1,000,771
1735	1,960	697	932,001
1736	4,311	1,302	1,296,000
1737	5,424	2,623	955,545
1738	4,875	3,701	1,116,500
1739	3,577	123	1,005,963
1740	3,002	0	1,124,240
1741	5,059	2,134	1,016,962
1742	4,710	1,257	962,000
1743	5,239	390	1,014,000
1744	5,170	0	1,210,000
1745	8,306	4,071	1,215,000
1746	6,315	898	1,354,000
1747	3,966	2,687	1,412,000
1748	7,432	8,317	1,368,000
1749	7,833	4.118	1,391,000
1750	4,940	1,175	1,554.000
1751	7,599	4.002	1,486.000
1752	7,787	31	1,603,000
1753	6,595	278	1,364,000
1754	10,239	4,863	1,364,000
1755	7,638	19,978	1,469,000
1756	9,684	10,293	1,447,000

Table 4 *Continued*

Year	Mercury (Quintales)		Silver (Marks)
	Dist.	Reserve	
1757	7,121	7,242	1,474,000
1758	6,614	2,296	1,500,893
1759	2,188	3.837	1,532,000
1760	7,467	9,561	1,408,000
1761	10,081	11,231	1,386,000
1762	7,175	9,704	1,189,940
1763	7,172	14,855	1,385,298
1764	10,178	9,724	1,152,063
1765	4,844	17,822	1,365,275
1766	11,913	24,121	1,318,829
1767	5,225	24,547	1,225,307
1768	7,991	18,960	1,444,583
1769	10,034	18,584	1,404,564
1770	8,841	21,532	1,638,391
1771	9,404	18,914	1,506,255
1772	8,678	17,009	1,996,689
1773	9,709	14,627	2,227,442
1774	10,796	11,336	1,516,714
1775	10,525	8,892	1,675,916
1776	12,744	2,637	1,936,856
1777	15,744	8,922	2,428,613
1778	11,284	6,040	2,334,765
1779	13,202	0	2,199,548
1780	5,961	8,885	1,994,073
1781	8,885	0	2,311,068
1782	24,998	4,970	2,014,545
1783	8,641	9,272	2,709,167
1784	10,887	10,339	2,402,965
1785	14,449	2,453	2,111,263
1786	10,444	6,518	1,978,844
1787	11,825	7,069	1,819,141
1788	16,488	4,152	2,293,555
1789	17,066	3,596	2,415,821
1790	11,464	3,022	2,045,951
1791	16,175	16,086	2,363,867
1792	19,003	21,846	2,724,105
1793	29,862	1,253	2,747,746
1794	11,654	6,659	2,488,304
1795	15,051	19,111	2,808,380
1796	18,752	12,419	2,854,072
1797	11,639	780	2,818,248
1798	7,656	412	2,697,038
1799	7,144	5,641	2,473,542
1800	7,541	2,074	2,098,712

Source: See Table 1.

The government struggled to keep the Mexicans supplied with mercury until 1750, when it was able to start building a reserve in Mexico again. But a fire followed by flooding devastated the principal mine at Almadén from 1755 to 1759,[22] and the colonial ministers had to draw down on reserves at Huancavelica in order to supply Mexico. Even with an increasingly vibrant Almadén, the crown was unable to accumulate much more than a year's reserve in Mexico before 1765. On the other hand, Mexico suffered no prolonged, serious mercury shortages during the 1760s, and it is curious therefore that silver output dropped so markedly during the decade.[23] In short, Mexican refiners stood ready to consume whatever mercury was supplied to them up to 1760, even at 82 pesos per quintal; the trend line for mercury distributed by the general administration in Mexico grew at 1.6 percent annual rate between 1716 and 1760.

But Mexican refiners naturally preferred the lower prices afforded them by Charles III's reformist ministers.[24] Mercury consumption, as reflected in the amount distributed by the general administration, grew annually at 2.8 percent between 1767, when the first price cut occurred, and 1796, the last year full mercury stocks were available before the onset of the British blockade. For the five-year period 1792–96, in fact, Mexico consumed an average of almost 19,000 quintales per year.[25] Over the 1767–96 period total silver output grew 2.2 percent compared with only 1.3 percent from 1716 to 1760.

Further proof of the strong impact that mercury availability had upon Mexican silver production is seen in table 5, which shows the coefficients of correlation between the amount of mercury distributed each year and the total silver produced that year, the following year, and the year after that. Judging by the coefficients, mercury explains approximately 20–25 percent of the fluctuations in silver output from 1714–1760 (see the r^2 values) and then jumps to 40 percent after the drop in mercury prices. Given the many other factors that enter into mining production—such as ore quality, entrepreneurship, and labor supply—that mercury by itself explains such a large portion of the variance in silver output underlines its crucial role in the colonial mining economy. A similar relationship between mercury consumption and silver amalgamation existed at the individual viceregal mining camps with the exception of Pachuca (table 6).

Yet mercury distribution is a poorer predictor of silver production for the entire century because of distortions caused by the price cut and the consequent shift from smelting to amalgamation by many operators. Because they had to pay less for mercury or because ore quality dropped to the point where it could no longer be profitably smelted, amalgama-

Table 5 Correlation Between Amount of Mercury Distributed by Mexican General Administration, and Total Marks of Silver Produced, 1714–1800

	Time Period		
	1714–1800	1714–60	1767–1800
In same year	$r = .2810$ $r^2 = .08$	$r = .4128$ $r^2 = .17$	$r = .6297$ $r^2 = .40$
Mercury lagged one year against silver	$r = .3625$ $r^2 = .13$	$r = .4907$ $r^2 = .24$	$r = .6545$ $r^2 = .43$
Mercury lagged two years against silver	$r = .3870$ $r^2 = .15$	$r = .5229$ $r^2 = .27$	$r = .6527$ $r^2 = .43$

Source: The mercury data were taken from the same sources as table 1; those for silver are from Humboldt, *Political Essay on the Kingdom of New Spain,* 3:292.
Note: The coefficients of correlation for each time period were calculated by subtracting the linear-trend value from the real value for each case and correlating the resulting residuals.

Table 6 Correlations Between the Amount of Mercury Distributed by the Provincial Treasury Offices and the Quantity of Silver Produced Through Amalgamation, 1751–1805

	Mercury Distributed	
	With Silver of Same Year	With Silver of Following Year
Bolaños	$r = .607$ $r^2 = .37$	$r = .556$ $r^2 = .31$
Durango	$r = .565$ $r^2 = .32$	$r = .496$ $r^2 = .25$
Guadalajara	$r = .647$ $r^2 = .42$	$r = .341$ $r^2 = .12$
Guanajuato	$r = .570$ $r^2 = .32$	$r = .679$ $r^2 = .46$
Pachuca	$r = .089$ $r^2 = .01$	$r = .040$ $r^2 = .00$
San Luis Potosí	$r = .403$ $r^2 = .16$	$r = .375$ $r^2 = .14$
Sombrerete	$r = .526$ $r^2 = .28$	$r = .502$ $r^2 = .25$
Zacatecas	$r = .767$ $r^2 = .59$	$r = .624$ $r^2 = .39$

Source: The data on mercury distribution and silver produced through amalgamation were taken from the mercury administration accounts in AGI, Contaduría 1043–48B; AGI, Mexico 2174–84.
Note: For methodology see table 5.

Table 7 Approximate Percentage of Silver Amalgamated in Mexico by Mining District, 1700–1800

District	1700	1720	1740	1760	1780	1800
Alamos, Rosario	—	—	—	—	78	73
Bolaños	—	—	—	98	90	88
Chihuahua	—	—	—	—	—	34
Durango	?	18	15	40	50	59
Guadalajara	65	53	72	91	52	86
Guanajuato	?	65	61	67	75	80
Pachuca	90	76	79	90	64	52
San Luis Potosí	?	5	8	42	57	100
Sombrerete	?	20	55	80	50	5
Zacatecas	56	70	?	?	85	73

Source: The percentages are calculated from the taxes received annually by the individual mining treasuries for *plata de azogue* and *plata de fuego,* as compiled by John J. TePaske and Herbert S. Klein. Their data, as yet unpublished, are contained in a computer printout deposited in the library of the Archivo General de Indias. Unfortunately, the treasury officials were not always consistent in their accounting procedures and sometimes combined the two taxes. In such cases, I have estimated the percentage when data were available for the years immediately preceding or following; otherwise, I have marked them with a question mark. In instances where the percentage for a given year is significantly different from those before and after it, I have given an average.
Note: The dashes represent that there was no registered mining production in the district.

tion became more prevalent by the end of the 1700s (see table 7). If perhaps a third of all silver was smelted early in the 1700s, the ratio had fallen by the end of the century. Humboldt estimated that smelting accounted for little more than 20 percent in 1803, and some placed the percentage even lower.[26]

Treasury data show, however, that the ratio of smelting to amalgamation varied widely from region to region, with mercury assuming greater importance in some districts and becoming less significant in others (see table 7). Nor was the adoption of amalgamation "largely caused by the royal decision to cut the price of mercury by half," as Brading asserts.[27] The transition away from smelting was well under way by 1760 at Durango, Guadalajara, San Luis Potosí, and Sombrerete. San Luis Potosí was one of the most extreme cases: it amalgamated almost no silver at the beginning of the century but did all its processing with mercury by 1800. On the other hand, smelting became more important at Pachuca, rising from 10 percent of output in 1700 to nearly half by century's end.[28] Guanajuato operators continued to amalgamate 65–70 percent of their ore until the late 1780s, when the combined shipments from Almadén and Idria made mercury so plentiful that Guanajuato's ratio surpassed 80 percent. It reached 93–95 percent from 1804 to 1806, when Almadén mercury flooded into Mexico following the war but before the French occupation of the peninsula.

Peru

In Peru the Spaniards initially found themselves doubly blessed by fabled Potosí and the mercury mines at Huancavelica. While Mexico depended entirely upon imports of quicksilver, Peruvian refiners rested secure with the guarantee of local mercury. Yet in the eighteenth century, imperial policy makers left Peru dependent upon decadent Huancavelica, dedicating most European mercury to Mexico. Their reasoning was logical: even without adequate mercury supplies, Mexican silver output had finally outstripped that of Peru in the 1670s, and once Almadén was able to supply large amounts of mercury after 1700, Mexico responded with the previously described explosion in production. Meanwhile, mining in the Andes languished, hindered by, among other things, high taxation and costly mercury. It is also likely that the lack of adequate mercury supplies limited Peruvian mining expansion until the late 1700s.

To trace the evolution of Spanish policy toward Huancavelica, especially as the Bourbon monarchs attempted to resolve the administrative and cost-of-production problems, would be beyond the scope of this chapter.[29] From my current research on Huancavelica, however, it is obvious that imperial policy makers failed to determine what their priorities should be regarding the mines. At one time or another their chief objective was to abolish the *mita*; to curb corruption at the mines; to limit or even eliminate Huancavelica's output to create a larger market for Almadén and consequently greater profits for the crown; to increase Huancavelica's output to supply the silver refiners; to check Huancavelica's production to fit the perceived demand of the refiners, so that as little government money as possible would be tied up in mercury reserves; and to cut the price charged for Huancavelica's mercury to stimulate silver production. These competing priorities and shifts in policy interfered with operations at the mercury mines and contributed significantly to the great Huancavelica cave-in of

1786. Government bureaucrats dithered when faced with Baron Nordenflicht's recommendations regarding Huancavelica in the 1790s, even though the crown had sent him to South America to modernize the industry's technology.

In short, the crown's handling of Huancavelica during the eighteenth century was neither coherent nor foresighted, and it left the Peruvian silver refiners dependent upon a declining source of mercury. To make the situation critical, smelting had never developed in Peru as it had in Mexico.[30] As a result, there was a substantial difference between the two regions in the amount of mercury expended and the total quantity of silver produced. Over the eighteenth century, for example, Peru averaged slightly less than 900 pesos of silver per quintal of mercury, whereas the Mexicans produced nearly 1,500 pesos per quintal.[31] Yet the expected ratio (*correspondencia*) of mercury used to silver produced through amalgamation was no different. In 1759 the Mexican correspondencia ranged from 80 marks per quintal at San Luis Potosí to 125 marks at Guanajuato.[32] The Peruvian ratio was roughly the same.[33] The efficiency of Peruvian amalgamation seems to have improved under Nordenflicht's influence.[34] One wonders whether the Peruvians might have smelted more ore had they lacked the security of Huancavelica or had easier access to fuel.

Demand for mercury seems to have declined substantially in Peru between the 1680s and the 1720s, although this may have reflected difficulties at Huancavelica to some extent. At any rate, consumption had risen to about 6,300 quintales per year around 1685, but thereafter it dropped to 3,500. TePaske's data show an accompanying decline in silver production over those decades. A lack of mines was part of the problem. While Potosí consumed 3,000 quintales per year during the late seventeenth century, Cailloma, the next largest, used less than a sixth of that amount. Labor also seems to have been in short supply even before the devastating epidemic of 1719–21.[35] But after the mid-1720s, the problems at Huancavelica diminished. Appointed by the king as general superintendent of Peruvian mercury in 1719 with a jurisdiction free from interference by the viceroy and audiencia, the Marquis of Casa Concha stabilized production, put the mine on a firm financial base, and largely ended mercury smuggling.[36] Mercury production slowly expanded (see table 8), reaching more than 5,300 quintales per year by 1740, when Jerónimo Sola y Fuente began a systematic use of blasting powder to mine ore. Annual output continued in the range of 6,000 quintales through 1769, enough to meet Peruvian demand but insufficient to stimulate much expansion. By

Table 8 Mercury Production in Huancavelica, 1690–1813

Period	Total Mercury Produced (in Quintales)	Average per Week
8/5/1690–31/8/1691	9,421	137
1/9/1691–31/8/1693	11,057	106
1/9/1693–28/2/1696	7,113	55
1/3/1696–31/8/1698	10,385	80
1/9/1698–31/8/1701	13,678	88
1/9/1701–31/8/1704	11,352	73
1/9/1704–31/8/1706	3,161	30
1/9/1706–31/8/1709	9,961	64
1/9/1709–28/2/1713	7,353	40
1/3/1713–23/2/1716	9,188	59
1/3/1716–31/8/1718	11,986	92
1/9/1718–28/2/1721	10,048	77
1/3/1721–31/8/1724	10,063	55
1/9/1724–28/2/1726	4,025	52
1/3/1726–28/2/1729	9,386	60
1/3/1729–28/2/1732	12,054	77
1/3/1732–28/2/1735	13,417	86
1/3/1735–23/2/1738	13,347	86
1/3/1738–31/8/1741	18,611	102
1/9/1741–3/8/1744	16,435	105
1/9/1744–4/5/1748	17,034	90
1748–52	17,564	81
1752–58	29,761	95
1758–59	8,316	82
1759	6,191	119
1760	6,721	129
1761	6,147	118
1762	5,322	102
1763	5,802	112
1764	5,511	106
1765	6,353	122
1766	6,586	127
1767	5,717	110
1768	6,847	132
1769	6,464	124
1770	4,543	87
1771	5,063	97
1772	4,719	91
1773	4,263	82
1774	4,834	93
1775	5,014	96
1776	3,742	72
1777	4,264	82
1778	2,848	55
1779	4,476	86
1780	5,804	112

Table 8 *Continued*

Period	Total Mercury Produced (in Quintales)	Average per Week
1781	3,063	59
1782	1,783	34
1783	2,463	47
1784	1,613	31
1785	4,493	86
1786	3,649	70
1787	2,400	46
1788	2,668	51
1789	1,620	31
1790	2,016	39
1791	1,788	34
1792	2,054	40
1793	2,033	39
1794	4,153	80
1795	5,725	110
1796	4,183	80
1797	3,927	76
1798	3,423	66
1799	3,571	69
1800	3,233	62
1801	2,557	49
1802	2,236	43
1803	2,622	50
1804	3,289	63
1805	3,130	60
1806	2,672	51
1807	2,438	47
1808	2,453	47
1809	2,281	44
1810	2,548	49
1811	3,263	63
1812	2,718	52
1813	188	4

Source: "Demostracion que manifiesta el azogue entrado en almacenes de estas Reales Caxas de Huancavelica desde el año de 1571 en que se empesaron á fundir los metales de la Real Mino de Santa Bárbara hasta 31 de mayo de 1805," AGI, Lima 1335; "Calculacion, que explica en extracto, el origen de lo que debe a su Majestad el Real Gremio de Mineros de Azogue de la Villa de Huancavelica," 20 June 1748, AGI, Lima 1326; "Azogue entrado en caja desde el año de 1571 en que se empezó a fundir el metal de la real mina de Huancavelica de cuanta del rey, hasta el de 1789, inclusive, Huancavelica, 5 Feb 1790," BNP, C3404; Libros mayores de la Real Caja de Huancavelica, 1793–1805, AGI, Lima 1323 A-B; John Fisher, *Government and Society in Colonial Peru: The Intendant System 1784–1814* (London, 1970), 257; Manuel de Mendiburu, *Diccionario histórico-biográfico del Perú,* 2d ed., 11 vols. (Lima, 1931–35), 6:454–56.

Note: The early accounts for Huancavelica were not kept on an annual basis until 1759. There is no way to determine annual production from them. These dates represent the time period in the accounts.

this time Potosí was using less mercury than in the late 1600s, but other districts, such as Oruro and Pasco, had emerged to push overall demand higher.[37] As in Mexico, mercury usage shows a strong statistical relationship to the amount of silver the refiners in a district produced. At Cailloma between 1720 and 1748, for example, the coefficient of correlation between the quantity of mercury distributed in one year and the amount of silver registered the following year is strong enough to explain 44 percent of the fluctuations in silver output.[38] Meanwhile, Andean silver output grew steadily but slowly, responding when the tax on silver dropped from 20 to 10 percent in 1736 and sustained in the 1770s by mercury imported from Almadén to supplement flagging production at Huancavelica.

Then in 1780 the industry suffered the twin scourges of the Tupac Amaru rebellion and mercury scarcity. The shortage resulted from the British interdiction of Spanish shipping during the American Revolution and was followed by the precipitous decline at Huancavelica once the crown began operating the mines in late 1781. With the crown running things, production costs jumped as high as 167 pesos per quintal in 1784, generating a huge deficit because the price to the refiners could not be raised.[39] Moved to action by difficulties at Almadén and the unacceptable situation at Huancavelica, Minister José de Gálvez finally brought himself to sign a contract with the Austrians to purchase up to 12,000 quintales of mercury per year from Idria at a cost of 53 pesos per quintal.[40] But refiners in Lower Peru received no shipments from Europe between 1779 and 1781.[41] After extremely optimistic reports from José Antonio Areche—the *visitador* whom Gálvez had appointed to raise Huancavelica's output and cut the price to the silver refiners—the crisis at Huancavelica took Gálvez by surprise, and he lacked the resources to make up the shortfall before the latter part of the decade.

Once the mercury from Almadén and Idria began reaching the Andean mines, the refiners responded by producing 86.8 million pesos of silver from 1791 to 1800, an increase of more than 30 million over the preceding ten years. This marked the all-time high, according to TePaske's data. While many factors entered into the surge—such as the new mining tribunal, the technological expedition of Nordenflicht, and particularly the expansion at Pasco—the European mercury was decisive. By this time, the Andean operators needed at least 8,000 quintales per year, a quota that Huancavelica could not meet. Unsure about what to do with the Santa Bárbara mine after its cave-in, the government closed this great mine at Huancavelica in 1791. The government permitted private individuals to exploit other deposits in the region, however, and they managed to produce 2,000–3,000 quintales per year without any subvention from the state.[42] Huancavelica's low output, coupled with the fact that from 1798 to 1801 war again deprived the amalgamators of European mercury, brought the boom of the 1790s to a halt. Furthermore, Gálvez's successors had allowed the contract with the Austrians to lapse in 1797, thinking that Almadén could meet the needs of the American colonies by itself.[43]

The reformers did not succeed in offering the Peruvian industry the stimulus of less costly mercury. Once the Mexican price had been cut, and once European mercury began arriving in the Andes, the crown showed interest in passing similar savings on to the Peruvian refiners. But Huancavelica stood in the way. Its guild argued that the mines were barely profitable. Yet it was impossible to lower the Almadén price without cutting the price at Huancavelica, because the crown feared that refiners would smuggle the European mercury to Huancavelica and sell it to the government for the higher price. When Areche abolished the guild in 1779 and turned the royal mine over to a monopolist operator, Nicolas Saravia, it was under the condition that he sell mercury to the government at 45 pesos per quintal. At the same time, the visitador intended to charge the refiners 55 pesos plus the customary costs of transportation from Huancavelica to the silver mines. But Saravia died, his heirs refused to assume the contract, and the government began operation of the mine with the aforementioned alarming rise in production costs. Areche's successor, Jorge Escobedo, consequently raised the price again to 79 pesos in 1785 and then rolled it back to the old level of 73 pesos.[44] To encourage the private distillers, the price rose to 85 pesos in 1799.[45]

Once the war ended and shipments to the Americas resumed in 1802, Peru found itself in a situation somewhat akin to that endured by Mexico in the mid-1600s.[46] No longer self-sufficient in mercury because of Huancavelica's difficulties and the tremendous increase in demand, the Andeans had come to depend upon European remissions. Yet Mexico now took priority when it came to distributing the quicksilver. To make matters even worse, Minister of Grace and Justice Miguel Cayetano Soler shortsightedly announced in 1802 that production was to cease altogether at Huancavelica. He believed Almadén was capable of distilling 30,000 quintales per year at a cost of about 15 pesos each. Thus, it made no sense to him to pay maintenance costs on the Huancavelica mines, nor should the government buy mercury at Huancavelica from private operators at the inflated price of 73 pesos. But Soler also had another motive: he hoped to curtail any sentiment among the Peruvians for independence by making them totally dependent upon Spain for mercury.[47] As it turned out, however, Almadén failed to deliver the promised 30,000 quintales per year,[48] and Napoleon invaded Spain. Meanwhile the Peruvians had managed to continue distilling at Huancavelica, but their production was meager compared to the amount lost when Napoleon's troops occupied the peninsula in 1808.

The Crisis of Bourbon Rule and Independence

The French seizure of Almadén battered the Spanish American mining industry. Mexico fortuitously had at least a three-year supply of mercury in 1809,[49] which permitted refiners there to continue operations, although they were beset with anxiety about what would happen when the stocks were gone. Lower Peru still had Huancavelica, where high-graders managed to produce 2,000 or 3,000 quintales per year with little assistance from the government. With stocks on hand when Almadén was seized, Peru also managed to keep refining. Probably Upper Peru suffered more from the French occupation than anywhere else. Less abundantly stocked than Mexico and without a local source of mercury such as Huancavelica, the amalgamators at Potosí and Oruro faced a more precarious situation, with shortages lasting from 1810 to at least 1817.[50]

Bowing less to American demands than to the mounting shortage of mercury in the New World, on 26 January 1811 the Cortes abolished the royal monopoly on mercury, removing the government entirely from the quicksilver trade. The decree officially recognized that the mercury monopoly impeded the search for new mercury mines because it placed the ownership of new discoveries in doubt. From that point onward, the discovery and exploitation of mercury mines and the commercialization of quicksilver were free from government control.[51] While the mining tribunal of Peru did everything possible to stimulate the discovery of new mercury mines, the Cortes made no specific proposals about how operations at Huancavelica might be financed, except to levy a small tax on silver.[52]

Had Almadén been lost permanently or even for several additional years, the crisis would have been much more serious, but as it was, the political predicament of the French invasion undoubtedly caused even more harm. The abdications of Charles IV and Ferdinand VII precipitated rebellions and eventually wars of independence throughout the colonies. Most serious was the Hidalgo Revolt in Mexico, which erupted in late 1810 and caused great destruction to the Bajío region where Guanajuato, Zacatecas, and other great mines were located. Although royalist forces defeated

Hidalgo by 1811, the rebellion continued to smolder with occasional flare-ups. These disruptions often made it difficult or impossible for refiners to obtain mercury from the central storehouse. The rebels impeded transportation between Mexico City and the Bajío for several years and harassed convoys traveling between Veracruz and the capital.[53]

When cut off from Mexico City, the amalgamators sometimes tried to bypass the capital and bring mercury directly from Veracruz or another port. But this flew against the centralizing policies of the monarchy, and bureaucrats impeded the operators.[54] Appeals to Spain were time-consuming. Even though the crown generally supported flexibility in the final analysis, months passed in the meantime, and new circumstances and problems arose. Thus, there were often local shortages of mercury at individual camps even though no shortage technically existed within the viceroyalty. The problem lay with the distribution network disrupted by the rebellions.[55] Rebel activity made even communications between Veracruz and the capital hazardous in 1813 and forced Viceroy Félix María Calleja to commit 2,000 soldiers and considerable resources to keep the road open.[56] Yet Almadén was back in Spanish hands by September 1812, at which time 17,000 quintales were ready for shipment to Spanish America.[57] Mercury supplies had been tight, but imminent disaster had not fully materialized.

In South America the turmoil did not uniformly disrupt either silver production or mercury distribution. At Potosí the rebels purposely stole the mercury or spilled it, trying to slash treasury revenues from mining.[58] Treasury officials shifted mercury from caja to caja to alleviate shortages.[59] At Huancavelica production by the *pallaqueros* dropped significantly by 1814: desperate for revenue to fight the rebellions that eventually culminated in independence, the treasury had stopped providing money to buy mercury from the Indian pallaqueros in 1812.[60] Merchants and other entrepreneurs, however, evidently stepped in to purchase the mercury from the pallaqueros.[61] They assumed the distribution role previously played by the viceregal government, and production rose to 2,500 quintales by 1816.[62] Although the Almadén mercury was not always available when needed by the *azogueros,* renewed shipments from Almadén after 1813 hampered production at Huancavelica, except by the Indians.[63] At the same time, the royal government continued to maintain the great Santa Bárbara mine even though it had been closed since 1791.[64] On 2 October 1814 the Indians of Huancavelica rioted, and in 1820 the city was invaded by rebels.[65] Despite the turmoil, demand for mercury in Peru remained high, suggesting that refiners continued processing silver ore in the midst of the revolts and wars. In 1815, for example, Peru still required 6,000 quintales per year. In the following year at Pasco the installation of a steam pump—the first used in Spanish American mines—touched off renewed activity.[66] Silver production undoubtedly declined, but the mines were not shut down. And in 1814 and 1815 the royal government dispatched 14,900 quintales from Almadén to Peru, more than enough to satisfy demand for two years.[67]

The second decade of the nineteenth century also brought important changes in the way Spain approached the task of delivering mercury to its colonists. In its desperation to provide the refiners with mercury during the French occupation, the Cortes of Cádiz decreed on 26 January 1811 that private parties could carry mercury to the New World, although such shipments were to be made in Spanish bottoms.[68] With the liberalization of policy, British interests began buying Idria mercury to send directly to Mexico, bypassing Spain altogether.[69] Besides trying to obtain mercury through third parties, the Spaniards also tried to bribe the French commander at Almadén to provide it. Neither attempt proved successful. In 1812 Spanish officials concocted secret plans to make a raid on Almadén and seize from 10,000 to 12,000 quintales. But the distribution network within Spain was so disrupted that no iron or sheepskin flasks were available to package the mercury. Miguel Lastarria, a Peruvian who had just been named *fiscal de Quito,* drew upon his experience shipping mercury in Chile to suggest the use of beer bottles. He recommended that the bottles should be only partially filled to allow the mercury to expand and should then be capped and wrapped in a sheep hide with the wool inside.[70] The French retreat removed the need for the plan, which had been delayed by lack of funds.

With the French gone, the Spanish government alternated between directing the commerce and turning distribution over to the Americans. By royal order of 30 December 1815 the crown authorized the refiners to purchase mercury in Seville, packaged in iron flasks, at 38 pesos per quintal.[71] It had apparently given up its attempt to dominate mercury distribution. Merchant houses filled the void left by the government, so well that at one point the mining tribunal of Lima had difficulty selling its stocks of mercury.[72] The primary difference between government and private shipments was that the prices of the latter varied greatly depending upon supply and demand. Occasionally the government did try to mount large shipments to the American colonies. In 1817 the crown responded to the war with the Peruvian rebels by deciding that all mercury to that viceroyalty should be shipped in men-of-war, but in two years none was sent in that manner.[73] Even so, there were apparently government shipments as late as 1821.[74]

Historians can debate the consequences of the Bourbons' emphasis upon the mining industry. John Coatsworth criticizes their policies, asserting that they propped up a moribund industry and sacrificed other sectors of the Mexican economy.[75] John Fisher, on the other hand, believes that the prosperity of mining rippled through the Peruvian economy.[76] In any case, the effect of mining upon monetary circulation in New Spain is noteworthy. At the beginning of the Bourbon period, Mexico rarely minted more than 4 million pesos per year; in 1804 it coined 27 million.[77] Whether or not the Bourbons' obsession with mining was misguided, the impact of mercury upon the industry was clear.

Independence, of course, removed the Spanish government entirely from the distribution of mercury in its former colonies, but the refiners there continued to amalgamate their ores throughout most of the nineteenth century. Huancavelica still produced some mercury—as much as 3,000 quintales (in 1847), perhaps more typically 1,000—with the bulk of its output undoubtedly going to Pasco and other nearby camps.[78] Mexico, Bolivia, and even Peru continued to depend primarily upon Almadén.[79] For the second quarter of the nineteenth century, mercury output at the great Spanish mine was roughly as much as it had been in the early 1800s, before the French invaded.[80] The former colonies continued to consume most of that mercury. Along with iron, mercury was the principal metal imported into Mexico during the nineteenth century.[81] The former colony apparently used about 10,000 quintales per year shortly after independence.[82] With Almadén mercury selling for 25–50 pesos per quintal in Peru, most activity at Huancavelica ceased, and only a few Indians continue to produce mercury.[83]

Then in 1830 the Spanish government decided to sell the total output of the mine to a merchant house and let it shoulder responsibility for marketing. Iñigo, Ezpeleta y Compañía held the first contract. In 1835 the British Rothschild family, which already controlled production from Idria, also won the contract for Almadén. The Rothschilds transferred the mercury to Great Britain, whence it was distributed to the New World. In Mexico, and probably Peru also, the monopoly led to increasingly higher prices. For example, at Real del Monte mercury cost 50 pesos per quintal in 1825, but the price rose as high as 154 pesos in 1846.[84] The Rothschilds largely monopolized American mercury distribution until 1849, when production from the New Almadén mines near Santa Clara, California, began to inundate the Pacific Coast of Mexico and South America, driving prices down.[85]

In assessing the Bourbon Reforms during the regin of Charles III, Charles Noel wrote: "Lacking any firm ideological base—they espoused mercantilist as well as liberal and physiocratic ideas in a pragmatic jumble—they never set clear priorities that could be widely agreed on and which could provide true insight into the needs of the Monarchy."[86] If that was true before 1790, it became even more the case after 1800, judging by the crown's handling of mercury production and distribution. Gálvez at least gave some coherence to the mercury policy, but thereafter vacillation, conflicting priorities, and imperial crisis took their toll. The ministers remained consistent in their emphasis upon silver production as the primary function of Mexico and Peru, but their determination to use mercury as a weapon of political control over the colonies actually interfered with silver output. They never really decided whether the crown's distribution of mercury should primarily facilitate silver refining or whether it should first generate a profit for the crown. Neither were they consistent as to whether the colonials should be permitted to exploit Huancavelica or other New World mercury mines. The availability of American mercury made the colonies less dependent on Spain, but on the other hand, it helped make silver production more secure.

And yet, given the difficulties in royal policy, it is significant that mercury shortages probably played only a small role in the decline of silver mining after 1810. In fact, that scarcity was not much more severe than the shortages that occurred from 1800 to 1802, when the British blocked access to the colonies. At that time lack of mercury idled many Mexican mines whose ores were too poor for smelting.[87] Minister of Grace and Justice Soler became so desperate to ship mercury to Mexico and Peru that he authorized North American ships to carry it.[88] As late as 1804, Soler had not managed to establish adequate stocks of quicksilver in Peru to alleviate anxieties about shortages.[89] At Pasco from 1800 to 1805 merchants exploited the shortage to sell mercury at 150–200 pesos per quintal.[90] In 1806 Mexico had only a six-month supply remaining, although Soler had 66,000 quintales awaiting shipment in Spain.[91]

In terms of mining production, the mercury crisis probably played a relatively minor role. Anxiety about whether mercury would be available hampered planning and depressed output to some extent, but other factors were more important. Strapped for money, the royal treasury could not always give the amalgamators credit on mercury purchases as it had traditionally done.[92] Sometimes it lacked funds to pay for the mercury arriving from Europe.[93] In addition, the turmoil of the 1810s in Mexico, according to Brian Hamnett, led to

> the elimination of the decisive role of the Spanish peninsular merchant-investor class. Loss of investments, withdrawal of capital and emigration of personnel accounted for the decline of this group: they, moreover, faced the brunt of insurgent hostility. Estimates of withdrawn capital vary from 80 million to 140 million pesos. . . . The events after September 1810 destroyed the intermediary position of the Spanish peninsular merchants in capitalizing the processes of silver production.[94]

Silver production at Guanajuato dropped by two-thirds between 1811 and 1825 compared to the previous fifteen years. Most other mining districts also suffered, although Tasco, little affected by the insurgents, maintained stable production, and Zacatecas expanded.[95] There is some indication that Mexican mining investment had begun to decline before the wars.[96] Throughout the colonial mining districts, the flight or migration of workers and the abandonment and destruction of mines and refining mills impaired the industry. Similar conditions held in the war-ravaged regions of Hispanic South America. In comparison to such upheaval, the mercury shortages were less critical.

Thus even though the defeat of Napoleon and the expulsion of the French invaders from the peninsula led to the restoration of the Bourbon monarchy, the Spanish government was unable to retain its monopoly over the sale of mercury to the American mines. Neither did it have a pressing interest in stimulating silver output once the colonies won their independence. Even before 1808 the efforts of the Bourbon rulers to deliver abundant and cheap mercury to the American refiners achieved only partial success. Vacillation, hesitancy, and conflicting priorities hindered their attempts to breathe new life into Huancavelica. But the Mexican silver boom of the eighteenth century and the more modest Peruvian revivial sprang in large part from the stocks of mercury the Bourbon ministers managed to gather from Almadén, Huancavelica, and Idria.

Notes

The author gratefully acknowledges the financial support of the National Endowment for the Humanities, which made possible the research for this paper.

1. Among the most important works on Mexico are David Brading, *Miners and Merchants in Bourbon Mexico, 1763–1810* (Cambridge, Eng., 1971); Brading and Harry E. Cross, "Colonial Silver Mining: Mexico and Peru," *Hispanic American Historical Review,* 52 (1972): 545–79; Richard L. Garner, "Silver Production and Entrepreneurial Structure in 18th-Century Mexico," *Jahrbuch für Geschichte von*

Staat, Wirtschaft und Gesellschaft Lateinamerikas, 17 (1980): 157–85; and John H. Coatsworth, "The Mexican Mining Industry in the Eighteenth Century," in Nils Jacobsen and Hans-Jürgen Puhle, eds., *The Economies of Mexico and Peru During the Late Colonial Period, 1760–1810* (Berlin, 1986), 26–45. The literature on the Andean region is less extensive. On Potosí, refer to Peter J. Bakewell, "Registered Silver Production in the Potosí District, 1550–1735," *Jahrbuch für Geschichte von Staat, Wirtschaft und Gesellschaft Lateinamerikas,* 12 (1975): 67–103; Enrique Tandeter, "La rente comme rapport de production et comme rapport de distribution: Le cas de l'industrie minière de Potosi, 1750–1826" (thèse de 3e cycle en histoire, Paris, 1980); and Rose Marie Buechler, *The Mining Society of Potosí, 1776–1810* (Ann Arbor, 1981). Although they focus on the latter part of the century, the works of John Fisher are valuable on Lower Peru, especially *Minas y mineros en el Perú colonial, 1776–1824* (Lima, 1977).

2. For quantitative data on mining production in both Mexico and Peru, see particularly the work of John TePaske, especially "Bullion Production in Mexico and Peru, 1581–1810" (unpub. paper, 1987). The most recent general summary of Spanish American mining is Richard L. Garner, "Long-Term Silver Mining Trends in Spanish America: A Comparative Analysis of Peru and Mexico," *American Historical Review,* 93:4 (October 1988): 898–935.

3. TePaske, "Bullion Production," 32.

4. Two basic introductions to the colonial mining industry are Brading and Cross, "Colonial Silver Mining"; and Peter Bakewell, "Mining in Colonial Spanish America," in Leslie Bethell, ed., *The Cambridge History of Latin America,* vol. 2: *Colonial Latin America* (New York, 1984), 105–51.

5. I have made no effort to address the production of gold, which was negligible in Peru and, compared to silver, relatively unimportant in Mexico also.

6. I have chosen to use TePaske's data because they make it possible to compare Mexican and Peruvian silver output. TePaske's figures do not always coincide with those compiled by Alexander von Humboldt (see note on sources for table 2), however, and the latter show a more rapid expansion in Mexico.

7. Peter Bakewell, *Silver Mining and Society in Colonial Mexico: Zacatecas, 1546–1700* (New York, 1971), 184, 192–93; and TePaske, "Bullion Production in Mexico and Peru, 1581–1810," 35.

8. Bakewell, "Mining in Colonial Spanish America," 145.

9. Brading, *Miners and Merchants,* 156–58; and Brading and Cross, "Colonial Silver Mining," 564.

10. Garner, "Silver Production and Entrepreneurial Structure," 157.

11. Regarding Almadén during this period, see M. F. Lang, *El monopolio estatal del mercurio en el México colonial (1550–1710)* (Mexico City, 1977), 66, 90–94. The standard history of Almadén to 1800 is Antonio Matilla Tascón, *Historia de las minas de Almadén,* vol. 1: *Desde la época romana hasta el año 1645* (Madrid, 1958), and vol. 2: *Desde 1646 a 1799* (Madrid, 1987).

12. Certificado de Gaspar de Pinedo, September 1708, Archivo General de Indias (hereinafter AGI), Indiferente General (hereinafter IG) 1787; and Consulta de la Junta de Azogues, 17 May 1710, AGI, IG 1774. Matilla Tascón (*Historia,* 2:53) says that the Castillo mine was discovered in 1697.

13. Made of ministers from both the Council of Hacienda and the Council of Indies, the Junta naturally showed more concern for Almadén (because of its interest in providing adequate mercury for the American refiners) than had been true when the Council of Hacienda ran the mines by itself. On 24 January 1717, however, Philip abolished the Junta and placed Almadén under the direct supervision of the Council of the Indies. That lasted only until March, when he created the General Superintendency of Quicksilvers, headed by Andrés de Pez, the governor of the council. A few years later, the crown decided to make the president of the council responsible for mercury matters and conferred the superintendency upon him. See Joseph Cornejo y Ibarra to Joseph Patiño, San Ildefonso, 27 August 1734, in Expediente sobre el nombramiento de Jerónimo de Sola como Gobernador de Huancavelica, 1734–1735, AGI, Lima 775; and Conde de Montijo to Crown, 30 March 1739, AGI, IG 1776. Increasingly, however, the secretary of the Indies and the navy began to oversee mercury matters and supervise the superintendency. Then in 1754 the superintendency was incorporated into the ministry of the Indies, and six years later, Charles III named Minister Julián de Arriaga general superintendent of mercury. Decree of 14 February 1760, AGI, IG 1745.

14. Consulta de la Junta de Azogues, 1 June 1710, AGI, IG 1774.

15. The basic account of the Mexican mercury administration is Antonia Heredia Herrera, *La renta del azogue en Nueva España: 1709–1751* (Sevilla, 1978).

16. Heredia Herrera, *La renta del azogue,* 241.

17. Duque de Arion to Crown, 26 August 1726, AGI, IG 1775; Conde de Montijo to Crown, 30 March 1739, AGI, IG 1776; Joseph de la Quintana to Conde del Montijo, 28 June 1739, AGI, IG 1779; Conde de Montijo to Crown, 30 March 1739, AGI, IG 1776; Royal decree of 28 September 1729, AGI, IG 1779.

18. Brading, *Miners and Merchants,* 141.

19. Consulta de la Junta de Azogues, 17 May 1710, AGI, IG 1774.

20. In the early nineteenth century, the crown incurred 35 pesos in costs to produce a quintal of mercury at Almadén and ship it to Mexico, compared with 40 pesos per quintal remitted to South America. Anonymous report, undated, AGI, IG 1783.

21. The difference in cost arose from the crown's suspension of the *quinto,* or fifth, on mercury. The government paid the guild members 73 pesos per quintal but until 1760 took back 20 percent through the quinto. This meant that the guild really received only 58 pesos until the quinto was suspended in 1760. Although this was intended as a temporary measure to assist the guild during difficult times, the crown never reinstituted the tax, making the suspension permanent. Consulta of the Council of the Indies, 7 May 1763, AGI, Lima 497.

22. M. H. Kuss, *Memoir on the Mines and Works of Almadén* [1852], trans. S. B. Christy (San Francisco, 1879), 46; and Matilla Tascón, *Historia,* 2:215–17, 479–81.

23. No one has yet offered an explanation, as far as I can tell, for the depression of the 1760s. Brading (*Miners and Merchants,* 157–58) addresses the factors involved in overcoming the crisis but says nothing about what caused it.

24. For a discussion of the difference the price cut made in profitability for the refiners, see Brading, *Miners and Merchants,* 155–56.

25. The general administration distributed even more mercury during 1802–5, a yearly average of 24,292 quintales, when supplies flooded into the viceroyalty

following the end of the blockade. Almadén had continued to produce and store great quantities despite the interruption in transatlantic trade, and once contact was restored, Mexico, Lower Peru, and Upper Peru received tremendous quantities.

26. Brading, *Miners and Merchants,* 139–40.

27. Ibid., 140.

28. For some reason, amalgamators at Pachuca required significantly higher grade ores to turn a profit than was true in most of the other mining districts. See Brading, *Miners and Merchants,* 156. This helps to account for Pachuca's predilection for smelting.

29. For a brief treatment, see Arthur P. Whitaker, *The Huancavelica Mercury Mine: A Contribution to the History of the Bourbon Renaissance in the Spanish Empire* (Cambridge, MA, 1941).

30. Far more smelting was done at Huantajaya than anywhere else in Spanish South America, although amalgamation became more important there also toward the end of the century. Report of Antonio de Ulloa to Crown, 14 September 1771, Biblioteca Nacional (Madrid) (hereafter BNM), MSS 19568, cap. 14.

31. These figures are drawn from tables 1 and 8.

32. See the mercury account for that year in AGI, Contaduría 1048A.

33. Brading and Cross, "Colonial Silver Mining," 556; Escobedo to Gálvez, 5 May 1795, anexo 1, AGI, Lima 1340; Escobedo to Sonora, 5 February 1787, AGI, Lima 1340; Biblioteca Nacional del Perú (hereafter BNP), MS C294.

34. Viceroy Osorno to Ministro de Hacienda, 22 June 1799, AGI, Lima 1333.

35. "Relación de Juan Luis López," f. 442, BNM, MS 2784; "Raçon y Computo ajustado de lo que se a gastado en todas las caxas deste Reyno del Perú," 1671–80, AGI, Lima 88; Informe del cabildo de Huancavelica, 15 April 1722, AGI, Lima 469; Governor of Huancavelica to the king, 23 September 1723, AGI, Lima 469; Certificación de Pedro de Larreta, Treasurer of Huancavelica, 22 September 1723, AGI, Lima 469; Marqués de Casa Concha, *Relación del Estado que ha tenido, y tiene la Real Mina de Guancavelica, Y los intereses de la Real Hacienda, en las dependencias del Azogue, que haze el Margues de Casachoncha al Señor Doctor Don Alvaro Cabero su succesor en los cargos de Governador de Guancavelica, y Superintendente de la R1. Mina y Caja* (Lima, 1726), cap. 46, AGI, Lima 469.

36. Consulta of the Council of the Indies, 27 July 1729, AGI, Lima 364.

37. In 1767, for example, Potosí required 2,250 quintales, compared to nearly 1,700 for Oruro and over 900 for Pasco. Expediente de la entrega del gobierno de la Real mina de Huancavelica por Carlo Beranguer, gobernador interino, a Domingo de Jáuregui, f. 22, 26 October 1767, AGI, Lima 840.

38. $r = .66$. Kendall W. Brown, *Bourbons and Brandy: Imperial Reform in Eighteenth-Century Arequipa* (Albuquerque, 1986), 66. The current lack of long series of data on mercury distribution hinders such calculations for other Peruvian districts.

39. Juan María de Gálvez to Diego de Gardoqui, 28 July 1797, AGI, Lima 778.

40. José de Gálvez to Intendant of Buenos Aires, 15 March 1785, AGI, Buenos Aires 434.

41. "Plan que demuestra los Azogues venidos de España a las Reales Cajas de esta capital con destino de consumirse en este Reino," AGI, Lima 1324; Libro

matrix de la real mina de azogues de Huancavelica, 1788, BNP, C3038; and John Fisher, *Minas y mineros,* 165.

42. Gálvez to Gardoqui, 31 January 1797, AGI, Lima 1335; and Libros mayores de la caja de Huancavelica, 1796–1801, AGI, Lima 1319–23B.

43. Carlos Alexandro de Lellis to Miguel Cayetano Soler, no. 6, 24 January 1804, AGI, IG 1790.

44. Areche to Gálvez, 5 August 1779, AGI, Lima 1328; Escobedo to Gálvez, no. 21, 16 December 1782, AGI, Lima 1340.

45. Marquis of Osorno to Minister of Hacienda, no. 236, 22 June 1799, AGI, Lima 1333; Representación de Lázaro Rivera, 12 October 1811, paragraph 11, AGI, Lima 1342.

46. See also María Dolores Fuentes, "El azogue en las postrimerias del Perú colonial," *Revista de Indias,* 46:177 (1986), 75–105.

47. Draft of royal order to Juan María de Gálvez, 28 November 1800, AGI, Lima 1334; Soler to Viceroy of Peru, 18 October 1802, AGI, Lima 1357; Carlos Alexandro de Lellis to Soler, no. 6, 24 January 1804, AGI, IG 1790; Juan Vives y Echeverría to Soler, 18 January 1808, AGI, Lima 778; and J. R. Fisher, *Government and Society in Colonial Peru: The Intendant System 1784–1814* (London, 1970), 144–45.

48. Only in 1801 and 1804 did Almadén meet the 30,000 quintal goal, and equally troubling, production costs were rising. "Estado que manifiesta los caudales recibidos en la Tesorería de estas Reales Minas," undated, AGI, IG 1783.

49. Draft of Pedro Catani to Marquis de las Hormasas, no. 5, ? May 1810, AGI, Mexico 2214, acknowledging that 56,322 quintales had been sent to Mexico in 1809, which should have been sufficient for three years.

50. Pezuela to Ministro de Hacienda, no. 120, 29 April 1817, AGI, Lima 1358.

51. Decree of the Cortes, 26 January 1811, AGI, Lima 1351.

52. Expediente sobre la libertad de trabajar las minas de azogue y poder venderle tambien libremente, 1810–11, AGI, IG 1791.

53. Brian R. Hamnett, *The Economic and Social Dimension of the Revolution of Independence in Mexico, 1800–1824,* Arbeit-spapiere no. 18 (Bielefeld, 1979), 26–27.

54. See, for example, the disputes between officials in Mexico City and Veracruz over control of mercury distribution in 1813, in Archivo General de la Nación (Mexico) (hereafter AGNM), Minería, vol. 199, expedientes 1 and 4.

55. These impressions of the mercury situation in Mexico around 1814 come from a number of documents found in AGI, Mexico 2215.

56. Timothy E. Anna, *The Fall of the Royal Government in Mexico City* (Lincoln, NE, 1978), 148. John TePaske, "The Fiscal Breakdown of Mexico and Peru During the Epoch of Independence" (unpublished paper, 46th International Congress of Americanists, 1988). TePaske argues that the difficulties in communications also resulted in a more pronounced fiscal crisis for the royal treasury in Mexico than in Peru.

57. Draft of letter to Viceroy of Mexico, 19 September 1812, AGI, Mexico 2215.

58. Pezuela to Minister of Hacienda, no. 120, 29 April 1817, AGI, Lima 1358.

59. Pezuela to Minister of Hacienda, Lima, no. 120, 29 April 1817, AGI, Lima 1358.

60. Vives to Minister of Hacienda of Ultramar, Lima, 1 December 1812, AGI, Lima 1335; and Representación de José Montenegro al rey, Madrid, 19 April 1816, AGI, Lima 1358.

61. Expediente relativo a la provisión de azogue para las minas de Potosí, BNP, D6131.

62. Lázaro de Ribera to Felipe Vallejo, Lima, 23 March 1816, AGI, Lima 1358.

63. Mining Tribunal to Secretary of State, Lima, 4 October 1813, AGI, Lima 1335; and Nelson Manrique, *Mercado interno y región: La sierra central 1820–1930* (Lima, 1987), 45–46.

64. Vives y Echeverria to Council of Regency, Huancavelica, 18 September 1813, AGI, Lima 1335.

65. El Intendente de Huancavelica sobre el abono de arrendamiento de casa que solicita el Contador de Azogues, 1815–16, ANP, Minería 34; Petition of José María Villarino, Madrid, 9 August 1821, AGI, Lima 1470; and Pedro Fernández Calienes to Pedro Fernando Trujillo, 20 February 1821, Lilly Library, Peru MSS.

66. Marquis de la Concordia to Secretary of State and of the Universal Dispatch of the Indies, no. 25, 17 April 1815, AGI, Lima 1358; and Guillermo Lohmann Villena, "Minería en el marco del virreinato peruano: Invenciones, sistemas, técnicas y organización industrial," in *La minería hispana e iberoamericana,* VI Congreso Internacional de Minería, Cátedra de San Isidoro, 8 vols. (León, 1970), 1:650.

67. Rafael Orozco to Felipe Gonzalez Vallejo, Cádiz, 5 December 1815, AGI, Lima 1335.

68. Decree of 26 January 1811, AGI, Lima 1351.

69. See, for instance, Eusebio de Bardaxi y Azans to Esteban Varea, 3 June 1811, AGI, IG 1791; and Venegas to Minister of Hacienda, no. 106, 20 March 1811, AGI, Mexico 2215.

70. Hacienda of Indies to Commanding General of 5th and 6th Armies, 11 February 1812, *muy reservado,* AGI, IG 1791.

71. Ibarra to Aparici, 30 December 1815, AGI, IG 1783.

72. Representación de José Montenegro al rey, Madrid, 19 April 1816, AGI, Lima 1358.

73. Minister of Hacienda to Interim Secretary of the Despacho de Marina, 5 December 1819, AGI, Lima 1358.

74. At any rate, there is reference in AGI, Lima 1358, to a *legajo* in the audiencia of Mexico materials regarding the shipment of mercury from Spain to Mexico and Peru in that year.

75. Coatsworth, "The Mexican Mining Industry," 41–43.

76. Fisher, "Mining and the Peruvian Economy." My own work on Arequipa tends to support Fisher's view. See Brown, *Bourbons and Brandy,* especially chapters 3 and 4.

77. Enrique Florescano and Isabel Gil Sánchez, "La época de las reformas borbónicas y el crecimiento económico, 1750–1808," in Enrique Cárdenas, comp., *Historia económica de México,* Lecturas, no. 64, 2 vols. (México, Fondo de Cultura Económico, 1989), 1:666.

78. José Deustua, *La minería peruana y la iniciación de la república, 1820–1840* (Lima, 1986), 180. For information on Huancavelica in the decades immediately

following independence, see also Reconocimiento, inventario y tasación de la mina de Santa Bárbara de Huancavelica [1829], BNP, D10363; Copia del informe y visitas que ha hecho la diputación a la mina de azogues del Estado sita en Santa Bárbara, 1840–42, BNP, D9510; and Ley expedida por el Congreso de la República del Perú, facultando al Ejecutivo para que arriende la mina de "Santa Bárbara" por término no mayor de 50 años, 26 January 1869, BNP, D2540.

79. See, for example, Johann Jakob von Tschudi, *Travels in Perú During the Year 1838–1842, on the Coast, in the Sierra, Across the Cordilleras and the Andes, into the Primeval Forests,* trans. Thomasina Ross (London, 1847), 333.

80. See the production figures appended to XIV International Geological Congress [Madrid, 1926], *Minas de Almadén* (Madrid, 1926); and Kuss, *Memoir,* 47.

81. Inéz Herrera Canales, "La composición de las importaciones y exportaciones," in Cárdenas, comp., *Historia económica de México,* 2:190–91.

82. "Memoria presentada por el Sr. Consultor Lic. Don José Garcés a la Junta General de Minería, sobre disminuir el consumo de azogue en el beneficio de amalgamación y modo de premiar a los inventores," undated, AGNM, Minería, vol. 28, expediente 7.

83. BNP, D9510.

84. Herrera Canales, "Importaciones y exportaciones," 192.

85. Inés Herrera, "El abastecimiento de mercurio para las minas mexicanas de plata durante el siglo XIX" (unpub. paper presented at the 46th International Congress of Americanists, Amsterdam, 1988), 5–10; and Antonio del Castillo, *Memoria sobre las minas de azogue de América* (Mexico City, 1871), 51–58.

86. Charles C. Noel, "Charles III of Spain," in H. M. Scott, ed., *Enlightened Absolutism: Reform and Reformers in Later Eighteenth-Century Europe* (Ann Arbor, 1990), 142.

87. Virrey Marquina to Soler, no. 543, 27 March 1802, AGI, Mexico 2213.

88. Soler to Juez de Arrivadas y Alzadas de Cádiz, reservada, 18 May 1801, AGI, Mexico 2213.

89. Aviles to Minister of Hacienda, Lima, 23 May 1804, no. 289, AGI, Lima 1334.

90. Informe del Tribunal de Minería, 4 October 1813, AGI, Lima 1358.

91. Virrey Iturrigaray to Soler, no. 1012, 26 June 1806, AGI, Mexico 2214.

92. Testimonio del Cuaderno Anterior de los Autos sobre arreglo de Derechos del Tribunal de Minería, 1817–21, AGNM, Minería, vol. 193 bis, f. 297r.

93. AGNM, Minería, vol. 199, expediente 7, f. 275r.

94. Hamnett, *Economic and Social Dimension,* 28.

95. Ibid., 29–30.

96. Laura Randall, *Mexico,* vol. 1 of *A Comparative Economic History of Latin America 1550–1914,* 4 vols. (Ann Arbor, 1977), 133.

8

The State and Dependency in Late Colonial and Early Republican Ecuador

KENNETH J. ANDRIEN

In recent years historians have begun reexamining the role of the state in guiding the socioeconomic life of Spanish America.[1] Much of this scholarship has been influenced to some degree by the dependency paradigm, which postulates a direct link between Spanish imperialism and economic backwardness. Dependency advocates have argued that the Spanish colonial system left Latin America with a legacy of domestic inequalities, economic subordination to the North Atlantic world, and structural underdevelopment.[2] Studies focusing on the colonial roots of this dependency usually emphasize the importance of the eighteenth-century Bourbon Reforms in "shoring up the gothic edifice" of Spanish colonialism, which served to block the autonomous development of regions within the Spanish American Empire.[3] According to Ian Roxborough, this process evolved over time as a result of "the transfer of resources from the periphery to the center" and the imposition of "blocking mechanisms which hold back or distort the economies of the periphery, thus preventing an allocation of resources which will produce economic growth."[4] By focusing on the link between colonialism and patterns of socioeconomic change, the dependency paradigm has done much to encourage the recent boom in scholarly literature on the political economy of Spanish America.

Despite its importance, few scholars of the colonial and early national periods acknowledge their intellectual debt to this dependency literature.[5] In large part, this stems from a central paradox of *dependencia*—it is not a theory to be proven, but a paradigm, which cannot be verified through empirical research. Thus, the dependency paradigm requires complete substantive and epistemological acceptance from its adherents. Some dependency writers have even questioned the legitimacy of criticism from those unwilling to accept the validity of the paradigm—a solipsism that many scholars find antithetical to the basic tenets of modern historical research.[6] This controversial position has led many critics to dismiss the dependency paradigm as a rigid, simplistic, and ineffective analytical tool for interpreting the past.[7] As a result, most historians of Spanish America—unwilling to embrace the basic intellectual and theoretical parameters of the dependency paradigm—have downplayed or even ignored its importance as an organizing framework for their scholarly work.

In his magisterial three-volume history of the world, *Civilization and Capitalism, 15th–18th Century,* Fernand Braudel remains one of the few historians to integrate the basic principles of the dependency paradigm with empirical research.[8] Braudel brings the *Annales* School's penchant for using economic theory and serial quantifiable evidence—such as prices, trade data, and vital statistics—to examine socioeconomic change over long time periods.[9] Moreover, Braudel's emphasis on the links between regional and global patterns of change provides an essential blueprint for scholars interested in placing dependencia within a historical framework. As more historians use this approach, their work can also contribute to the sharpening, elaborating, and even redefining of the dependency paradigm. Using the dependency perspectives in this way—even over the objections of the *dependistas*—can allow a deeper understanding and interpretation of socioeconomic changes, particularly in regions subject to colonial domination, such as Spanish America.

One needed contribution to refining the dependency paradigm involves examining the direct links between state policy and socioeconomic development in Spanish America. Most dependency advocates have underestimated the role of public policy, often treating the state as little more than a weak tool of the ruling classes. As many historians now understand, however, the colonial states profoundly influenced patterns of social and economic change in Spanish America. For this reason, I will provide an empirical examination of the role of the colonial and early national states in promoting the "transfer of resources" and in "imposing blocking mechanisms" in the Andean region that is now Ecuador. By 1700 this region was an economically diverse agricultural, grazing, textile-manufacturing, and commercial zone within Spanish South America. By the culmination of independence in 1830, however, its economy revolved around subsistence agriculture and the export of a single cash crop, cacao. This study, focusing on the critical period between the end of colonial rule and the early independence period, should yield some important answers to a fundamental question too often ignored by proponents of the dependency paradigm: Did the colonial and early republican *states* contribute directly to the problems of underdevelopment?

Any examination of the links between state power and dependency in late colonial and early republican Ecuador must rest on a detailed quantitative analysis of the fiscal records drawn from the major economic centers of Quito, Guayaquil, and Cuenca. These materials can reveal the financial parameters of the state and provide a wealth of information on the outcome of government policies. Despite their importance, some critics—for example, D. A. Brading—have argued that the uncritical use of these data can present a confusing mixture of "facts and figments," particularly about the economic evolution of the Spanish American Empire.[10] Others, like Jacques Barbier and Herbert Klein, have replied boldly that no other colonial records are so "voluminous," "well kept," and "reflective of the actual state of the economy."[11] The gaps in the data and the uneven quality of these fiscal materials for Ecuador, particularly during the independence era, make it doubtful that they reflect the "actual state of the economy." Nevertheless, the fiscal accounts do provide vital empirical evidence about the success or failure of state policies and their impact on regional economic dependency in the critical period between the Bourbon Reforms and the early national period.

The Bourbon Reforms and Public Finance in Ecuador

The Bourbon monarchs made few changes in the decentralized, patrimonial fiscal bureaucracy in Ecuador until the late eighteenth century.[12] Apart from establishing a royal monopoly on cane liquor (*aguardiente*) and ending tax farming for the sales tax (*alcabala*) in 1765, the crown did little to increase the fiscal power of the colonial state. Three separate treasury offices administered the royal revenues in Quito, Cuenca, and Guayaquil.[13] Although the treasury office (*caja*) in Quito was supposed to serve as a clearinghouse for surplus income from the other two offices, in practice Guayaquil and Cuenca seldom sent sizable sums to the capital.[14] There was no effective supervision over the collection and disbursement of royal funds, except for periodic audits by the Tribunal of Accounts in distant Lima and later Bogotá.[15] By the reign of Charles III, however, it became apparent that this fiscal apparatus had to be transformed into a more centralized bureaucracy if the crown hoped to realize its tax, commercial, defense, and administrative goals in the region.[16]

This process of reform reached its apex during the tenure of José García de Leon y Pizarro as *visitador,* president, and regent of the *Audiencia* of Quito. The foundation of García Pizarro's reform policies rested on a new centralized state fiscal bureaucracy headed, from 1783, by the Dirección General de Rentas.[17]. The reforms removed jurisdiction over the collection of lucrative taxes—such as Amerindian tribute, the sales tax, and several royal monopolies (*tabaco, naipes,* and *pólvora*)—from the treasury cajas and placed it under the control of the Dirección General and its subtreasuries scattered throughout the north-central highlands.[18] Only surplus income from these subtreasuries of the Dirección General was deposited in the local treasury cajas. The province of Guayaquil had its own network of offices controlling the collection of these same taxes, while in Cuenca the levies remained under the control of the treasury caja.[19] All these various tribunals, however, gave an annual accounting to the main office of the Dirección General de Rentas in Quito. The Tribunal of Accounts in Quito supervised the entire fiscal apparatus.

The number of fiscal offices increased dramatically during the tenure of García Pizarro, who ensured his control over the government by filling these new posts with kin, friends, and political allies. His brother Ramón held the governorship of Guayaquil, and his son-in-law, Juan Josef de Villalengua y Marfil, was the attorney (*fiscal*) of the audiencia.[20] The key position of *director de rentas* went to the personal secretary of the visitador, Agustín Martín de Blas, while another political ally, Pedro Josef de Franco, received the comptrollership.[21] Positions in important subordinate offices usually went to trusted peninsulars or well-connected creoles, such as Josef de Renxijo, a partisan of Villalengua who became *contador de tributos* in Quito.[22] García Pizarro further solidified his control by giving his allies officerships in the newly created disciplined militia regiments.[23] In this way, the García Pizarro clan exercised unparalleled political dominance in the audiencia district.

The fiscal reforms begun by José García de Leon y Pizarro represented a concerted effort to create a more centralized colonial state capable of extracting more wealth from these Andean regional economies. This was a difficult task because the highland textile industry suffered from a prolonged recession and the cacao economy of the coast experienced the beginnings of its export boom with the advent of comercio libre in 1778. The key problem before García Pizarro and his allies was how to use this reinvigorated state apparatus to increase the levels of taxation during a period of fundamental economic change.

Public Finance and State Power in Bourbon Ecuador

Despite these far-reaching economic changes, the rapid rise in revenues flowing into the three major treasury districts of Quito, Guayaquil, and Cuenca demonstrates the success of José García de Leon y Pizarro's reforms.[24] In Quito, for example, income rose from 127,196 pesos in 1778 to 497,807 pesos in 1803, an average annual growth rate of 5.5 percent.[25] Income in Guayaquil manifested a similar pattern of growth, from 78,909 pesos in 1777 to 213,107 pesos in 1804—a yearly growth rate of 3.7 percent. This trend also held for Cuenca, where the growth in treasury receipts started a few years earlier. Revenues in Cuenca began their uneven rise in 1775 from 41,463 pesos to 155,196 pesos in 1802, for an average annual growth rate of 4.7 percent.[26] In fact, public revenues in the audiencia of Quito grew even more rapidly than in much wealthier provinces, such as Mexico, a clear indication of the state's control over the rather modest economic output of this Andean region.[27]

The success of the colonial state in raising income in the Quito treasury district depended on new tax levies and more efficient tax collection procedures. As the data in table 1 indicate, levels of taxation and state power over the declining economy of the north-central sierra remained low until the reform period. Then income levels began to rise rapidly. Remissions from the Guayaquil and Cuenca treasuries played an important role in this process, rising from only 38,637 pesos in the period 1770–74 to over 700,000 pesos ten years later (see table 1). Significant increases in revenues collected in the Quito district itself also revealed the state's enhanced control over local resources. Clerical taxes, for example, increased 500 percent after the onset of the visita, largely because of the confiscation of Jesuit wealth after 1767. Likewise, royal monopolies accounted for between 5 percent and 15 percent of the total income in Quito.[28] Income levels from traditional taxes, like Amerindian tribute and levies on trade and production, also rose rapidly after 1778 (see table 1). In short, the figures in table 1 show the success of the colonial state in tapping local sources of wealth amid the prolonged economic downturn in the north-central highlands.[29]

Remittances from the Dirección General de Rentas also played a key role in the rising levels of public funds in the Quito treasury office. In 1778 the

Table 1 Income (in Pesos), Quito Caja, 1702–1803

Year	Commerce & Production	Indian	Bureaucratic	Clerical	Monopolies	Remittances	Loans	Mining	Misc.	Total
1702–1704	109,009	66,779	56,577	24,365	13,554		1,880		3,179	275,343
1705–09	41,129	25,286	3,607	18,670	9,808			8,852	1,547	108,899
1710–14	78,843	112,621	68,055	3,285	41,618				2,247	306,669
1715–19	57,551	123,401	36,937	10,472	16,769				8,930	254,060
1720–24	57,070	130,612	50,997	15,418	11,613			62	1,868	267,640
1725–29	70,495	132,053	26,685	22,685	17,645				10,222	279,541
1730–34	94,488	169,822	38,824	18,139	28,778			69	1,593	351,713
1735–39	95,697	262,524	61,482	6,032	27,649			276	572	454,232
1740–44	89,502	159,602	55,295	4,029	21,525	231,543			1,040	562,536
1745–49	164,768	330,961	98,607	14,197	42,876	65,876	25		30,340	747,71
1750–54	111,873	248,101	58,098	13,567	21,709	39,304			15,406	508,058
1755–59	151,562	261,923	38,356	55,669	37,970	17,179		5	40,823	603,487
1760–64	180,098	306,001	72,891	70,095	45,951	219,028			69,147	963,211
1765–69	226,547	209,532	66,517	135,744	33,386	70,236		2	3,863	745,827
1770–74	164,071	281,004	52,711	144,514	48,195	38,637			25,987	755,119
1775–79	173,588	331,291	87,231	122,315	44,845	89,327		9	14,023	862,629
1780–84	339,556	529,813	163,948	496,522	153,543	704,075	56,055	26	45,255	2,488,693
1785–89	295,006	526,959	97,978	710,235	381,523	453,031	15,464	70	28,104	2,508,370
1790–94	362,975	664,928	124,914	307,342	89,085	585,541	47,154	28	36,826	2,218,793
1795–99	308,211	751,039	120,255	255,856	155,326	356,059	50,923		146,781	2,144,450
1800–1803	290,069	644,643	88,463	347,029	105,592	343,598	115,471	52	105,627	2,040,544
All	3,449,191	6,313,357	1,476,187	2,860,090	1,356,412	3,213,494	286,972	370	598,927	19,447,524

Note: The following years are missing from the AGI, Seville, and the ANH, Quito: 1700–01, 1706–10, 1716–1717, 1733, 1740, and 1786. In several years, particularly early in the eighteenth century, some tax categories generated no income; in these cases blank spaces appear in the table under those categories.

Sources: ANH, Quito, Real Hacienda 10, 11, Cuentas de la Caja de Quito, 1702–05, 1739; AGI Contaduría, 1539–40, Quito, 140–44, 173, 175, 416–429, Cuentas de la Caja de Quito, 1711–1803.

new fiscal bureaucracy remitted 86,519 pesos to Quito; by 1803 officials from the various offices of the Dirección General sent 211,775 pesos. Much of this tremendous increase resulted from increased yields from Amerindian tribute and the cane-liquor monopoly. Tribute returns rose from 51,050 pesos in 1778 to over 195,000 pesos in 1801, while aguardiente taxes jumped from 14,952 pesos in 1778 to 44,246 pesos in 1803.[30]

The visita of José García de Leon y Pizarro dramatically strengthened state fiscal control in the Guayaquil region, as collections of tax revenues increased and became more predictable. As the data in table 2 indicate, before the reform period public revenues remained dependent on port taxes, but yields were erratic. García Pizarro's establishment of a new customs house (*aduana*) and the monopolies on cane liquor and tobacco in 1778 ended these problems. According to table 2, income from taxes on commerce and production increased from 130,174 pesos in the five years before the visita to over 600,000 pesos between 1800 and 1804. Contributions from the Dirección General also played an increasingly important role in total income levels, rising from only 28,774 pesos in 1778 (30 percent of total income) to 169,014 pesos by 1804 (79 percent of total income).[31] Increased yields from clerical taxes, as in Quito, stemmed from the crown's control over the former Jesuit properties, while rising tribute receipts resulted from the state's ability to tax the growing numbers of Andean migrants seeking work on coastal plantations.[32] In short, the reforms of García Pizaaro established firm governmental control over the coastal economy, just as the export boom commenced after 1778.

The development of state fiscal control was least successful in Cuenca, where the Dirección General de Rentas collected only Amerindian tribute. Government power had always been notoriously weak in the south highlands. As the figures in table 3 show, public revenues rose from only 37,598 pesos in 1755–59 to only 89,492 pesos in 1760–64, and most of these meager amounts came from Amerindian tribute.[33] After the reform period, however, remissions from the local office of the tribute administration rose from nearly 146,000 pesos (1775–79) to over 270,000 pesos (1795–99).[34] The only other lucrative levies were on regional commerce, which went from 30,739 pesos (1770–74) to nearly 90,000 pesos (1795–99).[35] In short, revenue increases in Cuenca were modest, and the tax base remained virtually unchanged from early in the century (see table 3). The state was able to collect revenues more consistently in the latter part of the century, but it was not able to extend fiscal control over any new economic sectors.

The dramatic rise in per-capita tax rates in the late colonial period provides graphic evidence of the growing fiscal control of the Bourbon

Table 2 Income, Guayaquil Caja, 1714–1804

Year	Commerce & Production	Indian	Bureaucratic	Clerical	Monopolies	Remittances	Loans	Mining	Misc.	Total
1714	4,810	3,060	67		63			26		8,026
1715–19	24,477	5,789	1,140		5,806			130	13,682	51,024
1720–24	33,618	2,497	1,455		1,688				53,880	91,138
1725–29	50,882	5,133	2,013		431				17,713	76,172
1730–34	47,506		3,771		1,796					53,073
1735–39	12,505		362		1,180					14,047
1740–44	63,389				3,945				57,760	125,094
1745–49	80,801	12,425			2,107				20,936	116,269
1750–54	18,848		364		498	75,000		630		95,340
1755–59	73,742	1,017	3,345	5,053	2,530	28,000		410	50,949	165,046
1760–64	74,598	15,375	21,004	7,797	3,327	1,645		120	11,525	135,391
1765–69	119,452	17,903	4,053	23,218	2,404	53,752		17,180	11,278	249,240
1770–74	130,174	16,344	6,272	15,782	5,554	68,966		800	5,003	248,895
1775–79	186,426	30,022	21,814	22,874	44,098	64,384		2,500	7,788	379,906
1780–84	449,571	38,080	46,452	52,602	181,581	97,032		1,924	25,824	893,066
1785–89	357,861	63,453	25,706	8,700	122,836	124,029	866	6	39,260	742,717
1790–94	423,069	61,651	17,681	1,822	130,288	9,932	9,786	20	25,157	679,406
1795–99	478,918	58,711	25,082	1,247	113,774	1,090	9,427	34	1,822	707,883
1800–1804	619,603	65,753	21,745	55,183	79,252	102,723	6,227	17	172,421	1,122,924
All	3,250,250	397,213	202,326	194,278	703,158	626,553	26,306	23,797	532,776	5,956,657

Note: The following years are missing from the AGI, Seville, and the ANH, Quito: 1710–1713, 1730, 1734, 1736–39, 1750–52. In several years, particularly early in the eighteenth century, some tax categories generated no income; in these cases blank spaces appear in the table under those categories.

Sources: AGI, Contaduría, 1377, 1576–77; Quito, 407, 469–75, 477.

Table 3 Income, Cuenca Caja, 1722–1803

Year	Commerce & Production	Indian	Bureaucratic	Clerical	Monopolies	Remittances	Loans	Mining	Misc.	Total
1722–24	5,970	29,024	12,411	114	265				3,128	50,912
1725–29	11,120	38,390	11,800		956			22	2,940	65,228
1730–34	10,348	26,099	10,448		1,662			30	308	48,895
1735–39	1,910	3,195	375					14	120	5,614
1740–44										
1745–49	1,517	10,334	137		14				30	12,032
1750–54	21,966	33,340	9,513					59	1	64,879
1755–59	10,143	22,846	4,003		466				140	37,598
1760–64	24,699	56,405	7,535		605			48	200	89,492
1765–69	18,928	36,975	7,054						1,672	64,629
1770–74	30,739	125,459	6,270	1,225	6,015	526		1,675	3,197	175,106
1775–79	66,054	145,999	15,000		8,412		28	1,889	18,157	255,539
1780–84	58,366	192,828	17,035		13,777		450	3,905	22,989	309,350
1785–89	68,005	208,386	13,747	882	14,566		4,791	3,236	18,373	331,986
1790–94	80,285	259,268	26,062	46,043	16,246		26,247	2,974	11,446	468,571
1795–99	89,030	271,872	24,774	52,010	36,106	30,000	19,347	2,808	14,914	540,861
1800–1803	67,785	207,479	45,776	18,490	65,012		39,508	1,049	81,348	526,447
All	566,865	1,667,899	211,940	118,764	164,764	30,526	90,371	17,709	178,963	3,047,139

Note: The following years are missing from the AGI, Seville, and the AHN, Quito: 1720–21, 1734, 1736–47, 1749, and 1772. In several years, particularly early in the eighteenth century, some tax categories generated no income; in these cases blank spaces appear in the table under those categories.

Sources: AGI, Contaduría, 1534, Quito, 453–58, Cuentas de la Caja de Cuenca, 1722–1803.

state. In the Quito district, for example, each citizen paid an average of 13 reales by the late eighteenth century.[36] At the same time, per-capita taxes on Amerindians doubled during the period from 4 to 8 reales.[37] Creoles, peninsulars, and *castas* paid approximately 22 reales. Tax levels in Cuenca remained significantly lower. Nevertheless, per-capita taxes rose from 2.5 reales to 3.3 reales. Taxes on Amerindians doubled, while the most significant increase fell on the European and caste populations, whose per-capita tax burden rose from under 1 real to over 6 reales annually.[38] The most dramatic rise, however, took place in the Guayaquil district, where per-capita taxes soared from 11 reales in 1765 to over 48 reales by 1780. Amerindians saw their per-capita tax burden increase from 4 to 6 reales, while the white and caste populations endured a tremendous expansion of their taxes from 13 to 75 reales by the turn of the century.

State control over local resources in the audiencia district reached stunningly high levels, particularly when compared to other European colonial systems. Despite its great economic and military power, England was never able to levy taxes so effectively in its prosperous North American colonies. Despite the decline of textile manufacturing in the north-central highlands, taxpayers in the Quito district paid twice as much in per-capita taxes as the English colonists in North America.[39] The amounts paid in Guayaquil dwarfed anything collected in the thirteen English colonies. In fact, the per-capita tax burden in Guayaquil reached nearly twice the amounts paid in England itself, which reputedly had the highest tax levels in western Europe.[40] By the late colonial period, the reforms of García Pizarro had created a state fiscal apparatus as powerful and exploitative as any in the world.

The remarkable financial success of the Bourbon Reforms rested upon the state's ability to draw taxes from regional economies, regardless of whether they experienced cycles of growth or recession. Although the crown imposed few new levies after 1778, the new state administrations extracted much higher levels of public revenues from local economies, particularly in Guayaquil and Quito. Guayaquil had paid relatively low taxes early in the century, but once the export boom commenced, the crown increased the tax burden tremendously. Quito, however, experienced no such prosperity during the century; instead the state drew markedly increased tax receipts from a declining regional economy. The overriding aim of Bourbon colonialism was to extract resources from the audiencia regardless of the cost.

Table 4 Expenditures, Quito Caja, 1702–1803

Year	Remittances	Clerical	Administration	Defense	Loans	Misc.	Total
1702–1704	109,299	11,459	124,635	18,389	6,300	22,085	292,167
1705–09	89,073	2,780	44,420	1,000	2,100	18,306	157,679
1710–14	91,039	23,832	188,225		7,700	12,407	323,203
1715–19	131,286	10,098	125,308		5,600	11,162	283,454
1720–24	100,475	26,476	134,237		8,400	9,641	279,229
1725–29	136,298	24,384	134,237		4,200	4,567	303,956
1730–34	171,914	42,039	207,360		10,500	9,077	440,890
1735–39	254,250	55,854	185,725		10,500	34,924	541,253
1740–44	339,020	3,950	47,810	151,834	8,400	2,408	553,422
1745–49	416,458	96,890	406,119		10,500	6,292	936,259
1750–54	265,481	64,788	187,659		11,200	11,951	541,079
1755–59	297,079	49,213	213,148	13,294	10,500	14,199	597,433
1760–64	584,480	60,131	198,279	24,729	10,500	30,851	908,970
1765–69	255,665	37,580	225,883	171,509	12,500	23,080	726,217
1770–74	297,831	46,248	253,551	115,065	11,400	53,606	777,701
1775–79	502,170	49,381	321,531	194,339	7,300	39,417	1,114,138
1780–84	1,381,856	71,246	402,590	329,747	26,350	113,010	2,324,799
1785–89	967,435	35,255	508,976	281,572	8,400	91,359	1,892,997
1790–94	1,230,930	101,149	508,927	385,688	9,654	66,422	2,302,770
1795–99	1,118,378	34,405	755,034	226,332	11,346	32,445	2,177,940
1800–1803	1,098,427	44,269	510,430	255,527	8,400	41,279	1,958,332
All	9,880,967	893,826	5,770,587	2,187,472	203,850	663,455	19,600,157

Note: The following years are missing from the AGI, Seville, and the ANH, Quito: 1700–01, 1706–10, 1716–1717, 1733, 1740, and 1786. In several years, particularly early in the eighteenth century, some tax categories generated no income; in these cases blank spaces appear in the table under those categories.

Sources: ANH, Quito, Real Hacienda, 10, 11, Cuentas de la Caja de Quito, 1702–05, 1739; AGI, Contaduría, 1539–40, Quito, 140–44, 173 175, 416–29, Cuentas de la Caja de Quito, 1711–1803.

State Expenditures and Public Policy

After the *visita general* of José García de Leon y Pizarro, the colonial state directed royal funds to meet imperial rather than local needs. Each year the colonial treasures spent whatever was necessary to meet the expenses of the local government and remitted the remainder to Cartagena, thence to Spain. During periods of expanding revenues, such as the late eighteenth century, state officials shipped increasingly large sums of money to Cartagena rather than spend it within the audiencia district (see table 4). Remittances to Spain increased from 109,299 pesos in the period 1700–1704 to 1,098,427 pesos between 1800 and 1803. Moreover, the percentage of total expenditures sent to Spain rose from 37 percent to over 56 percent during those same years. García Pizarro and his successors had changed the fiscal priorities in government spending markedly.

The only other major expenses of the Quito treasury were administrative and defense outlays. As the data in table 4 indicate, administrative costs rose steadily during the century, reaching a high of 755,034 pesos between 1795 and 1799. Nevertheless, their share of the total expenditures dropped from a high of 58 percent between 1710 and 1714 to an average of only 25 percent after the visita general. The money spent on local defense, however, grew from insignificant amounts early in the century to over 385,688 pesos when García Pizarro established the new disciplined militia system in the region (see table 4). Despite the increasing remittances to Spain, fiscal reform clearly exacted a heavy price in rising administrative and defense expenditures.

In both Guayaquil and Cuenca, remittances to Quito rose dramatically during the century. The sums remitted from Guayaquil to Quito were particularly impressive. According to table 5, the coastal treasury sent only 52,626 pesos to Quito between 1770 and 1774; after the García Pizarro reforms, however, remittances reached 531,784 pesos (1785–89). As the figures in table 6 demonstrate, the Cuenca caja also sent between 127,207 pesos (1775–79) and 359,293 pesos (1795–99) which averaged approximately 70 percent of the treasury's total expenses. These funds from Guayaquil and Cuenca formed a large portion of the annual subsidy sent from Quito to Cartagena.

Both the Guayaquil and Cuenca treasuries also allocated increasing sums for local administration and defense. According to the data in table 5, administrative costs in Guayaquil rose from only 46,023 pesos between 1770 and 1774 to over 433,823 pesos (1800–1804). Likewise, the cost of government operations in Cuenca nearly doubled between 1770 and 1795

Table 5 Expenditures, Guayaquil Caja, 1714–1804

Year	Remittances	Clerical	Administration	Defense	Shipyards	Loans	Misc.	Total
1714		615	2,089	1,651				4,355
1715–19		615	2,446	1,294				4,355
1720–24	11,545	2,460	16,782	2,417	29,932		853	63,989
1725–29	8,393	3,033	13,347	1,989	21,984		1,685	50,431
1730–34		1,845	4,767	57	27,678		125	34,472
1735–39	25,000	615	1,491	1,026	7,841		4,385	40,358
1740–44	15,000	2,209	10,544	48,285	44,676		24,762	145,476
1745–49	39,134	4,342	26,779	7,240	4,746		219	82,460
1750–54		11,020	6,429	1,011	86,696		1,446	106,602
1755–59	333	6,256	21,787	2,522	49,596		43,406	123,900
1760–64	67,194	1,920	17,918	12,953	308			100,293
1765–69	170,191	6,117	33,330	37,192	5,074		7,691	259,595
1770–74	52,626		46,023	55,190	89,987		4,000	247,826
1775–79	149,561		74,739	110,520			2,545	337,365
1780–84	509,267	809	111,748	219,862	16,967		9,821	868,474
1785–89	531,784	2,737	193,297	90,448	1,706	4,750	5,932	830,654
1790–94	339,803	4,136	98,850	85,642	864		16,758	546,053
1795–99	330,329		213,334	214,628			200	758,491
1800–1804	426,829		433,823	249,368			324	1,110,344
All	2,676,989	48,729	1,329,523	1,143,295	388,055	4,750	124,152	5,715,493

Note: The following years are missing from the AGI, Seville, and the ANH, Quito: 1710–13, 1730, 1734, 1736–39, and 1750–52. In several years, particularly early in the eighteenth century, some tax categories generated no income; in these cases blank spaces appear in the table under those categories.
Source: AGI, Contaduría, 1377, 1576–77, Quito, 407, 469–75, 477.

Table 6 Expenditures, Cuenca Caja, 1722–1803

Year	Remittances	Clerical	Administration	Defense	Misc.	Total
1722–24	30,468	10,525	13,845		794	55,632
1725–29	43,497	9,619	12,063	255	629	66,063
1730–34	32,064	2,101	8,031	1,000	4,187	47,383
1735–39	3,064		1,290	400		4,754
1740–44						
1745–49		2,636	2,332			4,969
1750–54	21,325	5,618	17,147		4,000	48,090
1755–59	35,100	4,184	12,797			52,081
1760–64	27,630	3,234	15,380			46,244
1765–69	45,150	2,064	7,115		4,625	58,954
1770–74	111,990		50,921	1,874	76,362	241,147
1775–79	127,207		75,819	4,620	18,594	226,240
1780–84	212,708		69,232		44,621	326,561
1785–89	248,485	6,156	62,017	6,501	14,569	337,728
1790–94	322,712	35,795	90,726	5,865	3,964	459,062
1795–99	359,293	56,815	83,542	540	11,041	511,231
1800–1803	260,107	50,611	81,974	6,848	3,106	402,646
All	1,880,800	189,358	604,231	27,903	186,492	2,888,784

Note: The following years are missing from the AGI, Seville, and the ANH, Quito: 1734, 1736–47, 1749, and 1772. In several years, particularly early in the eighteenth century, some tax categories generated no income; in these cases blank spaces appear in the table under those categories.
Sources: AGI, Contaduría, 1534, Quito, 453–58, Cuentas de la Caja de Cuenca, 1722–1803.

(see table 6). Defense spending, however, escalated most dramatically in Guayaquil. García Pizarro made the strategic port city the centerpiece of his military reforms, causing defense expenditures to rise to nearly 250,000 pesos between 1800 and 1804 (see table 5). On the other hand, military outlays were never extensive in Cuenca, which played an insignificant role in the strategic defenses of the realm.

Despite increased expenses, the treasury system in the audiencia of Quito became increasingly centralized and responsive to metropolitan needs by the late colonial period. The treasuries extracted escalating amounts of revenue, both from the booming coastal export zones and the declining regional economies of the north-central highlands. Moreover, the increased remittances from Guayaquil and Cuenca to Quito allowed the state to transfer ever larger sums to Cartagena and Spain. Funds were no longer retained to support local economies as in earlier years, except for defense and administration, which only increased the coercive power of the state.

The Bourbon Reforms in the audiencia of Quito demonstrate clearly that crown policy aimed to increase revenues, not to promote any lasting economic development in the colonies. Such policies primarily involved tightening administrative and fiscal controls. Crown policies clearly discriminated against manufacturing, trade, or agricultural centers, such as the north-central sierra. As Archbishop Antonio Caballero y Góngora, the viceroy of New Granada from 1782 to 1789, observed, the decline of Quito's textile industry was entirely fitting, because agriculture and mining were "the appropriate function of the colonies," while manufactures like cloth "ought to be imported from the metropolis."[41] As the fiscal accounts from the audiencia of Quito indicate, however, even favored regions, such as the coastal export economy around Guayaquil, paid exceedingly high taxes by the late colonial period.

Although the colonial treasury accounts provide little direct information on the growth or decline of the economy in the audiencia, they do show the evolution of a strong, activist state that attempted to direct, control, and exploit regional economies in the district.[42] The accounts for the Quito treasury, for example, show substantial revenue increases, but no contemporary observer would have argued that this indicated a vibrant regional economy. Instead, the revenue figures reflect a more exploitative and efficient state apparatus, capable of extracting wealth from the diminished highland economies. Such an interventionist colonial state succeeded only in draining investment capital from the declining north-central highlands and hindering the overall process of economic development. The spiraling level of taxation also did little good to the coastal export economies. In short, the Bourbon Reforms left a legacy of government intervention and dependency that severely limited the long-term economic prospects of the audiencia district of Quito.

The State and Dependency from Independence to 1861

The strong centralized state did not endure into the early national period.[43] The chaotic years of the independence struggle (1809–22) began the process of political disintegration in the audiencia. Before the incorporation of Ecuador into the republic of Gran Colombia in 1822, the fiscal bureaucracies in the Quito, Guayaquil, and Cuenca regions operated virtually independently. Even after joining the Colombian union, this fiscal decentralization continued apace. By the time of the founding of the republic of Ecuador in 1830, the strong activist state established by the Bourbons had essentially disappeared. As the new republic's finance minister complained in 1831, the nation was really three separate fiscal entities operating from Quito, Guayaquil, and Cuenca.[44]

The early history of the new republic was a long and generally inconclusive struggle between centralists and regionalists (who advocated creating local, autonomous, ad hoc juntas to collect and disburse government funds).[45] Amid this conflict, the state proved effective only in promoting minimal levels of public order and foreign security. As a result, the fiscal records are sporadic and do not reflect economic patterns in any meaningful way. The national government in Quito was never able to gain accurate data on the status of the economy, formulate a rational tax code, create a professional bureaucracy, or overcome the elite's intransigent opposition to paying even the minimal levels of taxation needed to run the government.[46]

The best, most comprehensive study of the political economy in the early republic, by Linda Alexander Rodríguez, indicates that taxes were regressive and perpetually inadequate. Total government income from 1830 to 1861 rose slowly from 554,000 pesos to 1,276,000 pesos. It was not until the 1850s that republican income levels matched those of the late Bourbon period. Despite these problems, important continuities with the colonial fiscal regime persisted. Customs duties collected at Guayaquil remained a crucial source of government funds, accounting for 34–64 percent of all public revenues.[47] The cacao economy of Guayaquil had recovered from the dislocations of the independence period, and exports from the port rose rapidly by the 1830s.[48] Traditional taxes, such as Amerindian tribute and the tithe, also remained important sources of national income.[49] Tithe revenues rose from under 40,000 pesos in 1832 to 117,723 pesos in 1861, but the tax never formed much more than 8 percent of the national income.[50] Amerindian tribute was a more lucrative levy, rising from 147,289 pesos to 205,652 pesos. It accounted for approximately 13–36 percent of all government receipts until its abolition in 1857.[51] Other direct imposts, such as the tobacco and cane-liquor monopolies, produced very little during these chaotic early years of the republic.[52] One significant departure from the colonial fiscal system was the reliance on foreign loans.[53] Nevertheless, the policies of the republican governments continued the colonial precedent of placing the bulk of the tax burden on the Amerindians and the export economy of the coast.[54]

The fiscal expenditures of the Ecuadorian state reflect the low income levels and chaotic political situation in the early nineteenth century. Until the 1840s, the military received between 47 and 74 percent of the public revenues; most of the rest went to defray administrative expenses.[55] The amounts spent on defense declined by the 1840s, but the cost of servicing the foreign debt and paying the bureaucracy more than compensated for these military savings. The republican government's fiscal priorities, however, differed markedly from those of the Bourbon state. The Bourbons never allocated more than 16 percent of total expenditures for defense, and loan repayments during the colonial period were insignificant outlays. The need to support the military establishment reveals the institutional weakness of the republican state and the endemic political disorders of the early nineteenth century. At the same time, the amounts spent on the bureaucracy matched the outlays during the colonial period. The monies expended on servicing the foreign and domestic debts also corresponded to the funds remitted to Spain during the late colonial era. Even after independence, the beleaguered Ecuadorian state still sent large allocations of public money to outsiders, proving that the drain of local capital continued through the early nineteenth century.

Leonardo Espinosa's study of state finances in Cuenca from 1779 to 1861 demonstrates the congruence of provincial and national trends in public policy. Income at the Cuenca treasury rose from 50,000 pesos to 110,000 pesos during the early republican era—still less than the 150,000 pesos collected in the best years of the late colonial period.[56] In addition, the weakness of the central government in Quito was apparent in the low level of remittances to the capital, which amounted to only 2 percent of the regional income in Cuenca. Even within the district of Cuenca itself, the administrative chaos of the period lessened control over the districts of Loja, Alausí, Gualaceo, Jaen, and Azogues, which sent declining yearly remissions of taxes.[57] The tax base of Cuenca also declined markedly from the colonial period. The only significant sources of revenue were Amerindian tribute, which produced over 40 percent of all income, followed by the sales tax at 7 percent, and loans at just over 5 percent.[58] The inadequacy of public revenues and the regressive nature of the levies, which fell disproportionately on the needy Amerindian villagers, again followed trends for the entire republic. Military and administrative expenses together accounted for over 70 percent of the provincial budget, with most of the rest going to pay the public debt.[59] In short, the early republican period in Cuenca was a reversion to the fiscal and political weakness characteristic of the region before the Bourbon Reforms.

The fiscal records of the national and provincial states indicate clearly the decline of the strong interventionist state established in the late colonial period. Amid this fiscal decentralization, the tax base and income levels of the state continued to shrink until the 1850s. Public finances came to depend largely on taxes levied against the coastal export economy and the Amerindian population. Government spending also went almost exclusively to service the military, the bureaucracy, and the burgeoning national and provincial debts. As a result, state intervention in the economy declined, but public policy also perpetuated regional and social inequities and foreign dependency, which did little to help the nation surmount its many socioeconomic difficulties.

Conclusion: The State and Dependency

The economic policies of the colonial and early national states interfered in certain specific and major ways with the autonomous development of Ecuador. The state directed public funds away from productive enterprises and sent large amounts of money first to Spain and later to foreign creditors. In addition to these transfers of capital, the state imposed fiscal and legal "blocking mechanisms" that impeded development. In short, the colonial and early national states failed to promote an institutional environment capable of sustaining enterprise and development.[60]

Colonial fiscal policies led to several important constraints on the socioeconomic development of Ecuador. The audiencia was divided by rugged geographical barriers, making transportation difficult and promoting thin and imperfect factor markets. The decline of the highland textile manufactures during the eighteenth century undermined the fragile economic integration of the north-central highlands, from Otavalo to Riobamba, and reinforced the daunting natural barriers to development. The state's rigid enforcment of the sales-tax regulations on the diminished cloth trade clearly raised the transaction costs in overland commerce, retarded the evolution of highland markets, and contributed to the isolation of regional trading centers. Indeed, the high levels of taxation per capita undoubtedly played a role in undermining colonial manufacturing throughout the highlands by the early nineteenth century.[61]

The regressive character of the Bourbon fiscal levies also hindered agricultural production in the highlands. The sales tax levied on rural estates and foodstuffs sold in the cities and towns undoubtedly raised food prices and interfered with the regional trade in rural produce.[62] Amerindian tribute, a burdensome head tax, also inhibited rural production because the fixed tax rates did not change in times of bounty or dearth.[63] Clerical taxes drained capital even from the church, which traditionally played an important role in the agrarian economy. The expulsion of the Jesuits and the state-run agency (Administración de Temporalidades) that administered their properties, for example, drew profits from these estates to Spain instead of reinvesting them in the sorts of regional socioeconomic enterprises formerly supported by the Society.

The onerous taxes levied in the Guayaquil region also cut into commercial and agricultural profits. The state imposed an alcabala of 5 percent on the sale of cacao, for example, and a customs duty of 1.25 percent when it left the port city. Cacao estates also paid the tithe and the sales tax, both levied against estimated rural production. Moreover, all imported goods paid the alcabala and a port duty ranging from 4 to 8 percent, depending on the origin of the product. Such goods paid an additional sales tax at each subsequent sale.[64] Royal monopolies on locally produced goods, such as tobacco, further raised prices and lessened the profit margins of coastal producers. In addition, the sales tax paid on foodstuffs and textiles from the sierra boosted prices in Guayaquil. Freer trade also brought the importation of European cloth, which damaged both highland cloth manufacturing and the export trade in quiteño woolens from Guayaquil to Lima. By the late eighteenth century, these fiscal policies had raised per-capita taxes for coastal residents to rates among the highest in the world. None of these policies proved devastating to the vibrant coastal export economy, but taken together they created an institutional environment concerned primarily with exploiting, not promoting, economic development.

The success of the colonial state in extracting resources from the audiencia district and shipping them to Spain also supports a basic premise of the dependency literature. Public investment in the economy was negligible, in contrast to the previous century when viceregal treasury officials routinely spent much larger sums in the colony than they sent to Spain.[65] This outflow of capital to the metropolis undoubtedly hindered capital accumulation and investment in the audiencia district.

In the first three decades of independence, the republican governments had the opportunity to remove many of these "blocking mechanisms" and end the transfer of wealth that had impeded economic progress from the late colonial period. Although the new governments did eliminate some constraints from the private sector, republican fiscal policies continued many onerous colonial levies and failed to create a markedly improved environment for development. Amerindian tribute, high customs duties, and levies on agriculture continued as the main sources of public revenues. Such regressive taxes drained resources from productive sectors, inhibited market expansion, and exacerbated the traditional communication and geographical barriers within the nation. Moreover, the transfer of resources to largely unproductive sectors, such as the military, the bureaucracy, and the burgeoning public debt, nullified the limited gains realized from the end of revenue transfers to Spain. The frequent collapse of the central government in the political disorders of the period—particularly the vacillation between centralism and federalism—created an ever more chaotic environment for investment, enterprise, and development. In short, the republican state proved weaker and less overtly exploitative than its colonial predecessor but equally unenlightened.

Despite justifiable criticism, the dependency literature has provided a useful framework for analyzing the economic role of the state in Ecuador from 1700 to 1861. The methodological problems inherent in using the colonial and early national fiscal accounts, however, make it difficult to measure with any precision the impact of these state policies on economic development. What they do indicate is the level of state intervention in the economy and its overall failure to provide an institutional environment conducive to any autonomous economic growth. In preindustrial societies growth in aggregate demand is vital for sustained development. This usually requires an expansion of consumer demand and foreign trade, sufficient capital accumulations to promote investment, and the direction of some public monies to support key enterprises. The fiscal policies of the Bourbon and early republican governments did none of these things. Instead, state policies hindered Amerindians from participating in key elements of the market economy, contributed to raising consumer prices and retarding demand, discouraged investment, and even limited many potential salutary effects of the export boom after 1778. In short, the state promoted economic policies that created a discriminatory, arbitrary, and irrational economic environment for promoting sustained, autonomous development. While most dependency advocates that emphasized the late nineteenth and twentieth centuries as the critical periods in the formation of economic dependency, these problems actually began much earlier, and the colonial and early national states played a central role.

Notes

1. One compilation of such studies of the colonial state is Karen Spalding, ed., *Essays in the Political, Economic, and Social History of Colonial Latin America* (Newark, DE, 1982).

2. The most articulate dependency analysis for colonial Latin America appears in Stanley J. Stein and Barbara H. Stein, *The Colonial Heritage of Latin America: Essays on Economic Dependence in Perspective* (New York, 1970). Most dependency studies, however, focus on the late nineteenth and twentieth centuries. Two standard works are Andre Gunder Frank, *Capitalism and Underdevelopment in Latin America* (New York, 1967); and Fernando Henrique Cardoso and Enzo Faletto, *Dependency and Development in Latin America* (Berkeley, CA, 1979 [1971]). The dependency argument has been extended by Immanuel Wallerstein and Fernand Braudel from a focus on the exploited peripheries, like Latin America, to the discussion of a single world system linked by the expanding forces of European capitalism. Like the Steins, Wallerstein and Braudel trace the roots of dependency in the peripheries of the world system to the fifteenth century. Both men have published voluminously, but their major works outlining the historical formation and evolution of the world system are the following: Immanuel Wallerstein, *The Modern World-System I: Capitalist Agriculture and the Origins of the World-Economy in the Sixteenth Century* (New York, 1974); Wallerstein, *The Modern World-System II: Mercantilism and the Consolidation of the European World-Economy, 1600–1750* (New York, 1980); and Wallerstein, *The Modern World-System III: The Second Era of Great Expansion of the World-Economy, 1730s–1840s* (New York, 1989); Fernand Braudel, *Civilization and Capitalism, 15th–18th Century,* vol. I, *The Structures of Everyday Life: The Limits of the Possible,* trans. Sian Reynolds (New York, 1979 [1981]); Braudel, *Civilization and Capitalism, 15th–18th Century,* vol. II, *The Wheels of Commerce,* trans. Sian Reynolds (New York, 1981 [1979]); and Braudel, *Civilization and Capitalism, 15th–18th Century,* vol. III, *The Perspective of the World,* trans. Sian Reynolds (New York, 1984 [1979]). A useful survey and analysis of the dependency literature may be found in Ian Roxborough, *Theories of Underdevelopment* (New York, 1979), 42–69; and William B. Taylor, "Between Global Process and Local Knowl-

edge: An Inquiry into Early Latin American Social History, 1500–1900," in Olivier Zunz, ed., *Reliving the Past* (Chapel Hill, NC, 1985), 115–90.

3. Stein and Stein, *Colonial Heritage of Latin America,* 104.

4. Roxborough, *Theories of Underdevelopment,* 63.

5. Prominent historians, such as John Lynch, Peter Bakewell, and John Coatsworth, have published studies clearly influenced by the paradigm, but none of them has even listed references to the dependency literature in their notes. See, for example, John Lynch, *Spain Under the Hapsburgs, 1598–1700,* Vol. II (Oxford, 1982 [1969]), 160–228; Lynch, *The Spanish American Revolutions, 1808–1826* (London, 1973), 1–36; P. J. Bakewell, *Silver Mining and Society in Colonial Mexico: Zacatecas, 1546–1700* (Cambridge, Eng., 1971), 221–36; and John Coatsworth, "The Limits of Colonial Absolutism: The State in Eighteenth-Century Mexico," in Spalding, ed., *Essays in the Political, Economic, and Social History,* 25–51; and Coatsworth, "Obstacles to Growth in Nineteenth-Century Mexico," *American Historical Review,* 83 (February 1978): 80–100.

6. This point is made clearly in the following articles: Robert Packenham, "Holistic Dependency," *New World: A Journal of Latin American Studies,* 2 (1987): 12–48. These criticisms also extend to Wallerstein's work. See, for example, Daniel Chirot and Thomas D. Hall, "World-System Theory," *Annual Review of Sociology,* 8 (1982): 81–106; and Charles Ragan and Daniel Chirot, "The World System of Immanuel Wallerstein: Sociology and Politics as History," in Theda Skocpol, ed., *Vision and Method in Historical Sociology* (Cambridge, Eng., 1979), 276–312.

7. Several scholars have tested the basic precepts of the dependency paradigm empirically and found them wanting. See, for example, Patrick O'Brien, "European Economic Development: The Contribution of the Periphery," *Economic History Review,* 2nd ser., 35 (November 1982): 1–21; D. C. M. Platt, "Dependency in Nineteenth-Century Latin America: A Historian Objects," *Latin American Research Review,* 16 (1980): 113–29, 147–49; and Steve J. Stern, "Feudalism, Capitalism, and the World-System in the Perspective of Latin America and the Caribbean," *American Historical Review,* 93 (October 1988): 829–72, 886–97. Some Marxist critics of dependencia have faulted its alleged overemphasis on the importance of the international market over class structures. See, for example, Robert Brenner, "The Origins of Capitalist Development: A Critique of Neo-Smithian Marxism," *New Left Review,* 104 (1977): 27, 92. Dependency advocates such as Wallerstein have added to this debate by merely dismissing most criticisms—particularly any attempts to "test" empirically the validity of the paradigm—as wrongheaded or irrelevant. For example, see Wallerstein's reply to Stern's criticisms in "Comments on Stern's Critical Tests," *American Historical Review,* 93 (October 1988): 873–85.

8. Braudel, *Civilization and Capitalism,* vol. 1: *Structures of Everyday Life;* vol. 2: *Wheels of Commerce;* and vol. 3: *Perspective of the World.*

9. Braudel uses a massive base of empirical evidence to trace the rise of a European-dominated world system as it incorporated new areas of the globe from the fifteenth to the eighteenth centuries. Like Wallerstein, Braudel divides this world system into core, semiperipheral, and peripheral zones (such as Spanish America). Braudel also explains how the vast, isolated, self-sufficient peasant economies across the world were linked by small but growing regional markets to the emerging global economy dominated by Europe. For a concise summary of

Braudel's basic theories, see Fernand Braudel, *Afterthoughts on Material Civilization and Capitalism,* trans. Patricia Ranum (Baltimore, 1977).

10. D. A. Brading, "Facts and Figments in Bourbon Mexico," *Bulletin of Latin American Research,* 4 (1985): 61–64. Other vehement criticisms appear in Henry Kamen and Jonathan Israel in "Debate: The Seventeenth-Century Crisis in New Spain: Myth or Reality," *Past and Present,* 97 (November 1982): 144–56. Other critics have simply urged using greater care with the accounts. See, for example, Samuel Amaral, "Public Expenditure Financing in the Colonial Treasury: Analysis of the Real Caja de Buenos Aires Accounts," and Javier Cuenca Esteban, "Of Nimble Arrows and Faulty Bows: A Call for Rigor," both in *Hispanic American Historical Review,* 64 (May 1984): 287–95, and 297–303.

11. Herbert S. Klein and Jacques A. Barbier, "Recent Trends in the Study of Spanish American Colonial Public Finance," *Latin American Research Review,* 23 (1988): 304–9.

12. This system was founded by the Hapsburg monarchs in the late sixteenth century. For a theoretical discussion of patrimonial forms of authority, see Max Weber, *The Theory of Social and Economic Organization,* trans. Talcott Parsons (New York, 1968), 352–58.

13. The jurisdictional lines of these three treasuries (cajas reales) varied over time and depended on the taxes collected, but generally the Quito office controlled the provinces of Ibarra, Otavalo, Quito, Latacunga, Ambato, and Riobamba. Cuenca controlled Chimbo, Guaranda, Cuenca, Loja-Zaruma, and Alausí. Guayaquil exercised jurisdiction over Guayaquil, Puertoviejo, Punta de Santa Elena, Machala, Baba, Yaguache, Babahoyo, Daule, and Puná.

14. In Guayaquil treasury remissions to Quito ranged from nothing to a high of 75,691 pesos which was reached in 1766, one year after the Quito Insurrection. Archivo General de Indias (hereafter cited as AGI), Contaduría, 1377, 1576, 1577, and Quito, 407, 469–75, and 477, Cuentas de la Caja de Guayaquil, 1714–1804. Remissions from Cuenca ranged from nothing to 46,445 pesos, reached in 1774. AGI, Contaduría, 1534, and Quito, 453–58, Cuentas de la Caja de Cuenca, 1722–1803.

15. From the creation of the Tribunal of Accounts in Lima in 1605 until the establishment of the tribunal in Bogotá (the capital of the newly created Viceroyalty of New Granada) in 1740, the cajas in the audiencia of Quito remained under Lima's jurisdiction. The Bogotá tribunal's authority continued until 1776, when the crown created a separate audit court in Quito, independent of the viceregal capital. María Luisa Laviana Cuetos, "Organización y funcionamiento de las cajas reales de Guayaquil en la segunda mitad del siglo XVIII," *Anuario de Estudios Americanos,* 37 (1980): 314.

16. The crown was moving from a patrimonial system to what Weber has termed a "rational-legal" form of authority. A rational-legal order is usually circumscribed by a strict legal code and clearly established jurisdictional lines, each official having a specified sphere of influence. Officials must be appointed on the basis of talent and technical training, and they must have fixed salaries, no outside socioeconomic ties, and a strong sense of discipline and authority. See Weber, *Social and Economic Organization,* 329–41.

17. This new fiscal bureaucracy was established by royal decree on 10 March 1777. See Douglas Alan Washburn, "The Bourbon Reforms: A Social and Eco-

nomic History of the Audiencia of Quito, 1760–1810" (Ph.D. diss., University of Texas at Austin, 1984), 129.

18. The visitador created separate tribunals in Quito to supervise the sales and cane-liquor taxes, the collection of tribute, and the royal monopolies. Each tribunal comprised a comptroller, administrator, and several clerks. These three offices supervised subtreasuries (*recepturías*) in Alausí, Latacunga, Ambato, Riobamba, and Guaranda. AGI, Quito, 407, Razón de los empleos de R1 hacda que hay establecidos en Quito y sus provincias y los sujetos destinados en ellos, según proviene la Real Orden de 12 marzo de este año de 1783, Quito. This information is summarized in Washburn, *The Bourbon Reforms,* 129–32; and Laviana Cuetos, "Organización y funcionamiento," 314; AGI, Quito, 411, Juan Antonio de Asilona to José de Gálvez, Quito, 18 October 1778; AGI, Quito, 409, Instrucción y ordenanza para el régimen y govierno de la Dirección General de Rentas de Tabacos, Alcavalas, Aguardiente, Pólvora, y Naipes de Quito y provincias comprehendidas en el distrito de sus reales cajas, Quito, 3 July 1783.

19. The jurisdiction of tribute revenues in Guayaquil remained separate from the Quito office and did not begin operating until 1785. Ibid.

20. Villalengua was also a cousin of the new bishop of Cuenca, José de Carrión y Marfil. See Federico González Suárez, *Historia general de la república del Ecuador* 7 vols. (Quito, 1970), 2:1206, 1219, 1247.

21. AGI, Quito, 267, Pesquisa contra José García de Leon y Pizarro. This legajo contains many documents providing details about the way García Pizarro abused his patronage appointments. See also, AGI, Quito, 264, José García de Leon y Pizarro to José de Gálvez, Guayaquil, 19 March 1778.

22. AGI, Quito, 232, Hoja de servicio de Josef de Renxijo, Quito 1795.

23. Allan J. Kuethe, *Military Reform and Society in New Granada, 1773–1808* (Gainesville, FL, 1978), 118–25.

24. I have chosen to use the accounts of the treasury districts rather than the Dirección General de Rentas to evaluate the effectiveness of the reform policies. These records provide a more extensive time series and facilitate comparisons both with the prereform period and with other revenues not under the jurisdiction of the Dirección General de Rentas. Although the amounts remitted from the treasuries of the Dirección General de Rentas represent surplus income rather than the gross amounts collected, they still show the profits of these agencies, and they are a good measure of the outcome of the reforms.

25. Although some scholars have criticized recent studies of the treasury accounts for failing to adjust for fluctuations in basic commodity prices, the figures presented in this study are not deflated. Compete price data have simply not been compiled for the entire period from 1700 to 1861. The preliminary price figures that I have collected for the period from 1750 to 1790 from the records of rural estates, commercial sales, and tax materials, however, show no inflationary trend, in marked contrast to Mexico. In fact, these data (using 1755 as the base year) show a slight deflationary trend: The price index—compiled from figures for cane liquor, beans, corn, blue cloth (*paño azul*), and potatoes—actually declines 11 percent by 1790. While hardly conclusive, these figures suggest that prices remained relatively static or even declined slightly during the late colonial period. As a result, changes in the nominal figures for treasury receipts were apparently not influenced signifi-

cantly by price fluctuations as they were in Mexico. The price data used to compile this index come from the following sources: ANH-Q, Haciendas, Caja 3, Estado de las haciendas de Chaquibamba y Lloa, Caja 5, Libro de recivos de la hacienda de San Antonio de Quaxara desde 1 agosto hasta fin de septiembre 1767; Caja 8, Libro de recivo de estas haciendas de San Yldefonso del Colegio Mayor de Sn. Luis, que empieza a correr desde 1 dic. 1759; Caja 14, Cuentas de las haciendas de San Xavier, El Palmar, y San Pedro, 1774–80; Cuentas ajustadas a dn Francisco Auzeco Echea de las haciendas de Santiago, Carpuela, Chaluayaco, Caldera, Concepción, Chamanal, y Tumbaviro, desde 12 junio 1776 hasta 28 marzo 1778; Cuentas ajustadas a dn Simon Fuentes y Vivero, Comisionado de las Temporalidades de Tacunga desde 31 diciembre 1776 hasta 5 mayo 1778; Caja 20, Cuentas del obraje y haciendas de San Ildefonso desde 30 marzo 1780 hasta 31 enero 1787; ANH-Q, Temporalidades, Caja 8, Cuentas dadas por dn Joaquín de Merizalde y comisionado de las Temporalidades de Cuenca, añ 1772; and Robson Brines Tyrer, "Demographic and Economic History of the Audiencia of Quito: Indian Population and the Textile Industry, 1600–1800" (Ph.D. diss., University of California at Berkeley, 1976), 188.

26. In these calculations of total income, I have subtracted the amounts listed as carryover funds, such as *debido cobrar, depósitos, existencia, fianzas,* and *reintegros.* These amounts sometimes reached over 50 percent of the total income in certain years, thus dramatically distorting the amounts of money actually flowing into the treasuries each year. AGI, Quito, 419, 429, Cuentas de la Caja de Quito, 1778, 1803; AGI, Quito 469, 471, Cuentas de la Caja de Guayaquil, 1777, 1804; AGI, Quito, 453, 458, Cuentas de la Caja de Cuenca, 1775, 1802.

27. According to figures provided by John J. TePaske and Richard Garner, the rate of growth in public revenues in the treasury office in Mexico City ranged from 2.9 percent to 3.3 percent annually from 1775 to 1809. See Richard L. Garner, "Further Consideration of Facts and Figments in Bourbon Mexico," *Bulletin of Latin American Research,* 6 (1986): 59.

28. I have included the returns from the aguardiente monopoly with the levies on commerce and production rather than with royal monopolies. The funds were profits from the manufacture and sale of cane liquor, made from locally grown sugar cane. As a result, they represented local production and trade more directly than any other monopoly in the Quito district.

29. For an interesting account of the links between increased fiscal pressures and Amerindian revolts in the highlands, see Segundo Moreno Yánez, *Sublevaciones indígenas en la Audiencia de Quito, desde comienzos del siglo XVIII hasta finales de la colonia* (Quito, 1985 [1976]).

30. These figures are compiled from the following legajos: AGI, Quito, 418–29, Cuentas de la Caja de Quito, 1778–1803.

31. These data are compiled from AGI, Quito, 469, 472–77, Cuentas de la Caja de Guayaquil, 1778–1804.

32. Michael T. Hamerly, *Historia social y económica de la antigua provincia de Guayaquil, 1763–1842* (Guayaquil, 1973), 65–79; and María Luisa Laviana Cuetos, *Guayaquil en el siglo XVIII: Recursos naturales y desarrollo económico* (Sevilla, 1987), 104–13.

33. Amerindian tribute accounted for between 51 and 86 percent of the total income in the Cuenca district before the reform period. Cuenca's small European population paid virtually nothing in taxes until 1770, apart from minor exactions on regional trade and production. AGI, Contaduría, 1534, Quito, 453, Cuentas de la Caja de Cuenca, 1722–1775.

34. These remittances normally accounted for between 50 and 60 percent of total income. See, AGI, Quito, 453–58, Cuentas de la Caja de Cuenca, 1775–1803.

35. Bureaucratic and clerical taxes experienced only modest increases, while royal monopolies were an insignificant source of funds until 1799, when they began to yield over 13,000 pesos annually. See table 3.

36. I calculated the amount of taxes per capita by using the population figures taken from the following sources: AGI, Quito, 381, 412, Numeración de Juan Josef de Villalengua, 1780; Martin Minchom, "Demographic Change in Eighteenth-Century Ecuador," in M. Delaunay and M. Portais, eds., *Equateur 1986* 3 vols. (Paris, 1989), 1:179–96; Laviana Cuetos, *Guayaquil en el siglo XVIII,* 77–159. I then divided these figures by the income from taxes in each treasury district after subtracting the carryover funds.

37. I used the ethnic breakdowns in the census materials and divided each racial-ethnic group by the amount collected from the taxes levied against them. In the case of the Amerindians, I assumed that they paid only tribute; thus, their per-capita tax burden is a bare minimum figure. I also subtracted the figures for the slave populations from the totals for the Europeans and castes, assuming that the bondsmen paid no taxes.

38. This rise clearly reflects the minimal levels of taxes paid by non-Amerindians in the south highlands before the reform period.

39. Taxpayers in Cuenca paid approximately the same amounts in per-capita taxes as the English colonists, but the economic output of the south highlands was hardly comparable. For sources indicating the tax burdens in English North America, see Edwin Perkins, *The Economy of Colonial America* (New York, 1980), 124–43. Information on the necessary currency conversions needed to make these comparisons may be found in John J. McCusker, *Money and Exchange in Europe and North America, 1600–1775: A Handbook* (Chapel Hill, NC, 1978), 3–12.

40. Perkins, *The Economy of Colonial America,* 129; Peter Mathias, *The First Industrial Nation: An Economic History of Britain, 1700–1914* (London, 1969), 32–50.

41. Quoted in John Lynch, "The Origins of Spanish American Independence," in Leslie Bethell, ed., *The Independence of Latin America* (Cambridge, Eng., 1987), 16.

42. Although tax rates are known, flaws in the records and changes in the efficiency of tax collection over time are virtually impossible to measure. In addition, the treasury accounts in many cases represent only remissions from the Dirección General, not gross receipts. As a result, the accounts provide a flawed view of economic performance.

43. The fiscal data for Ecuador are sporadic for the early nineteenth century. As a result, I chose to end this section in 1861, rather than 1850, in order to get an adequate sample of the accounts, capable of illustrating the basic fiscal trends.

44. At this time Cauca was also included in the republic and was cited as the fourth fiscal district. See Linda Alexander Rodríguez, *The Search for Public Policy: Regional Politics and Government Finances in Ecuador, 1830–1940* (Berkeley, CA, 1985), 56.

45. Ibid., 55.

46. Ibid., 54.

47. Ibid., 187.

48. Hamerly, *Historia social y económica,* 121.

49. Rodríguez, *Search for Public Policy,* 62.

50. Ibid., 66.

51. Ibid., 63.

52. Ibid., 215.

53. Ibid., 75–78.

54. For a discussion of the failures of coastal elites to protect their regional economic interests during the independence era, see David J. Cubitt, "Economic Nationalism in Post-Independence Ecuador: The Commercial Code of 1821–1825," *Ibero-Amerikanisches Archiv,* 11:1 (1985): 65–82.

55. Rodríguez, *Search for Public Policy,* 223.

56. I arrived at these figures for income by subtracting carryover funds from Espinosa's total income figures. See Leonardo Espinosa, "Política Fiscal de la Provincia de Cuenca: Reseña histórico—presupuestaria—1779–1861," in *Segundo encuentro de historia y realidad económica y social del Ecuador,* 3 vols., (Cuenca, 1978), 1:1–75.

57. A further manifestation of this chaotic situation was the changing geographical jurisdiction of the Cuenca district. See ibid., 18.

58. Ibid., 8, 36–37, 61–62, 65–66.

59. Ibid., 9, 27–34.

60. For an intriguing examination of this process in Mexico, see Coatsworth, "The Limits of Colonial Absolutism," 25–51 and Coatsworth, "Obstacles to Growth," 80–100.

61. For an examination of the decline in Cuenca's cottage textile industry by the early nineteenth century, see Silvia Palomeque, "Historia económica de Cuenca y sus relaciones regionales (desde fines del siglo XVIII a principios del XIX)", in *Segundo encuentro,* 77–129.

62. For a discussion of how this problem promoted economic dislocation and popular discord in the Quito region, see Kenneth J. Andrien, "Economic Crisis, Taxes, and the Quito Insurrection of 1765," *Past and Present,* 129 (November 1990): 104–31.

63. For a discussion of the problems caused by head taxes in peasant communities, see James C. Scott, *The Moral Economy of the Peasant: Rebellion and Subsistence in Southeast Asia* (New Haven, CT, 1976), 99–110.

64. For a detailed discussion of the sales tax reforms in Quito, see Montserratt Fernández Martínez, *La alcabala en la audiencia de Quito, 1765–1810* (Cuenca, 1984), 35–68.

65. By the period from 1681 to 1690, for example, Lima treasury officials remitted only 5 percent of their outgo to Spain and spent the remainder in the viceroyalty. See Kenneth J. Andrien, *Crisis and Decline: The Viceroyalty of Peru in the Seventeenth Century* (Albuquerque, 1985), 67.

9

Distribution of Wealth in Nineteenth-Century Buenos Aires Province: The Issue of Social Justice in a Changing Economy

LYMAN L. JOHNSON

Great historical transformations are always bought dearly, often after one has already thought that one got them at a bargain price.

Jacob Burckhardt

In this essay I present the basic outline of my ongoing work on changes in the distribution of wealth in the province of Buenos Aires during the Rosas era, and I offer the first tentative results of my statistical analysis. Two measures of wealth inequality are presented here: the Gini coefficient and the percentage of all wealth held by the wealthiest 1 percent of the population. Although I am primarily interested in measuring this component of economic performance for the period 1829–55, I have also estimated wealth distribution for 1800 based on a separate data sample. All the conclusions presented here are preliminary, and much work needs to be done before reliable findings can be presented. Nevertheless, I am confident that both the direction and scale of changes in wealth distribution presented here are reliable indicators of the era's socioeconomic reality.

Perhaps because the conflict between authoritarianism and democracy has yet to be finally resolved in Argentina, Juan Manuel Rosas has attracted more attention than any other figure in Argentine history. Yet despite the depth and breadth of this historiographical legacy, the economic history of this important period is known only in outline. Studies written following Rosas's defeat and exile traced the basic character of the regime and suggested the direction of economic development during this tumultuous era. More recent work by historians less tainted by the partisan loyalties that suffused late nineteenth-century analyses has filled in some of the missing detail. There is little disagreement among scholars on the basic character of the early national economy. The half century following independence clearly witnessed a dramatic expansion in the wealth and power of the grazing sector in Argentina, especially in Buenos Aires province.

The territorial expansion and increased economic power of the grazing sector coincided with, and depended on, an increased region-wide reliance on British and North American commercial ties. By the 1825–30 quinquennium, the United States was the destination for 26 percent of Argentina's hide exports. With the rapid development of Argentine wool production after 1830, the United States became an even more important trading partner. From 1840 to the end of the Rosas period, the United States imported twice as much Argentine wool as did Great Britain.[1] As the grazing sector's frontier was pushed to the south and east at the expense of indigenous peoples, the province's export of hides, salted and dried beef, tallow, and wool increased significantly. In turn, earnings from this expanding export sector helped pay for an enlarged volume and expanded array of imported manufactures and agricultural goods. Over the long term these changes undermined the viability of the interior's traditional producers of textiles and of many artisanal industries in Buenos Aires and secondary cities.[2]

These changes were documented by the early statistical services of both provincial and national governments and by astute contemporary observers, such as the English consul Woodbine Parish.[3] These sources, other governmental sources, and the often polemical accounts of contemporary participants in the political struggles provided the primary sources for Miron Burgin's still indispensable study of fiscal and monetary policy during the first half of the nineteenth century.[4] More recently these same sources provided the basis for general histories of the period and a few specialized monographs dealing with the economy. With interpretive and narrative power, scholars such as Tulio Halperín, John Lynch, and Jonathan Brown, have described in rich detail the basic structure of the grazing economy. They have provided convincing, if somewhat contradictory, arguments about how these changes were connected with the political process of the early national period.[5] Mark Szuchman's recent work has pushed beyond these arguments to identify the conjuncture of economy, society, and ideology.[6] Yet despite the value of these studies, scholars still lack even rudimentary measures of economic performance during the Rosas period.

My current project is an effort to expand our understanding of the nineteenth-century Argentine economy by generating a data base and asking new questions. I have undertaken the task of creating a reliable statistical basis for estimating the direction and scale of changes in the size of the provincial economy, in the distribution of wealth, and in the sectoral allocation of wealth. That is, I am ultimately interested in measuring both economic growth—the economy's performance—and changes in the distribution of wealth—the economy's achievement of social justice. In this essay, I will address the second issue and offer two statistical measures of wealth inequality for the province of Buenos Aires.

The probate records of the province of Buenos Aires provide the basic evidentiary resource for my analysis. Although seldom used systematically by Latin American historians, probate records have proven a useful tool for North American economic historians interested in the prestatistical era. Certainly no other records provide a similar level of comprehensiveness, detail, or reliability.[7] Probate records take three major forms: wills, inventories, and accounts of administration. For my purposes, estate inventories have proven most valuable.

In the normal course of the judicial supervision of the probate process in the nineteenth century, court-appointed expert assessors produced detailed inventories of all wealth held by a decedent at the time of death. Assessors were generally drawn from a pool of master artisans regularly employed by the courts in the probate process. In the provincial towns and countryside, local alcaldes (usually *estancieros*) undertook the inventory. Assessors' compensation was paid from fees imposed on estates by the courts, or, in the case of an indigent decedent, it was paid directly by the state. When the estate included real estate, it was examined separately by a mason, a carpenter, and a blacksmith. Depending on the mix of goods found in an estate, other experts—such as a jeweler or someone capable of assessing the value of crops and livestock—would be appointed as needed. Artisan shops, small manufactories, and retail shops were also subject to detailed inventories. These inventories provide, therefore, a remarkably specific summary of both accumulated wealth and ongoing economic activity.

The vast majority of surviving probate records for the province of Buenos Aires include a complete inventory. In those few cases where inventories did not provide assessed values, I assigned average values drawn from all other inventories. It must be made clear that estimates provided in probate inventories are not reliable indicators of market values. In approximately 20 percent of the probate cases examined for this study, real estate, livestock, and other possessions were sold under court supervision to satisfy the claims of heirs. It is clear from these records that values estimated by probate assessors were often greater than the market values established through sale. In all but a few cases, these discrepancies were quite small.

Nevertheless, they would present a problem if the records were being used to create a price series. That is not my objective. Because there were few changes in assessors during this long period and because their evaluations demonstrate high levels of internal consistency, their inventories provide a reliable basis for estimating both wealth distribution at a given historical moment and changes in wealth distribution over time.

Most inventories are remarkably detailed. In the case of real estate, separate assessments were made for land and for improvements. The value of each property was disaggregated to provide separate values for land, masonry, woodwork, and hardware. Household furnishings, tools, and other utensils were itemized and evaluated. Also assessed were consumption goods, such as silverware, clothing, books, and—in the few cases where they were found—paintings, porcelains, and other luxuries.

Because a similar level of specificity was applied to producer goods, these records are of particular value to historians interested in the process of economic development. Commercial and factory inventories, livestock, tools, machinery, carts and wagons, buildings used in rural and urban production—even fruit trees, unharvested crops, and unsold rural products such as hides—were counted and assessed. For the early years of the period studied here, slaves were also evaluated.[8] Financial assets—such as loans owed the decedent; cash, both metallic and paper; stocks and bonds; and debts—were also regularly included in inventories. For each decedent, therefore, we can calculate both total wealth and net worth. We can also estimate with some confidence for both individuals and the society the distribution of wealth among categories of production and consumption goods.

Since I had no assistance in coding these records, I was compelled to surrender some of their rich specificity. I selected and coded fifty-five variables: twelve to fix the decedent's geographic location and economic and social position; thirty-three to summarize the quantities and types of wealth held at death.[9]

Despite the relative comprehensiveness, reliability, and rich detail of these records, there are inherent problems in using them in the ways proposed here. Obvious age and class biases are built into the probate process. The probate population in any society is always older and therefore richer than the general population. There is a natural tendency in all populations for maximum property accumulation and earnings to be associated with the later stages of life. As people age, they acquire skills and sometimes inherit wealth. The more mature, more affluent sectors of the population are more likely to write wills and have their estates go through the probate process.[10] The very poor, often single and living alone, are much less likely to have heirs interested in involving the courts—with their fees and little-understood rules—in the division of an estate. For this sector of the population, more informal mechanisms were used to divide property among heirs.

I anticipated two additional problems related to the representativeness of these sources. In similar studies of the United States investigators found few probate records outside urban centers, and they discovered underrepresentation of many occupational groups. In my research I found adequate geographic and occupational coverage. The probate records for the period yielded inventories for fifty-three provincial towns plus the city of Buenos Aires and for fifty-one separate occupations. There was, however, a slight underrepresentation of women and of residents of provincial towns in the countryside. And, as has been the case in other analyses of probate records, members of the urban and rural lower classes were not found in representative numbers for either the city or the countryside.

This problem of bias—inadequate coverage for the young, the poor, and rural dwellers—is not disabling, however. Statistical weights derived from contemporary censuses, burial records, and other contemporary sources can be used to adjust for biases in location, age, and sex. As expected, there was a slight underrepresentation of women in both the city and the countryside. In the preliminary results presented here I corrected raw data with a single weight based on age distributions found in contemporary census records. The probate process did not require the precise indication of a decedent's birth date or age. In some cases, however, this information was provided. Where specific age information was missing, I used life-cycle cohorts (such as married with minor children and married with adult children) as age proxies. I then associated these with age distributions drawn from the censuses of 1810, 1827, and 1855.[11]

Often there is circumstantial evidence that portions of an estate were removed by heirs, neighbors, creditors, or others before the inventory. In both the city of Buenos Aires and the countryside (even in the largest estates), the consistently low values recorded for cash, jewelry, and especially clothing suggested that some of these items may have been distributed outside the probate process. I have not yet decided whether some estimate of preinventory loss will be necessary. The probable insignificance of these amounts in relation to total estates, especially in larger estates, and the apparent universality of this characteristic across all class and age groups suggest that this problem is not likely to distort my current task, which is the estimation of wealth distribution.

I initially intended to collect a stratified random sample of probate records for each year of the Rosas period. I have abandoned this strategy because the surviving population counts from this period do not permit me to design annual samples confidently and because the low number of probate records for many years makes sophisticated sampling impossible. I am also aware that questions about the appropriateness of sample design provoked the most telling criticism of Alice Hanson Jones's ambitious effort to use probate inventories to estimate wealth holding in 1774 for the thirteen North American colonies.[12]

Instead, I have designed an alternative research method that provides predictably reliable results. Because I want to identify and measure large economic changes over a long period, I have decided that two data sets based on a universe of cases found in two-year cohorts at both ends of the Rosas era meet my needs. I have therefore coded and analyzed every probate inventory for the years 1829–30 (N = 179) and 1855–56 (N = 263).

The number of inventories found for these two-year cohorts may appear a weak foundation for an effort to measure changes in wealth holding in a provincial population that rose from approximately 135,000 in 1829 to 275,000 in 1855. Yet Jones used a sample of only 919 cases in her study of the thirteen British North American colonies, a region with a population in 1774 of approximately 2,300,000.[13] A more important consideration in assessing the utility of these inventories is the actual coverage of the population of decedent wealth holders found in the probate records. My analysis of contemporary burial records suggests that probate inventories survived for 58 percent of all wealth-holding decedents in 1829–30 and for 65 percent in 1855–56.[14] The parish burial records provided no evidence of systematic bias in the probate accounts. The parish records show clearly that the very young and very poor were underrepresented in the probate documents.

The most important results presented in this essay are based on a statistic known as the Gini coefficient. The Gini coefficient conveniently summarizes inequality in a number ranging from 0.0 to 1.0. A zero value indicates perfect equality, a value of 1.0 indicates maximum inequality. This statistic is based on the Lorenz curve, which displays graphically the cumulative percentage of wealth owned from the poorest to the wealthiest in comparison with a 45° line of hypothetical perfect equality. If all wealth holders had equal wealth, all points would be on this 45° line. The Gini coefficient is the ratio of the inequality area (between the 45° line and the concave or upper side of the Lorenz curve) to the total triangular area (enclosed by the 45° line and the boundary lines at the base and right side of the graph).

The Gini has some limitations as a measure of inequality. Of particularly importance for this analysis of early national Argentina is that it ignores the effects of age on wealth distributions. Societies with youthful populations have higher levels of wealth inequality than societies with older populations. This was convincingly pointed out by Robert Gallman in the context of wealth distributions in the United States.[15] Since Argentina in the nineteenth century had a youthful population (as shown in table 1, approximately 62 percent of the population was under thirty years old in the census years of 1827 and 1855), I assume that at least some of the inequality identified by the Gini coefficient resulted from demographic and not economic characteristics. This may be particularly true if Szuchman is correct about the demographic effects of the era of civil war. When I have completed the final stages of this study, I will report the results using both the Gini and a more age-sensitive statistic, the Paglin-Gini.[16]

At the outset of the Rosas period, Buenos Aires and its rural hinterland was suffering from more than twenty years of political chaos, fiscal mismanagement, and periodic military violence. However, this was also a period of economic expansion—particularly in the grazing sector, which was newly tied to Europe and North America as a result of liberalized commercial regulations at the port of Buenos Aires. Stimulated by increased export demands, the settled regions of the province of Buenos Aires grew by 42 percent and the Indian frontier was pushed south. As Andrés M. Carretero points out, this expansion coincided with an increase in the average size of estancias and with the appearance of a few *latifundia* measuring over 120,000 acres. By 1852, 28 percent of all estancieros owned 60 percent of the largest holdings (estates of ten square leagues or larger).[17] Wealth in the grazing sector was clearly becoming concentrated.

Table 1 Age Distribution in Argentina, 1810, 1827, 1855

Years of Age	1810 (%)	1827 (%)	1855 (%)
Under 20	42.8	40.9	40.8
20–34	33.3	31.4	31.1
35–49	13.7	16.6	17.5
50 and over	10.1	11.3	10.5

Note: Percentages may not add to 100 due to rounding.
Source: Mark D. Szuchman generously provided these age distributions based on his sample of the three censuses.

There was also some diversification in the grazing sector as Argentine wool found a place in the European market.[18] By 1865 the value of wool exports far exceeded the total value of cattle products.[19] During the Rosas period the value of wool exports grew from a marginal position in 1830 to 1.1 million gold pesos in 1851, putting wool behind only tallow (1.2 million) and hides (6.9 million) in importance.[20]

My preliminary analysis of the 1829–30 probate records produced a Gini coefficient of 0.61 (see table 2). This level of wealth inequality for the province of Buenos Aires compares favorably with the Gini coefficient of 0.73 that Jones found for Britain's thirteen North American colonies in 1774.[21] Texas on the eve of the Civil War provides a better comparison. Although Texas in 1860 had a more dispersed pattern of urbanization and a larger slave population than the province of Buenos Aires in 1829–30, there were many similarities. Both had an important grazing sector, abundant and inexpensive land, and similar population densities. Using wealth information from the 1860 U.S. census, Randolph Campbell and Richard Lowe found a Gini of 0.74 for Texas.[22] What explains the difference? The lower level of inequality found for the province of Buenos Aires was clearly not the result of a more dispersed landholding pattern. In fact, by 1830 sixty large-scale estancieros held 76 percent of the province's settled area.[23] Landholding was more concentrated in the province of Buenos Aires than in Texas. Evidence drawn from studies of the period suggests that labor shortages and high wages combined with political violence, especially in the city of Buenos Aires, to retard the pace of wealth concentration despite the expansion of latifundia.[24]

Table 2 Changes in Levels of Wealth Inequality (Gini Coefficient) for Province of Buenos Aires, 1800–1855

Year	Gini Coefficient
1800	0.71
1829–30	0.61
1855–56	0.80

Note: In the analysis for both this and table 3, slaves were included as property, not as potential wealth holders. If slaves were counted as wealth holders, then both measures of inequality would show slightly greater levels of concentration.

The extensive literature on the economic history of the United States suggests that wealth holding there became more concentrated during the nineteenth century. Both Robert Gallman and Lee Soltow have demonstrated this for 1860 using estimated wealth provided by census schedules. Soltow found a Gini coefficient of 0.83 for all adult free men in 1860.[25] He argues that this high level of wealth inequality remained fairly stable to the end of the century, despite economic expansion, industrialization, and urbanization. Gallman and others are in general agreement with the 1860 estimate but argue that there was a second round of wealth concentration near the end of the century.[26] In the case of Argentina, both Burgin and Lynch have suggested that the combined effects of tariff and monetary policy worked to redistribute wealth from the lower classes to the landowning elite beginning in the Unitarian period and continuing at least until the fall of Rosas. My data base allows me to use the Gini to test this hypothesis and provide a quantitative description of these changes.

For the probate cohort 1855–56, my analysis produced a Gini coefficient of 0.80 (see table 2). In other words, wealth was much more unequally distributed at the end of the Rosas period than at the beginning. At the end of the period wealth distribution was similar to that found by Soltow for the United States in 1860 or by Soltow, Gallman, and others in succeeding census years. Evidence from the United States in the nineteenth century appears to demonstrate that wealth holdings tended to be more concentrated in the older cities and towns of the East and Midwest than in the West and South.[27] National-level studies of the United States appear to demonstrate that the patterns of concentrated wealth associated with industrialization and urbanization were somewhat offset by the opening of new communities in the West, where low land values promoted a more equitable wealth-distribution pattern. That is, in the United States wealth inequality appears to have been strongly associated with the proliferation of commercial and manufacturing activities and with the growth of urban populations in the East and Midwest. My analysis of estate inventories from the province of Buenos Aires suggests a pattern distinct from that found for North America. Although the city of Buenos Aires grew by more than 60 percent during the Rosas era, the city's rural hinterland grew much more rapidly, as one can see in table 3. Buenos Aires province was becoming more rural as the level of inequality grew. In the countryside there was a clear tendency toward increased wealth concentration despite the southward push of the frontier and a proliferation of new settlements. Put simply, the frontier seems to have worked quite differently in Argentina than in the United States.

Table 3 Population of the Province of Buenos Aires, 1822 and 1855, and Average Annual Growth, 1822–55

	1822	1855	Average Annual Growth, 1822–55 (Percent)
City	55,416	90,076	1.9
Countryside	63,230	183,861	5.8

Source: Ernesto J.A. Maeder, *Evolución demográfica de Argentina de 1810 a 1869* (Buenos Aires, 1969).

To better understand the scale and direction of these changes in wealth distribution during the Rosas period, I created a streamlined probate file for 1800, a year arbitrarily selected to represent the late colonial period. I found eighty-two probate records with complete inventories for 1800. For these records I calculated the net wealth of decedents rather than coding the entire array of category-specific data used for the later periods. I then adjusted the data for age bias using the census of 1810. As expected, the probate records for 1800 provided much less comprehensive coverage of the countryside and provincial towns than the cities. Therefore my analysis reflects the economic and social realities of the city of Buenos Aires in the late colonial period. Analysis of the 1800 group of records produced a Gini of 0.71 (see table 2)—a level of inequality nearly identical to that found by Jones for the thirteen colonies of North America in 1774. Jones provides regional-level analyses as well. As one would expect, the Gini for Buenos Aires is lower than that found for New England with its well-developed network of towns and broad commercial links. The North American region that in 1774 was most like late colonial Buenos Aires was the slave-holding South, where Jones found a Gini of 0.68.[28]

In addition to Gini coefficients for 1800, 1829–30, and 1855–56, I have calculated a second statistic for measuring levels of wealth concentration. The percentage of all wealth held by the richest 1 percent of the population illustrates even more dramatically than the Gini Coefficient the tendency toward increased levels of inequality during the Rosas period (see table 4). The measure shows the same pattern indicated by the Gini coefficient. By the fall of Rosas, nearly 50 percent of the province's total wealth was concentrated in the hands of a small elite. The land policies of the Rosas government obviously promoted this tendency toward increased inequality, but, as noted earlier, rural property was already highly concentrated before Rosas. The military campaigns against the Amerindian populations

Table 4 Changes in Levels of Wealth Inequality (Percentage Share of Wealth Held by Top 1 Percent), 1810–55

Year	Percentage
1800	32
1829–30	24
1855–56	47

Note: Percentages rounded to nearest whole number.

in the south of the province in the 1830s allowed Rosas to distribute vast new estates to allies and kinsmen. However, rural landownership alone cannot account for this significant increase in inequality. Rather, the increased profitability of raising livestock allowed the rural elite to invest heavily in urban real estate and, to a lesser extent, in commerce. As a result, by 1855 rural and urban elites had coalesced into a single rentier class.

As pointed out by Burgin and Lynch, fiscal and monetary policies also played a role. Port duties remained the government's primary source of revenues through this period. They provided 82 percent of the provincial government's revenues in 1829, rising to 93 percent in 1850.[29] Since port duties were not adjusted for inflation in the Rosas era, rural producers were little inconvenienced by these assessments. A property tax introduced in 1822, *contribución directa,* placed heavier burdens on urban commercial sectors than on rural producers. As Burgin points out, capital invested in goods imported on consignment paid 56 percent of all the revenues obtained from this tax in 1849. The monetary policy of the Rosas government was second only to its policies on land distribution as a contributor to wealth concentration. Unwilling to cut expenditures, especially for the military, the government papered over its revenue shortfalls with currency issues. Between 1836 and 1851 the provincial government issued 109,980,854 pesos in paper money.[30] Livestock producers who operated in the hard currency export market were clearly better off than members of the urban commercial and manufacturing sectors who received paper pesos for their goods and services while making their essential purchase of imports in gold.

The consequences of these policies are manifested in the probate inventories of the rural elite. Tables 5 and 6 show the composition of wealth for two representative estates. Both José Joaquín Arana and Ygnacio Galindez had accumulated great riches during their lives.[31] Their wealth was based primarily on extensive rural holdings and vast herds. To diversify invest-

Table 5 Composition of Wealth in Estate of José Joaquín Arana, 1856 (in *Moneda Corriente*/Paper Pesos)

Wealth Components	Value	Percentage of Total Estate
All producer goods	2,735,836	58.8
Tools and equipment	7,716	0.3
Inventory (includes unsold rural products)	3,960	0.1
Livestock	2,724,160	58.4
All real estate	1,131,452	38.2
Primary residence	180,305	6.1
Business property (urban)	–	–
Rental property (urban)	192,478	6.5
Rural property	758,669	25.7
All consumer goods	74,256	2.5
Household goods	32,123	1.1
Clothing	4,700	0.2
Jewelry and silverware	37,433	1.3
Financial assets	10,919	0.4
Cash (paper and coin)	10,919	0.4
Claims	–	–
Financial liabilities	66,105	2.2
Total estate	3,952,463	
Net estate	3,886,358	

ment they acquired urban real estate, including rental properties. These investments provided some protection against the potentially devastating consequences of drought, animal diseases, and disruptions of the export market. In Galindez's estate there were unusually large amounts of cash (including gold coin), unminted bullion, and credits extended to neighbors and the government. Arana's estate, with relatively small amounts of cash and without active loans, was more representative of his class.

In neither estate was there significant investment in tools, machinery, and other such producer goods. The small amounts for this category shown in tables 5 and 6 were mostly devoted to wagons, carts, and harnesses. Note also the small amounts of wealth maintained in inventory. Consumer goods also represented only a small percentage of the total estate. Even among the richest members of this society there was relatively little investment in either comfort or display. Ygnacio Galindez, a man worth nearly 7 million pesos in 1856, did not own a coach or expensive clothing. Neither estate included books or paintings. Wealth was invested in land and livestock or,

Table 6 Composition of Wealth in Estate of Ygnacio Galindez, 1856 (in *Moneda Corriente*/Paper Pesos)

Wealth Components	Value	Percentage of estate
All producer goods	1,591,156	23.0
Tools and equipment	6,589	0.9
Inventory (includes unsold rural products)	99,462	1.4
Livestock	1,485,105	21.5
All real estate	1,468,002	21.3
Residence (urban)	400,746	5.8
Business property	–	–
Rental property (urban)	308,210	4.5
Rural property	759,046	11.0
All consumer goods	5,343	0.08
Household goods	4,958	0.07
Clothing	385	0.01
Jewelry	–	–
Financial assets	3,842,733	55.6
Cash (paper and coin)	1,886,511	27.3
Claims	1,956,222	28.3
Financial liabilities	206,225	3.0
Total estate	6,907,234	
Net estate	6,701,009	

[a]This includes 5,197 ounces of gold valued at 363 paper pesos = 1 ounce.

in the case of Galindez, conservatively in gold, the most portable and predictable investment of all.

The inventory of Género Lázaro provides a fitting counterpoint to the estates of these two beneficiaries of the Rosas era. Lázaro was an unmarried Italian immigrant who worked as a laborer in Buenos Aires. Following his suicide in 1856, his possessions were inventoried by the *alcalde de barrio*. His material legacy included his clothes (47 pesos), his watch (98 pesos), and 50 pesos in paper money. His possessions were auctioned to pay his landlord.[32]

Summary of Results

At this stage of my analysis, I can suggest a periodization for changes in wealth concentration during the first half of the nineteenth century. At the end of the colonial era my analysis finds a high level of inequality—levels similar to those of England's North American colonies on the eve of independence. This pattern of wealth distribution appears to have been associated—as in North America—with the expansion of long-distance trade, with the relative growth of urban population, and with the articulation of commercial marketing and credit networks that increasingly linked and subordinated the interior to the capital city. This association of increased wealth concentration with the development of urban networks and economic specialization has been found in studies of both North America and Great Britain, and I expected to find it for Buenos Aires in 1800.

In the two decades that followed the *cabildo abierto* of 25 May 1810 this tendency toward increased inequality was temporarily reversed. Although students of the period find strong evidence of economic growth in the grazing and agricultural sectors of the province after 1810, the city of Buenos Aires experienced a period of stagnation or at best slow growth. In the city it appears that wealth was redistributed away from traditional commercial and government elites toward new middle and skilled working groups. Novel fiscal mechanisms, altered commercial arrangements, and the vagaries of the political process all played a role in this transfer. During the long period of regional conflicts, civil war, and political instability that followed the events of 1810, confiscatory taxes and direct expropriations were used by various governments to punish enemies as well as to generate needed revenues. The loss of some traditional regional commercial links—Potosí and Paraguay among others—and the many difficulties associated with substituting Great Britain and the United States for Spain as dominant trading partners led to the loss of economic power—and wealth—by wholesale merchants. The combined effects of these forces explain most of the reduction in the Gini coefficient by 1829–30. Bureaucrats, Spanish and criollo merchants linked to the traditional trade with Spain and Potosí, and ultimately artisans and small manufacturers all lost wealth to new groups, such as revolutionary officials, the military, and especially rural landowners.

The Rosas era reversed this trend toward greater wealth equality. The relative stability of Rosas's long rule permitted the maturation and diversification of the grazing sector and led to significantly increased levels of inequality (a Gini of 0.80). Although frontier expansion, particularly in Frederick Jackson Turner's interpretation of North American history, is often presumed to coincide with social mobility, studies of U.S. census samples demonstrate that in some cases frontier regions had very high concentrations of wealth. For example, four small cities in Texas had a Gini coefficient of 0.85 in 1860. In 1860 Texas, however, the ownership of slaves was an important determinant of wealth concentration. The entire state of Texas with its free-labor agricultural and grazing regions included had a Gini coefficient of 0.74. Wisconsin, another frontier area in 1860, had a Gini of 0.75. That is, relative to these two very different frontier states in the United States in 1860, the province of Buenos Aires had a more concentrated pattern of wealth holding in 1855–56.

Frontier expansions in the Americas were both economic and political phenomena in which government played a crucial role. Government controlled the distribution of the primary frontier resource, land, and provided institutional support for the distribution of scarce labor. The southern expansion of the Rosas era was characterized by the creation of enormous estancias as well as by governmentally sanctioned efforts to create a disciplined, subordinate rural labor force. The social costs of this process are suggested by the two measures of inequality offered in this essay. Of all frontier areas in the Western Hemisphere studied to date, the province of Buenos Aires at the end of the Rosas era had the highest level of wealth inequality.

The economic and social policies of the Rosas period promoted inequality by redistributing wealth from the rural and urban masses, urban commercial and artisanal sectors, and small farmers to the rural grazing elite. These economic and social policies depended upon the antidemocratic political policies of the period. The strong trend toward wealth concentration after 1830 identified in this essay exceeded levels established at the end of the colonial period. I conclude therefore that the transition from the commercial- and public-sector-dominated economy of 1800 to the grazing economy of 1855 was accomplished at a substantial cost in terms of social justice. My future analyses will concentrate on establishing measures of economic performance and a close scrutiny of investment and consumption patterns.

Notes

1. Jonathan C. Brown, *A Socioeconomic History of Argentina, 1776–1860* (Cambridge, Eng., 1979). For hide exports see table 2, p. 59. For wool exports to Great Britain and the United States see table 3, p. 66.

2. It is clear now that this decline began in the late colonial period rather than with the free traders of the independence era. Rosas was willing to provide some protection for provincial manufacturers (e.g., the Tariff of 1835), and his inflationary issues of paper money also retarded the progress of imports. Nevertheless, by 1852 little manufacturing remained in the province. See Miron Burgin, *The Economic Aspects of Argentine Federalism, 1820–1852* (Cambridge, MA, 1946), especially chap. 10.

3. See, for example, *Registro oficial de la provincia de Buenos Aires* (Buenos Aires, 1821–51); *Registro estadistico de provincia de Buenos Aires,* (Buenos Aires, 1821–23); *Gaceta mercantil* (Buenos Aires, 1830–52); and Woodbine Parish, *Buenos Ayres and the Provinces of the Rio de la Plata . . .* (London, 1852).

4. Burgin, *The Economic Aspects.* An important recent addition to the discussion of fiscal policy is Tulio Halperín Donghi, *Guerra y finanzas en los orígenes del estado argentino, 1791–1850* (Buenos Aires, 1982).

5. Tulio Halperín Donghi, "La expansión ganadera en la campaña de Buenos Aires, 1810–1852," *Desarrollo Económico,* 3:1–2 (1963), pp. 57–110; John Lynch, *Argentine Dictator, Juan Manuel de Rosas, 1829–1852* (Oxford, 1981); and Jonathan C. Brown, *A Socioeconomic History of Argentina, 1776–1860.*

6. Mark D. Szuchman, *Order, Family, and Community in Buenos Aires, 1810–1860* (Stanford, 1988).

7. See Lois Green Carr and Lorena S. Walsh, "Inventories and the Analysis of Wealth and Consumption Patterns in St. Mary's County, Maryland, 1658–1777," *Historical Methods,* 13:2 (Spring 1980), pp. 81–104; Alice Hanson Jones, "Wealth Estimates for the American Middle Colonies, 1774," *Economic Development and Cultural Change,* 18:4 (July, 1970), pp. 1–48; and Gloria L. Main, "Probate Records as a Source for Early American History," *William and Mary Quarterly,* 33:1 (January 1975), pp. 89–99.

8. For a short summary of the abolition process, see Leslie B. Rout, Jr., *The African Experience in Spanish America, 1502 to the Present Day* (Cambridge, Eng., 1976), pp. 185–96.

9. The personal variables are sex, birthplace, primary occupation, birth legitimacy, marital status, age, race, secondary occupation, number of children, location of primary residence, location of secondary residence, and membership in lay brotherhood. The economic variables (coded in paper pesos) are value of slaves, number of slaves, value of clothing, jewelry, gold and silver furnishings, furniture, household utensils, urban residence (land), urban residence (improvements), business (land), business (improvements), rental property, tools and machinery, raw materials, inventory, cash (paper), cash (coin), rural residence (land), rural residence (improvements), livestock, farm and ranch tools and machinery, corrals, rural inventory, trees, wagons and carts, boats, stocks, bonds, debts, credits, books, paintings, area of rural estate.

10. See Carole Shammas, "The Determinants of Personal Wealth in Seventeenth-Century England and America," *The Journal of Economic History,* 37:3 (September, 1977), pp. 675–89.

11. The age cohorts used are presented in table 1. The distributions were provided by Mark D. Szuchman.

12. See, for example, the review of Jones's *American Colonial Wealth: Documents and Methods,* vols. 1–3, by Gloria Main in *Business History Review,* 52:3 (Autumn, 1978), pp. 408–10; and the review of Jones's synthesis, *Wealth of a Nation to Be,* by John J. McCusker in *The Journal of American History,* 68:1 (June, 1981), p. 113. Jones responds in "Estimating Wealth of the Living from a Probate Sample," *Journal of Interdisciplinary History,* 13:2 (Autumn 1982), pp. 273–300.

13. Alice Hanson Jones, *Wealth of a Nation to Be* (New York, 1980). See especially app. A.

14. Unfortunately, some of these parish records were destroyed. I examined copies of the surviving records held by the Genealogical Library of the Church of the Latter Day Saints, Salt Lake City, Utah. These parishes are Merced, Piedad, Balvanera, Pilar, San Telmo, Socorro, Monserrat, San José, and Concepción.

15. Robert Gallman, "The 'Egalitarian Myth,' Once Again," *Social Science History,* 5:2 (1981), pp. 223–34; and Gallman, "Blumin on Age and Inequality: Ante Bellum America," *Social Science History,* 6:3 (1982), pp. 381–84.

16. Alice Hanson Jones, *Wealth of a Nation To Be,* pp. 166–67.

17. Andrés M. Carretaro, *La propiedad de la tierra en la época de Rosas* (Buenos Aires, 1972), pp. 13–15. See also Miguel A. Cacano, *Evolución histórica del régimen de la tierra pública 1810–1916* (Buenos Aires, 1972), chap. 3.

18. Hilda Sabato, *Capitalismo y ganaderia en Buenos Aires: La fiebre del lanar, 1850–90* (Buenos Aires, 1989). A somewhat dated but still useful summary is found in chap. 5 of Horacio C. E. Giberti, *Historia economica de la ganaderóa Argentina* (Buenos Aires, 1954).

19. Sabato, *Capitalismo,* p. 39.

20. Burgin, *The Economic Aspects,* p. 271.

21. Jones, *Wealth of a Nation to Be,* p. 169.

22. Randolph B. Campbell and Richard E. Lowe, *Wealth and Power in Antebellum Texas* (College Station, TX, 1977), p. 127.

23. Lynch, *Rosas,* pp. 68–69.

24. Hilda Sabato et al., *Los trabajadores y el mercado del trabajo en Buenos Aires, ciudad y campaña, 1850–80* (Buenos Aires, 1981), and Burgin, *The Economic Aspects,* p. 27–28.

25. Lee Soltow, *Men and Wealth in the United States, 1860–70* (New Haven, 1975), p. 103.

26. Robert Gallman, "The Social Distribution of Wealth in the United States of America," in the *Third International Conference of Economic History, Munich, 1965* (The Hague, 1905), pp. 320–21.

27. Robert Gallman, "The Effects of Changes in Economic and Demographic Structure on the Size Distribution of Wealth in the Antebellum U.S.," comment on the session "Historical Implications of 19th Century Wealth Data," Social Science History Association, 2–3 November 1979. For the Boston data see Edward Pessen, *Riches, Class, and Power Before the Civil War* (Lexington, MA, 1973), pp. 30–40. For Baltimore and other cities, see Robert Gallman, "Trends in the Size Distribution of Wealth in the Nineteenth Century," in Lee Soltow, eds., *Six Papers on the Size Distribution of Wealth and Income* (New York, 1969), pp. 22–23.

28. Jones, *Wealth of a Nation to Be,* p. 316.

29. Burgin, *The Economic Aspects,* pp. 49, 195.

30. Ibid., p. 216.

31. Archivo General de la Nación, Sucesiones no. 3516, Sucesión de Don José Joaquin Arana, and no. 5949, sucesión de Don Ygnacio Galindez.

32. Archivo General de la Nación, Sucesiones, no. 6525, Sucesión de Don Genaro Lazaro.

10

Paraguayan Commerce with the Outside World, 1770–1850

JERRY W. COONEY AND THOMAS L. WHIGHAM

From the Conquest in the sixteenth century until only a generation ago, people and trade goods passed through the littoral of the Río de la Plata principally by way of its great rivers. This riverine connection was essential to the development of the upriver region of Paraguay. Finished goods passed to this agricultural land from the outside by river trade, and to pay for manufactures, Paraguay's export merchants sent tobacco, hides, and the green tea, yerba maté, down the Paraguay and Paraná rivers to the port cities of Montevideo and Buenos Aires. This pattern of trade was altogether natural for an interior region such as Paraguay. Yet in the late colonial as well as the early national period, politics constantly affected the extent and direction of this vital commerce. The interplay of politics and trade gave the infrastructure of river traffic, called the Carrera del Paraguay, a complex and precarious character. The transitional era between 1770 and 1850 provides a fine test of the resiliency of the commerce, for it was in that period that we find an interventionist state, working in conjunction with merchants—or sometimes against them—in reconstructing the Carrera.

For Paraguayan and other *comerciantes* on the littoral, the period from 1770 to 1810 was the Golden Age of the colonial Carrera del Paraguay. Native-born merchants expanded their activities, and Paraguay, in common with the rest of the Río de la Plata, experienced a large immigration of peninsular merchants attracted to the economic opportunities.[1] The creation of the Viceroyalty of the Río de la Plata in 1776, the Edict of Free Commerce two years later, and the creation of intendencias in 1782—all in response to imperial perceptions of needed economic and political reforms—liberated latent economic forces that produced an explosion of economic growth in the province of Paraguay and throughout the Plata.[2] Later, with the establishment of the Real Consulado de Buenos Aires in the mid-1790s and the resultant appointment of *diputados consulares* at critical points along the Carrera, business became even more regularized, and merchants had a body to represent them before royal authorities.[3]

By 1780 Paraguay dominated the commerce of the littoral. Demand for that region's products was high, increasing throughout the viceregal era. The province, with its yerba, tobacco, timber products, *dulces,* and sugar, supplied better than 80 percent of all products shipped downriver. Exports from that *intendencia* were hardly affected by the international problems of the empire in the 1790s and early 1800s because commodities from Paraguay were destined for internal viceregal consumption. Yerba maté then had no competitor, and as a reasonably cheap luxury, it remained in high demand. All legal tobacco consumed in the littoral, and much that was illegal, came from the province. Moreover, timber and dulces from the north had no rivals. Nearly all the craft on the Carrera were built in Paraguay and had Paraguayan crews.[4] At the same time, the Upper Plata also consumed a large portion of the manufactured goods shipped north to pay for those exports.

To understand the export commerce of Paraguay, market theory considerations must be set aside. Not only did politics play a major role, but also personal relations between merchants assumed great importance. This commerce of the late colonial period had a traditional nature and was associated with the era of preindustrial, premodern finance capitalism. Credit supported by trust fueled business, and that trust resulted from such nonmarket factors as kinship, prior friendship or business association, and even common provincial origins in Spain. The trade consisted of a long commercial chain stretching a thousand miles from Villa Real de la Concepción near the Mato Grosso frontier south to Buenos Aires and Montevideo in the estuary. Even with a good postal service established in 1770, a *porteño* merchant-capitalist depended on his associate upriver to treat him fairly. In fact, partners might not see each other for years on end. Those in Buenos Aires were as much in need of trust as those upriver. For if the latter defaulted on commitments, platine merchants found themselves with serious problems that might lead to bankruptcy.

Mutual confidence was evident in various instruments of commerce used on the Carrera. While most were relatively short-lived—two or three years with definite agreed-upon ends—trust was essential because partners held liabilities in common. In addition to partnerships, merchants used the common *poderes* (powers of attorney) to conduct business on behalf of friends, associates, relatives, partners, or anyone else granting that right.

Poderes could address specific or general ends, but in any case, one simply had to trust the *apoderados.*[5]

Another example of such confidence and trust was the common practice of consigning goods to be sold. The consignee generally received only a nominal 3 or 4 percent fee on the sale of these items.[6] Such a small percentage reveals much about the nature of the instrument. By consigning yerba to a creditor in Buenos Aires, for example, the Asunción merchant had to trust the porteño to sell it at the best price possible in order to apply all the proceeds or a portion against the Paraguayan's outstanding debt. If there was no debt to be paid, the proceeds were commonly used to purchase goods for the upriver trade. At other times those proceeds were carried on the porteño's books, earning interest for the Asunceño. In the provincial capital, that merchant had the power to sell consigned goods from his porteño creditor and associate and then invest the proceeds in yerba for shipment south or remit the profits to Buenos Aires after extracting a consignment fee—or transact any and all combinations.[7]

Often as many as seven or eight different transactions at any one time existed between creditor and debtor, and the Asunceño was not always the debtor in this web of credit, sales, and remittance. Commonly a mere 5 percent interest charge on goods purchased on credit fueled this trade, and as in the case of consignment fees, the low interest rate was more a symbol of commitment than a device to gain profit.[8]

But what of the nature of profits in this commerce of the rivers? No great money was made on consignment fees or interest. It was the profit from each sale that kept business alive. Overwhelmingly, the power of mark-up was the prime determinant of gain on the Carrera del Paraguay. Mark-ups of 70 to 80 percent at retail points on both up and downriver goods were common. Yet transportation charges, interest payments, spoilage losses, storage costs, and, of course, taxes ate away at profits. Taxes on a single transaction of goods shipped either up– or downriver were about 30–40 percent.[9] And though the profits may appear high to the modern eye, one must remember that not only were there great risks, but also realization of profits could be long delayed because of the credit-driven nature of this commerce.

In the late 1700s it became evident that the great expansion of yerba maté, tobacco, and timber exports from the Upper Plata depended upon an additional crucial factor—the plenitude of inexpensive, salaried *mano de obra.* In the eighteenth century Paraguay had witnessed a demographic shift in its population as the number of persons classified as *criollos* or *españoles-americanos* rose dramatically while those still counted as Indians fell. At the same time the provincial population was expanding. One result by the 1770s was that salaried labor displaced traditional *encomienda* labor.[10] The greatest increase of criollos occurred in nuclear Paraguay, the region of the Cordillera and Asunción districts, and agricultural land became hard to obtain. There, *pueblos de indios,* the Church, the landed elite, even the state, inevitably controlled the best land. During the late colonial period the best that many criollos could hope for in those districts was a precarious *arrendatario* or lessee status. By the 1770s there was a definite outflow of *desarraigados y vagos* who flocked to the northern yerba-gathering areas, became *peones* on the new cattle ranches of the frontiers, settled the new towns of the Paraguayan littoral, and provided crews for the boats of the Carrera.[11] No lack of young Paraguayan males existed to do hard, dirty, and hazardous work.

In the preindustrial era the advantages of water transport over transport by land were obvious. Yerba, tobacco, and timber were all high-bulk, relatively low-profit commodities. Without cheap river transport the yerba of Paraguay, for example, would have been a curiosity confined to that region. Tobacco and timber for Montevideo and Buenos Aires could have been imported from Cuba or Brazil. River transport made all the difference, and the traffic increased dramatically throughout the viceregal era. About 20 craft departed Asunción in 1776.[12] In 1808, a record year, 502 craft left Asunción for the journey south.[13] Another indication of the expansion of the yerba trade in this period is that in 1776 about 26,500 *arrobas* of this commodity were exported from Paraguay while thirty-one years later, in 1807, the yearly total amounted to 278,262 *arrobas.*[14] By 1804 the magnitude of the yerba trade from Villa Real de la Concepción—a recently founded town on the Río Paraguay about three hundred miles north of Asunción—was so great that the viceroy appointed a *diputado consular* to Concepción to handle mercantile disputes.[15]

Volume was the key to profits on the Carrera. Freight charges from Asunción to Las Conchas in the estuary (the river town serving Buenos Aires) were a mere 2 reales per arroba in the 1790s.[16] By 1800, because there were more vessels on the rivers and more competition for cargoes, an astute Asunción merchant could often pay 1.5 reales per arroba for the same voyage.[17] The overland wine trade from the Cuyo region offers a comparison. By cart from San Juan to Buenos Aires—roughly the same distance as from Asunción to Buenos Aires—freights were about two and a half times more expensive by weight, and about five or six times by volume.[18] From Jujuy to Buenos Aires, again roughly comparable in distance to the route from Asunción to the viceregal capital, the land freight per arroba was 8 reales.[19]

Paraguay's internal economy also underwent a revolution in this same period as the establishment of the Real Renta de Tabacos in the province in the early 1780s fostered the use of silver and the transfer of money by paper instruments. Before that monopoly's purchase of tobacco with silver, barter characterized the province's economy. Growers, after the delivery of tobacco to the Asunción *factoría,* purchased goods in the capital with hard cash.[20] Merchants then used those pesos to finance provincial production of yerba, boat building, timber extraction, and other business enterprises. The *giro,* or circulation of silver, had a multiplier impact upon the local economy.[21]

Eventually accounts with porteño associates or creditors had to be settled. The merchant in Asunción simply took his accumulated money to the treasury of the factoría and there purchased a *libranza,* payable on sight against the treasury of the renta in Buenos Aires in the name of the payee. This instrument was dispatched by post, and the treasury in Buenos Aires received a separate confirmation through the post of that transaction.[22] In 1809 the Asunción treasury of the real renta issued more than 100,000 pesos of libranzas.[23] While the most common flow of libranzas was toward the viceregal capital, their direction could be reversed, and they could even be exchanged between Asunción and other river towns. The real renta was more than happy to provide this service because it meant silver with which to pay tobacco growers would be on hand in Asunción, thus reducing the need for upriver shipment of specie.

Nonetheless, even with the introduction of a money economy into Paraguay in the 1780s, the old barter system of the province survived. Contracts in the province were still drafted to call for payment in tobacco or yerba based upon the old, imaginary provincial peso of 6 reales.[24] The desire to use this old peso de la provincia was natural because that cheaper money benefited those purchasing extractive products.[25] At the same time, it signified a dual economic system in Paraguay as merchants dealt in silver with each other, their downriver creditors, and the government. On the other hand, they attempted and often succeeded in using the imaginary pesos de la provincia, or outright barter, with their suppliers.

A partial application of Gresham's Law occurred in Paraguay as a consequence of tension between silver and kind. While silver did make its way into the rural regions of the province, much of it was hoarded. The acquisition of plate by private individuals grew rapidly from the 1770s onward, and the province's favorable balance of trade encouraged retention.[26] Félix de Azara, probably the most astute visitor to the province in the 1780s and 1790s, declared that Paraguay experienced an average yearly "extraction" of goods worth 327,646 pesos with a yearly average "introduction" of merchandise worth only 136,000 pesos.[27] A similar assessment of the province's balance of trade in the early 1800s came from Miguel Lastarria, personal secretary to the viceroy, the Marqués de Avilas. Lastarria declared that Paraguay's trade surplus of exports over imports stood at about 153,000 pesos a year.[28]

When all was said and done, however, much of the base for Paraguay's prosperity in this era rested upon its ships and their crews. And for sailors on the Carrera some hazards always existed. Overloading of craft (often with secretly acquired contraband), poor maintenance of boats, and generally poor judgment on the part of pilots were the primary causes of shipwreck.[29] Still, because of the nature of wrecks on the Carrera, many of their cargoes were salvageable.

More common than wrecks were spoilage and delay. The use of undecked craft contributed to spoilage through dampness, and inordinate delay worsened the problem. If the Asunción merchant-shipper did not provide the master-pilot with a portion of the voyage's profits—a common practice to ensure care—the pilot would see little need for deadlines and would put in at other ports to do a little business of his own. Some voyages south took nearly a year to complete. In the words of one concerned but sarcastic observer this was "enough time to circumnavigate the globe."[30]

An investigation into wrecks, spoilage, and delay by the consulado de Buenos Aires in 1798 prompted Governor Lázaro de Ribera of Paraguay to take precautionary measures. He ordered various inspections at the port of Asunción:

> When any owner of a boat presents himself to the Intendant, requesting permission to load cargo, that permission will not be given until the *Alcalde de Primer Voto,* the *Diputado de Comercio,* and the *Comandante de Ribera* have concluded an exact inspection of the craft—assuring that it is well caulked and will not take water anywhere.

When the vessel was loaded another inspection was made of the cargo, masts, rigging, anchors, sails, and oars. The boat had to be well provisioned and have two canoes and a lighter. Governor Ribera further ordered that a *derrotero,* or guide to the rivers, be compiled "for the precise direction of the *Patrones* of the *Carrera,*" in order that "dangerous passages" be avoided. Hours for night anchorages were determined, and peones were warned that new regulations were to be issued to keep them in good discipline and subordinate to their masters during the voyages. Finally he ordered that southward bound boats could "make port at Ñeembucú [Pilar], Corrientes, and Santa Fe to discharge cargo but not to receive it." The latter order was designed to reduce delay on the part of the pilots. The governor then selected an experienced river captain, merchant, and peninsular favorite, Juan de Machaín, to be *sargento mayor de la ribera* and gave him orders to enforce all these reforms.[31]

Paraguayans were heavily engaged in the upriver trade as well, but unfortunately more is known about the flow of goods downstream than about the importation of European manufactures. Visitors to the Carrera in the late 1700s, Félix de Azara and Francisco de Aguirre in particular, were always more interested in the yerba traffic and the odd craft used in that commerce than they were in the import trade. Today, the few historians who delve into the history of the Carrera del Paraguay are Paraguayans, and they naturally tend to stress their country's exports over foreign imports.[32] Much remains to be done in investigating this topic, but it is obvious that the two-way Paraguayan sailing craft and their personnel were as characteristic of the Carrera as were the clumsy one-way *balsas, garandumbas,* and *piraguas* that carried yerba to markets.

At Las Conchas at the mouth of the Paraná, European manufactures in demand upriver were loaded aboard keeled sailing craft capable of tacking upriver against the current.[33] By the late 1790s sophisticated, decked, Paraguayan-built *sumacas* appeared in greater numbers.[34] A cargo bound for the north in 1791 reveals the extent to which consumers in the Upper Plata had become accustomed to finished goods. Items aboard ranged from hats to axes, buttons to knives, silk to "false pearls."[35] Again, the entire system of poderes, consignments, and credit still held.

The ships that plied the two-way river trade were different from those of the one-way southbound traffic and so were the crews. Peones aboard the sailing craft were better paid because they were considered to be more skilled.[36] They deserved their higher salary because winds often failed, and the crew, debarked onto the banks, were often forced to tow the ship upriver.[37] The greatest difference, however, was found in the owner-pilots of the two-way craft. An examination of the upriver traffic suggests that a high proportion of these small entrepreneurs were Spanish immigrants. Many of these Spanish owner-pilots became merchants. Ambitious Spanish newcomers to Paraguay, such as Juan Gellí, José de Astigárraga, Antonio Sánchez, Juan de Machaín, and Carlos Genovés, all began as owner-pilots. Their skill and reliability, as well as official bias in favor of Europeans, brought them lucrative transport contracts with the Real Renta de Tabacos. By 1796 this aggressive, commercial-minded immigrant element had seized control of the Asunción cabildo. From that vantage point they profited monetarily and enjoyed the favor of governors. A few Paraguayans profited along with the *peninsulares,* but the domination of Asunción society and economy by these former loggers and master-pilots was quite striking.[38]

At the same time upriver backland towns, such as Curuguaty, Yuty, and Villarrica, now boasted local merchants with close ties to their Asunceño counterparts. In return for hides, tobacco, and especially yerba maté, European-made *géneros,* such as clothing, hats, tools, knives, and firearms, found their way as never before into these rustic areas. This new commerce brought about a revolution in consumer habits. In the absence of studies on that great increase in the consumption of finished goods, we can only speculate on its impact. Nonetheless, that consumer revolution may have signaled the demise of the traditional colonial way of life in the Upper Plata.

The old Carrera del Paraguay and the external commerce of the province depended upon the political unity of the Río de la Plata. Let that territory be rent apart by the different independence movements and civil wars, then the old Carrera would disappear. Even so, trade survived through the troubles of the independence era. Certainly, the post-1810 commerce operated on different terms than that of the colonial period. It required different responses to the dangerous and ambiguous state of affairs along the rivers. Still, the rest of the Río de la Plata needed yerba, timber, and tobacco, and Paraguay needed manufactures. That part of the old equation remained intact, and merchants in Asunción continued to supply consumers' needs.

Paraguayan independence came as an offshoot of the May 1810 revolt by which patriots in Buenos Aires cast off Spanish authority. Immediately after that porteño action, trade upon the Carrera fell prey to hostility between Asunción and the port city and continued to suffer for the rest of 1810 and much of 1811. The capital of the former viceroyalty demanded the allegiance of all the interior provinces and sent out emissaries to the hinterland to effect that subordination. In Paraguay proponents of a nascent nationalism rejected the overtures of Buenos Aires, and the province mobilized behind its last royal governor. A porteño military expedition sent to crush that resistance headed upriver in late 1810, but in early 1811 the provincial criollo militia defeated the invading army. In negotiations after the Paraguayan victory, Manuel Belgrano, commander of the invaders, played upon Paraguayan dissatisfaction with Spanish rule. As one would imagine during this "war," both sides took measures to curtail commerce with each other.

In a bloodless coup of May 1811, militia officers, discontented with recent actions of the royal governor, cast off Spanish authority. Paraguay then began its often tragic history as an independent nation.[39] The ties of commerce remained strong, and after a congress met in 1811 to select a junta to rule Paraguay, trade tentatively resumed. To be sure, one of that new body's members, Dr. José Gaspar de Francia, represented a highly nationalistic faction within the new nation, which greatly distrusted the motives of Buenos Aires. Nonetheless, in October of that year Dr. Francia and the rest of the junta regularized relations with that city. Manuel Belgrano and an associate traveled to Asunción, where they concluded a "treaty" with the junta. The agreement promised Paraguay full autonomy in exchange for a vague promise to support the patriot cause in the Río de la Plata.[40] Commerce resumed its normal status, or at least as normal as could be expected in this period.

The years 1811–13 were marked by Dr. Francia's rise to complete power in the new nation. By 1814 he had acquired absolute control over the new republic and two years later became "dictator for life."[41] He alone ruled Paraguay from 1814 until his death in 1840. Throughout his tenure, his one overwhelming obsession was a fanatical, nationalistic defense of Paraguayan sovereignty. But this austere lawyer had no ambitions beyond the boundaries of his land, and in the mid-1810s he did nothing to disturb the river traffic.

Notwithstanding the resurgence of river trade by 1813, the events of 1810–18 proved paradoxical for Paraguay's external commerce. On one hand, trade revealed a great vitality—and even grew—in the face of adversity and rapidly changing conditions. On the other, it became obvious that this commerce was now subject to political pressures never encountered when the Carrera del Paraguay was under one authority.

The first commercial casualty of the independence movements was the viceregal infrastructure that had nourished commerce. Libranzas and common treasuries rapidly became a thing of the past. The postal service connecting Paraguay with the littoral and the estuary fell into disrepair. The consulado de Buenos Aires no longer appointed deputies for Asunción or Concepción. Political turmoil interrupted passage on the rivers. In 1810, during the period of armed resistance to porteño demands, Paraguay had to dispatch a naval expedition to Corrientes to rescue detained merchant vessels bound for Asunción. And few craft sailed south until relations with Buenos Aires improved in 1811. Until 1813 royalist craft, operating out of Montevideo, harassed river commerce, causing the Paraguayan junta to prohibit voyages temporarily. And no sooner had the royalists abandoned

Montevideo than the forces of the gaucho leader, José Gervasio Artigas, erupted into the littoral and began to prey upon river shipping.

By 1812 relations between Buenos Aires and Asunción had worsened because Paraguay refused any meaningful aid to the porteño military effort against the royalists in Upper Peru and elsewhere. By way of retaliation, and in complete violation of an earlier 1811 agreement that forbade Buenos Aires to collect more than a moderate tax on Paraguay's exports downriver, the porteño government began to levy severe taxation upon tobacco from the north—double that on tobacco produced in territory subject to Buenos Aires.[42] In 1813 all pretense of normal relations between Paraguay and Buenos Aires ended when a provincial congress adamantly rejected any subordination to the former viceregal capital. The congress elected Dr. Francia as one of the republic's consuls knowing that he would defend Paraguay's interests to the utmost.[43] Not until 1852 could relations between Asunción and Buenos Aires be regarded as amicable—and for most of the preceding four decades relations were very bad indeed.

For all the porteño harassment of commerce, yerba and tobacco flowed out of Asunción in these years in quantities that matched and even surpassed the best years of the colonial era. Tobacco exports, for example, totaled 33,196 arrobas in 1816 with a value of some 82,990 pesos.[44] Of course, since the royal tobacco monopoly had been abolished in Paraguay upon independence, much of the apparent increase in exports of this crop may be due to the fact that growers at that time reported their production. Before 1811 it was obvious that much of the province's tobacco production was not reported because it fell into the hands of smugglers. Yerba exports for 1816 revealed a similar expansion to 289,920 arrobas.[45] How did this occur in the face of political uncertainty and intermittent harassment of riverine trade?

Undoubtedly the best explanation lies in the demand for Paraguay's products even during a period of social and political turmoil on the littoral of the Paraná. During this period, Paraguay surrendered none of its desire for the finished goods of the outside world. Yet one must also give credit to the tenacious survival of those instruments of trust and confidence between merchants that had characterized colonial commerce. Without libranzas, an efficient postal service, and viceregal support, that trust was even more important than before. Peninsular merchants in Buenos Aires may have been harassed by patriot governments. No matter. Their criollo sons, sons-in-law, nephews, and associates assumed responsibility for trade upon the Carrera. Essentially the same occurred in Asunción. Credit was still advanced even though payment of debts might be more problematical.

The turmoil of independence notwithstanding, merchants were still merchants, and most realized that excellent profits still could be made. Demand for Paraguayan yerba and tobacco was as great as before. People do not surrender their pleasures just because they find themselves immersed in a revolutionary struggle.

Another explanation for the vigor of river trade in the 1810s lies in the new international situation of the Río de la Plata. British manufactures now flooded the markets of this region, drawing specie out of retirement into circulation. Those same imported manufactures were accompanied by aggressive, imaginative British merchants who, by paying cash for local products rather than relying on the traditional credit system, also pumped specie into local economies.[46] Inevitably, as that silver fled to Britain, hard money became scarce, and the Plata fell into a depression. But for the palmy days of the 1810s, silver in circulation encouraged commerce of all types.

Yet for all the power of supply and demand in the 1810s, Dr. Francia placed political considerations far above economic ones. At one time he favored a vigorous, export-oriented policy as long as it was not subordinated to Buenos Aires and posed no threat to the independence of the republic. In a remarkable interview with the Scottish merchant, John Parish Robertson, who had extensive commercial operations in Paraguay from 1812 to 1815, Dr. Francia proposed a trading arrangement between his republic and Great Britain:

> I invite England to a political and commercial intercourse with me; and . . . I am ready and anxious to receive in my capital, and with all the deference due to diplomatic intercourse between civilized states, a minister from the court of St. James's; I also will appoint to that Court an envoy of my own.
>
> Such a treaty of commerce and political alliance may then be framed, as shall comport at once with the dignity and interests of the great empire of England, and with those of the rising state which I now rule.[47]

To be sure, nothing came of this overture to Great Britain.

Always foremost in Dr. Francia's foreign policy was his desire to preserve Paraguay from porteño machinations. He knew that Buenos Aires continually conspired against his authority. The forces of Artigas kept rampaging up and down the rivers with resultant anarchy coming close to Paraguay's borders. To save his nation, as well as his government, from the turmoil and threat of the outside world, Dr. Francia decided in the late 1810s to close Paraguay's borders to foreigners.[48] In so doing, he changed the entire complexion of Paraguay's external commerce.

Politics had triumphed. Dr. Francia no longer allowed merchant ships free passage to and from Asunción. By the early 1820s the harbor of the capital resembled a maritime graveyard as the "port of Assumption [*sic*] literally resembled a coast where a hundred ships had run aground."[49] Still, the isolation decreed for Paraguay after 1818 was political and diplomatic—never commercial. From that year to the death of the dictator in 1840, Paraguay continued to participate in the regional trade of the Río de la Plata. This commerce flowed at a much lower level than it had during the golden days of the colonial era. What now characterized Paraguay's commerce with the outside world was the high degree of state control imposed upon it. Yet at the same time that Dr. Francia was constructing his rigid, nationalistic dictatorship, peninsulares resident in Paraguay retained a precarious interest in both the internal and external commerce of the new republic. They, and criollo and non-Paraguayan American merchants, kept private trade alive in Paraguay, uncertain as they always were about the whims of the dictator.

Three means of commercial outlet existed for Dr. Francia's Paraguay after 1818. The best known was the Itapúa-São Borja vent by which trade occurred between Paraguay and the empire of Brazil. Two other trade connections to the outside world led out of Pilar de Ñeembucú, south of Asunción. One was simply a local commerce with neighboring Corrientes. The other was by way of Pilar to Buenos Aires by river craft with special permits from the dictator. All these commercial outlets, controlled though they were, reveal the paramount importance of politics relative to trade. At the same time, however, the Pilar–Buenos Aires route revealed that personal attitudes on the part of the dictator also played a role in Paraguay's external commerce.

José Tomás Ysasí was a Paraguayan businessman who became active in the river trade around 1800 and was part of the mercantile power structure in Asunción. As did so many *comerciantes* of the era, he busied himself in the export of yerba, conducting business as far away as Chile and associating with immigrant peninsular merchants.[50] During the confused era of 1811–14 he ingratiated himself with the patriot cause. He was a fervent supporter and close associate when, in 1814, Dr. Francia attained full dictatorial power. As a measure of Dr. Francia's trust and appreciation, Ysasí became his agent for trade in Buenos Aires after 1818. The merchant appeared to justify this trust as he managed to obtain firearms for the Paraguayan Army in Buenos Aires—even in the face of porteño hostility to Asunción.[51]

The dictator should not have trusted Ysasí. The merchant became implicated in a plot against him in 1826 and fled Paraguay. It was discovered, moreover, that Ysasí had taken advantage of the government's favor to extract specie illegally from the republic and to take out goods upon which he had paid no duties.[52] The dictator seized Ysasí's property but did not forbid others from engaging in the special ship trade with Buenos Aires.

In the same year as Ysasí's betrayal, Miguel de Guanes, a peninsular merchant resident in Asunción, received a load of goods from Francisco Fernández Dozal of Buenos Aires. The latter remitted these goods, worth some 1,648 pesos, to Guanes at his "account and risk," revealing an association that continued beyond the era of independence.[53]

The cases of Guanes and Ysasí place in doubt the common supposition that Dr. Francia took an intransigently anti-Spanish and antimerchant view and drove those elements into the ground. Certainly foreigners and comerciantes lost political power at independence, and throughout Dr. Francia's long dictatorship, peninsular and other merchants faced capricious fines and even imprisonment for frivolous reasons. The state also confiscated the worldly goods of foreigners unfortunate enough to die in Paraguay during Dr. Francia's rule.[54] Nonetheless, some Spanish merchants continued their business operations long after Dr. Francia's assumption of power. Alexandro García Díez, a peninsular resident of Asunción, continued to engage in commerce and acted as the financial guardian of the Spanish-born bishop of Asunción as late as the 1830s.[55] The records of Emeterio Velilla, another Spaniard, reveal an active business into the 1830s as a money lender and general merchant.[56] Other Spaniards and Europeans did likewise. They had to watch themselves quite carefully, and when they were unable to meet the dictator's sudden and exorbitant exactions they sometimes found themselves in jail. Still, a few preferred to remain in Asunción and in business rather than leave the country or retreat to estates in the countryside. It is remarkable, but understandable, how in the fragmentary commercial records of the 1820s and 1830s the Recaldes, Baldovinos, Hadeos, Bedoyas, Decouds, Domecqs, and Machains—all sons or grandsons of peninsular merchants—are mentioned time and again.[57]

The trade in permitted ships to Buenos Aires, however, was always much less than the local trade between Corrientes and Pilar. There had been a flourishing commerce in cattle and salt between Paraguay and Corrientes in the colonial era, and even the political tensions of the 1820s and 1830s failed to destroy the natural trading patterns between these two river port towns. Most of Paraguay's products shipped to Pilar were ultimately transshipped to Corrientes, and the opposite held true for manufactures bound for the latter port. Dr. Francia knew that his nation needed this outlet, so he placed no insurmountable barriers before it. He nonetheless watched the activities of the peninsulares, Paraguayans, and Correntinos who either resided in or frequented Pilar on a regular basis.

Paraguayan products bound for Pilar traveled downriver in small craft under a naval escort. In this southernmost Paraguayan port they were warehoused along with items that arrived by cart from Pilar's hinterland. From Curupayty, near the mouth of the Paraná on the northern bank, small naval vessels escorted Correntino merchant ships upriver to Pilar.[58] Often merchants sent samples of their goods from these vessels anchored at Pilar all the way to Asunción so that the dictator might satisfy himself as to the quality. He then set his arbitrary price in yerba or tobacco on those imports. Merchants could take it or leave it, but from all indications most were quite satisfied with his prices.[59] They should have been; there was commonly a 100 percent price differential in yerba between Pilar and Corrientes. By way of this Correntino connection, Paraguay received cloth, clothing, iron, shoes, paper, and other finished and semifinished goods.

The Paraguayan government alone purchased arms and ammunition. Dr. Francia also strictly controlled the import of printed matter. For its purchases through Pilar, the government used products from in-kind taxation and from the state-owned and operated ranches. All other items remained in private hands. Private involvement inevitably invited contraband, and in 1826–27 an investigation into that problem at Pilar resulted in many arrests. Seven peninsular merchants were imprisoned for involvement and stripped of their property. Even a government official was charged with being an accomplice in that smuggling.[60] But commerce, foreign merchants residing at Pilar, and discreet smuggling all continued. The trade was too lucrative for the Paraguayan treasury to halt. Export duties on yerba and tobacco shipped through Pilar constituted a substantial part of the national income. Paraguayan yerba and tobacco retained their hold on platine tastes just as they had in colonial times. Upon the death of Dr. Francia and the tentative liberalization of Paraguayan commerce in the 1840s, Correntinos maintained their key role thanks to their knowledge of the Pilar trade.

As useful and important as the Pilar outlet was, commerce through that port focused mainly on Corrientes. And that city and province in the 1820s and 1830s was loosely subject to Buenos Aires. The former viceregal capital had never surrendered its claim to Paraguay, and Dr. Francia desired an alternative trade route. For that reason the dictator opened commerce southward through Itapúa, a small town on the Alto Paraná. From there, exports moved through Candelaria and over the old Jesuit Missions land bridge to the Uruguay and the Brazilian port of São Borja. The consolidation of the lieutenant governorship of Misiones in 1805 into the person of the governor-intendent of Paraguay had given the new republic a vague claim to this territory.[61]

In 1817 Paraguayan armed forces crossed the Paraná and occupied Candelaria. That former Jesuit capital had been a no-man's land since Artiquista and Paraguayan troops had fought for it in 1814. Now the Paraguayan occupation made possible a relatively secure overland passage and trade for Paraguayan merchants to the southeast. To ensure Paraguayan authority over this trade nexus, Dr. Francia ordered a series of fortifications to be constructed in the Candelaria and Itapúa region, and he ordered the region to be garrisoned.[62] Since these fortified positions alone were insufficient to dominate the disputed areas between the Alto Paraná and the Uruguay, the dictator also marshaled resources to patrol the zone and to escort merchant caravans. A small garrison was stationed in the ruins of Candelaria along with even smaller temporary way-stations at Santo Tomás, San Carlos, and, periodically, Santo Tomé. This placed the Paraguayans in an excellent position to maintain trade contacts with the Brazilian port of São Borja on the Uruguay River. While none of these steps assured absolute Paraguayan sovereignty over Misiones, they did make trade feasible, and the region benefited accordingly.

Interested merchants from Brazil's Rio Grande do Sul operated in Itapúa as early as 1819. Their activities were strictly regulated by Dr. Francia, who wished to limit contacts between Paraguayans and foreigners and thus protect his regime from foreign (especially porteño) influence. The Riograndense presence in Itapúa represented a deviation from Dr. Francia's general predilection for a closed Paraguay, but at the same time the link with São Borja served the republic well. This commercial safety valve permitted an alternative to Pilar for the passage of tobacco and yerba in exchange for needed armaments, paper, and manufactured goods.

Unlike the commercial network associated with Pilar, the Itapúa network received some sanction through diplomatic channels. In January 1822 Pablo Machado, an envoy of the new Brazilian empire, arrived in Asunción to discuss the possibility of formal commercial relations. The dictator was well pleased with this de facto recognition and agreed to a one-year opening of Itapúa to Brazilian commerce—but he restricted trade to that one port.[63] Since the empire had rendered São Borja safe for the Paraguayan merchants who earlier took their wares to Brazil, Dr. Francia decided to allow the trade to remain open indefinitely. Commerce grew quickly.

The major diplomatic aim of the empire in the Plata was to prevent the consolidation of a United Provinces of Argentina under porteño aegis. To accomplish this, the Brazilians wooed Paraguay with promises of expanded commerce and official recognition. The promise of recognition went unfulfilled, but the Itapúa commercial connection remained strong.[64] Brazil's involvement in the Cisplatine War of 1825–28 and later the Farrapo Rebellion of 1835–45 in which the empire's southernmost province rebelled against Rio de Janeiro did little to disturb that trade. For example, tobacco and yerba exports to Brazil through Itapúa were as high for the war years of 1838 and 1839 as they had been for many peace time periods.[65]

The Itapúa commerce was important to eastern Paraguay between the 1820s and the 1840s because the better part of the tobacco and yerba maté exchanged in the trade was drawn from the Yuty region some 62.5 miles to the north of the Alto Paraná.[66] Several state ranches in the same locale provided the livestock and hides for much of the state's share in this commerce. Yuty, however, was so isolated from the rest of the nation as to invite smuggling on the part of both outsiders and its own inhabitants.[67]

Although Itapúa possessed only some 2,000 inhabitants in the mid-1820s, it became a key entrepôt of the republic and a scene of great mercantile activity. It handled a large portion of the imports of the republic, which included armaments, paper, cloth, ponchos, vinegar, oil, wine, hats, drugs, and iron goods. Dr. Francia even arranged for the importation of gaily painted children's toys for sale at the state store in Asunción.[68]

The Brazilian merchants resident in Itapúa were a favored lot. Although they were few, they exercised great influence over the affairs of the region. Their influence was such that Portuguese quickly became the lingua franca of Itapúa, displacing even Guaraní in its utility.[69] As for their personal lives, the Brazilian traders enjoyed an official toleration not normally allowed the Paraguayan residents of this town. In 1831 Dr. Francia admonished the chief Paraguayan official in this district to ignore the women that accompanied some of the merchants. The merchants were not Paraguayan citizens and had come only temporarily to Itapúa. Paraguay did not have the right, therefore, to judge their morals. The official's ill-advised actions had already caused one merchant to abandon Itapúa—much to the dictator's vexation. Dr. Francia concluded his reprimand by stating that the official's action "only cheats the Treasury out of customs receipts and the populace of an abundance of wares. See the trouble you have caused with your imprudence and thoughtlessness!"[70]

The dictator's favor did not go unnoticed by the merchants, who generally accorded him every support. They reported regularly, for example, on the movements of Correntino troops in that region, for Corrientes also claimed the entirety of the Misiones. The merchants' regard for Dr. Francia was based on the common interest in keeping Itapúa and the Misiones open to trade. In general, their combined efforts proved successful.[71]

Strangely, we know more about the activities of Brazilian merchants in this trade than we do about Paraguayan traders. The comandant of Itapúa kept track of Brazilians there, but the materials recording Paraguayan activities seem either to have disappeared from the Asunción archives or never to have arrived there. Nonetheless, enough is known to state that this commerce involved many Paraguayans, particularly in the transport of goods into Itapúa from the hinterland. More than the Pilar trade, the Itapúa commerce offered even humble Paraguayans a chance to better themselves economically. For instance, Eucebio Pereyra, a free *pardo* of Asunción, carried trade all the way to Itapúa, and Paraguayans of higher social stature did the same.[72] This internal trade of Paraguay which fueled the Itapúa commerce is almost completely unknown, but it, like the Pilar trade, indicates the existence of an active group of private merchants in Dr. Francia's Paraguay. At the same time Paraguayan merchants, with passports from the dictator, traveled to São Borja in pursuit of wares.

Many impediments existed, however, to a safe passage across Misiones. Often the Paraguayans provided military escorts for merchant caravans, but sometimes the traders had to fend for themselves. And this, after all, was bandit-infested territory.[73] The fundamental drawback to the trans-Misiones traffic, however, was political. As long as the border between Paraguay and Corrientes remained unclear, commerce could not proceed smoothly. In the beginning Paraguay had the upper hand in this area, but Correntino expansion to the east ultimately challenged Paraguayan authority.

In the 1820s Paraguay dominated the land bridge. However, hostilities erupted in the early 1830s at roughly the same time that rumors spread about a curious scheme conceived by the porteño leadership to sell Misiones land to certain British investors for settlement and exploitation. When informed of this plan, Dr. Francia left no room for doubt as to his position:

> The lands between the Aguapey and Uruguay belong to Paraguay and not to Buenos Aires which for the past twenty years has not

> even thought about them. It is now clear that [Buenos Aires] has conspired to appropriate this territory and feign its sale to these Englishmen only to impede and cut the Brazilian trade with Paraguay, which has hurt them as much as they envy it.[74]

The colonization did not occur, but Governor Pedro Ferré of Corrientes did move troops into the disputed territory.

The events of 1832–34 never went beyond a few skirmishes. Apparently, Ferré was anxious to exaggerate the Paraguayan threat to obtain political and material aid from the lower provinces for other ends.[75] Paraguayan resistance was totally ineffectual, and after a brief campaign the Correntinos occupied the Candelaria region in September 1832.[76]

The Correntino occupation lasted only two years. Although the Correntino government attempted to tax the transit of goods across the Misiones, its efforts were ineffectual. At that time the Misiones was relatively useless to Corrientes since both the population and the commerce of the province were located far from the area in contest. On the other hand Paraguay needed it. It was only a matter of time before an avenging Paraguayan military expedition crossed into Misiones and expelled the invaders. By 1834 the critical points of passage were again under Paraguayan control, and commerce with Brazil resumed even in the face of the Farrapo Rebellion.

The death of Dr. Francia in 1840 left Paraguay in a temporary state of political confusion. Eventually Don Carlos Antonio López dominated the government of the republic. He desired a cautious reopening of relations with the nations of the Río de la Plata and other powers.[77] However, he could not contend with the strength of Juan Manuel de Rosas of Buenos Aires. That porteño caudillo never acknowledged Paraguayan independence, and López was forced to secure the Misiones route. On the other hand, Paraguay under his leadership in the 1840s took a more active role in coalitions against the porteños. At one point in 1845 the Paraguayan government sent an expeditionary force to Corrientes to aid that province in a rebellion against Rosas.[78] The rebellion and the expeditionary force were utter failures. In consequence, López ordered the strengthening of defenses on Paraguay's southern borders in mid-1847.[79]

In framing a plan of defense, López did not differentiate between Rosas himself and Rosas's new clients in Corrientes. Nor did the Paraguayan leader sit idle when the Itapú trade seemed threatened. In 1849, just as Dr. Francia had done many years before, López moved to assure Paraguayan sovereignty over the Misiones by military means. In June of that year an expedition under the command of Hungarian mercenary, Francisco Wisner de Morgenstern, advanced into the disputed territory with instructions from López to secure the territory all the way to the Uruguay.[80]

Don Carlos clearly meant the expedition to assure that the lines of trade between Itapúa (after 1846 called Encarnación) and São Borja remained open. The Brazilians, however, did not wish at that time to endanger their status as neutrals in the smoldering platine conflict.[81] Therefore, the commerce desired by Paraguay did not revive, and Wisner did not tarry in Misiones for long. He limited his offensive to several minor forays against the Correntino Rosistas and their Entreriano allies. These engagements proved inconclusive, and by the early part of 1850 the Paraguayans had returned to the Paraná, making only occasional raids against the Correntinos over the next two years.[82] Indeed, López appeared to have foreseen the eventual lessening of importance of the Itapuáa trade as the political complexion of the Río de la Plata changed. Only if armaments from Brazil needed to be imported did he appear to deem it worthy of revitalization. In the end, Paraguay decided to retain the Candelaria district, but not primarily for commercial reasons.

The 1849 Paraguayan expedition to the Río Uruguay was for all practical purposes the last serious utilization of this "vent" for trade, and ironically it resulted in such destruction that even had a revitalization been desired, it would have proven difficult. The retreating Paraguayans decided they could no longer hold various villages in the land bridge and burned them to the ground. They also seized large quantities of livestock and drove them back to Paraguay.[83] Political reasons in the 1810s had prompted Dr. Francia to construct the Itapúa–São Borja trade route in the first place. Now, as the López saw quite clearly, the overall political situation in the Río de la Plata was on the brink of rapid change.

The abandonment of the Itapúa route coincided with the creation of the alliance that eventually toppled Juan Manuel de Rosas. Paraguay, after Rosas's fall in 1852, no longer needed the Río Uruguay outlet. The new Argentine government recognized Paraguayan independence. The subsequent reopening of the traditional Paraguay-Paraná river route to Asunción restored the old Carrera del Paraguay—or at least a good imitation of it. Merchant vessels again moved freely along the rivers as trade reverted to its earlier pattern.

Adverse political conditions had destroyed the Carrera del Paraguay; now political conditions also restored it. Much had changed since the colonial period, but Paraguay's traditional markets yet remained in the south, and the quickest, most efficient way to those markets was by the rivers. The republic needed finished goods just as much as in the colonial era, and the traditional river route was still the most efficient way to supply those needs. It is remarkable how much the commerce of Paraguay in the decade before the Great War of 1864–70, resembled that of the colonial Carrera. Only in one consideration—a higher degree of state control over such commerce—was there any lasting legacy of the Dr. Francia era. To be sure, even on this point, a certain parallel with colonial times was manifested. The Bourbon administrators of the intendancy of Paraguay had always favored an activist role for the state. Dr. Francia simply followed their lead, expanding the state prerogatives when he felt it necessary. The unstable political situation to the south led him to intervene in all facets of the economy, but in matters of foreign trade there was much in the old order that he would have preferred to restore. He never had the opportunity to do so. More than a decade passed after his death before Paraguay again enjoyed an open commerce—but then it looked much as it had before. Politics may have distorted the workings of the traditional trade route after independence, but given a fair chance it reasserted itself with surprisingly little fuss.

Notes

1. The economic impact of the immigration of Spaniards to the Río de la Plata, beginning around 1760, awaits study. We need to know more about the origins, economic rise, and associations of these newcomers.

2. Still the best overview for the changes in the Río de la Plata in the late 1770s is John Lynch, *Spanish Colonial Administration, 1782–1810: The Intendant System in the Viceroyalty of the Río de la Plata* (London, 1958). The rise of commodity prices for Paraguayan products in the last two decades of the eighteenth century was marked. See Governor Bernardo de Velazco of Paraguay to Real Dirección de la Real Renta de Tabacos, Asunción, 19 December 1807, in Archivo Nacional de Asunción (Paraguay), Sección Histórica (hereafter cited as ANA-SH), vol. 203.

3. For the matter of diputados consulares, see Germán Tjarks, *El Consulado de Buenos Ayres y sus proyecciones en la historia del Río de la Plata,* 2 vols. (Buenos Aires, 1962), 1:80–91 and 2:574–78, 944–45. Unfortunately, Tjarks is somewhat weak in his discussion of the diputados of the littoral.

4. For the great changes in the economy of Paraguay during the viceregal era, see Rafael Eladio Valázqez, *El Paraguay en 1811* (Asunción, 1966). For production of timber, tobacco, and other Paraguayan products in this period, as well as a discussion of life on the Carrera, see Jerry W. Cooney, *Economía y sociedad en la intendencia del Paraguay* (Asunción, 1990).

5. An excellent example of the commercial and legal use of poderes is Pleito de Gregori de la Cerda, apoderado de Basilio Sorante, Asunción, 26 July 1809,

ANA–Sección Judicial y Civil (hereafter cited as ANA-SJC), vol. 1961. Also see Joseph Díaz de Bedoya, apoderado de D.n Nicolás de Ygareda, Asunción, 13 December 1790, ANA–Sección Nueva Encuadernación (hereafter cited as ANA-NE), vol. 288.

6. See consignment of goods in Noticia de la carga que conduse la Garandumba de D.n Salvador Cavanas y Ampuero . . ., Asunción, 27 August 1780, in "Guías 1780," ANA-NE 445; and Cuenta de vista y liquido producto de una angada de maderas que remite a mi consinuacion . . ., Diego Antonio Pombo y Comp. a, Buenos Aires, 14 August 1804, ANA-SJC 1949.

7. An excellent source for littoral business dealings in the 1780s that illustrates this type of continual association is the Gaspar de Santa Coloma papers in the Archivo General de la Nacion in Buenos Aires. See Libro de Cuentas corrientes con las Provincias del Tucumán i Paraguay, Documentación Donada, Archivo General de la Nación (hereafter cited as AGN), legajo 7-6-5-9. For consignment of 178 tercios of yerba by a longtime Paraguayan associate, see "Guía" to Manuel Pérez Isquirido que de quenta, costo y riesgo de D.n Gregorio Lopez de Vigo, a consignacion de don Gaspar de Santa Coloma, Asunción, 10 March 1783, in "Guías 1783," ANA-NE 11.

8. See the running credit in the account of José de Casal, a merchant-rancher and yerba-promoter of Paraguay who in 1789–93 received 6,961 pesos and 6 1/2 reales credit from Gaspar de Santa Coloma and repaid it in the same period by shipments of yerba, libranzas, and consignments. Cuenta de José de Casal, Documentación Donada (Libro de Caja no. 1, 1787), AGN 7-6-5-13.

9. For an indication of the mark-up at Buenos Aires, see Susan Migden Socolow, *The Merchants of Buenos Aires, 1778–1810: Family and Commerce* (London, 1978), 60. For mark-up and profits on shipments of Paraguayan goods downriver, see Jerry W. Cooney, "Forest Industries and Trade in Late Colonial Paraguay," *Journal of Forest History,* 23:4 (October 1979): 195; and Cuenta gral. q.e rindo yo D. Mariano Claucel como Apoderado de D. Ant.o Ros y Roura . . ., Asunción, 23 October 1800, ANA-NE 2894.

10. Difficulties encountered with the use of encomienda labor in Paraguay by the 1770s are mentioned in Agustín Fernando de Pinedo, Informe al Rey de España acerca de la pobreza de la Provincia y de la opresión de los indios, Asunción, 29 January 1777, *Revista del Instituto Paraguayo,* 6:52 (1905): 3, 12–13. For the shift to salaried labor, see Juan Carlos Garavaglia, *Economía, sociedad y regiones* (Buenos Aires, 1987), 239–45.

11. Renée Ferrer de Arréllaga. *Un siglo de expansión colonizadora: los orígenes de Concepción* (Asuncion, 1985), 27.

12. "Hacienda que salió del Paraguay el año de 1776," in Juan Francisco Aguirre, "Diario de Capitán de Fragata d. Juan Francisco Aguirre," *Revista de la Biblioteca Nacional* (Buenos Aires), 17:43/44 (1949): 372.

13. "Guías 1808," ANA-NE 1159.

14. Efraím Cardozo, *El Paraguay colonial: Las raices de la nacionalidad* (Buenos Aires, 1959), 106; and Razón de los Tercios de Yerba que salieron de esta Provincia en el ultimo quinquenio . . . , Ministros de R.1 Hacienda del Paraguay Pedro de Oscariz and José de Elizalde, Asunción, 28 November 1808, ANA-NE 1790. The arroba was equal to approximately twenty-five English pounds.

15. Viceroy marqués de Sobremonte to Minister of the Treasury Miguel Cayetano Soler, Buenos Aires, 29 August 1804, Archivo General de Indias, Audiencia de Buenos Aires (hereafter cited as AGI-BA), legajo 135.

16. Consular Deputy Gregorio Thadeo de la Cerda to Governor Lázaro de Ribera of Paraguay, Asunción, 27 July 1798, AGN 9-4-7-4.

17. Governor Ribera to Viceroy Antonio Olaguer Feliú, Asunción, 19 August 1798, ANA-SH 173.

18. Don Francisco Pinto to Viceroy Manuel Vertiz, Buenos Aires, 20 December (?) 1783, in Recursos que hace a esta Superioridad . . . sobre el Flete de unas Carretas, año de 1784, AGN 9-37-8-2.

19. Concolorcorvo, *El Lazarillo: A Guide for Inexperienced Travelers Between Buenos Aires and Lima, 1773* (Bloomington, IN, 1965), 93.

20. Garavaglia, *Economía, sociedad y regiones,* 245–48; and Superintendent Francisco de Paula Sanz to Director General of the Real Renta de Tabacos Pedro Dionisio Gálvez, Buenos Aires, 6 February 1786, AGI-BA 421.

21. Ibid. Superintendent Francisco de Paula Sanz to Director General of the Real Renta de Tabacos Pedro Dionisio Gálvez, Buenos Aires, 6 February 1786, in AGI-BA 421.

22. Subdelegate of the Corrientes Treasury Joseph Fernández Blanco to the Director General of the R.1 Renta de Tabacos D.n Francisco de Urdaneta about a libranza to D.n Eugenio José Balbastro by D.n José Riera in the sum of 533 pesos and 5 5/7 reales de plata, Corrientes, 2 October 1793, Archivo General de la Provincia de Corrientes, Documentos de Gobierno (hereafter cited as AGPC-DG), legajo 47. Governor Ribera to Viceroy Joaquín del Pino, Asunción, 19 April 1803, ANA-SH 192; and Viceroy the Marqués de Sobremonte to Governor Ribera, Buenos Aires, 17 December 1804, ANA-SH 427.

23. Cargo de caudales a la Tesoreria de esta Factoria y Administracion General en el año de 1809, Ministros de R.1 Hacienda Pedro de Oscariz y José de Elizalde, Asunción, 31 December 1809, ANA-NE 3088.

24. Contrato público of Juan Duarte de Goyrí with Juan Francisco Decoud, Asunción, 27 July 1790, ANA-NE 288.

25. This is an extremely complicated financial issue, but the best discussion about how local merchants manipulated the six-real peso to their benefit is Director General de la Real Renta de Tabacos Francisco de Paula Sanz to el Cabildo de Asunción, Asunción, 10 April 1779, ANA-SH 144.

26. In the 1770s Asunción possessed no *plateros.* By 1797 seven such silversmiths practiced their trade in the city. Velázquez, *El Paraguay en 1811,* 84. For the private hoarding of silver, see Charles Washburn, *The History of Paraguay,* 2 vols. (Boston, 1871), 1:443.

27. "Tabla de comercio del Paraguay," in Félix de Azara, *Descripción e historia del Paraguay y del Río de la Plata,* 2 vols. (Madrid, 1847), 1:313–14.

28. Miguel Lastarria, *Colonias orientales del Río Paraguay o de la Plata,* in Facultad de Filosofía y Letras, *Documentos para la historia argentina* (Buenos Aires, 1914), 3:177.

29. Causas que influyeron a los reiterados naufragos que se experimentan en las naves de este trafico, Disputado Consular Fermín de Arredondo y Lobatón to Consulado de Buenos Aires, Asunción, 19 March 1798, AGN 9-4-7-4.

30. Sindico Juan Ygnacio de Ezcurra to the Consulado of Buenos Aires, Buenos Aires, 20 March 1797, AGN 9-4-7-4.

31. Governor Ribera to the Consulado of Buenos Aires, Asunción, 19 August 1798, AGN 9-4-7-4.

32. For example, see Velázquez, *El Paraguay en 1811*. What is sad, but not surprising, is the near total slighting of the Carrera del Paraguay by Argentine historians of the colonial period. Even though this commerce was an important part of the economic activity of Buenos Aires, the best documentation on it lies in upriver depositories. Porteño historians are all too prone to believe that anything that concerns Buenos Aires can only be found in the depositories of that city—or perhaps in the Archivo General de Indias, but hardly in the interior. Then too, the tragic state of historical research in Argentina today undoubtedly contributes to the disregard of the Carrera.

33. Scholars know surprisingly little about Las Conchas. Still, see Aguirre, "Diario," 357–59; and Enrique Udaonda, "Reseña histórica del Partido de las Conchas" in vol. 21 of *Contribución a la historia de los pueblos de la Provincia de Buenos Aires* (La Plata, 1942), 20–22.

34. See the relevant chapter on shipbuilding in Cooney, *Economía y sociedad.*

35. Guía de la R.1 Aduana de Buenos Aires no. 3706 fecha 2 de Diz.re de 1790—a D.n Miguel Xeronimo Ferragut . . . Buenos Aires . . ., in "Guías 1790–1791," AGPC-DG 57.

36. Félix de Azara to the Consulado of Buenos Aires, Buenos Aires, 15 December 1798, AGN 9-4-7-4.

37. Aguirre, "Diario," 404–7; and J. P. Robertson and W. P. Robertson, *Letters on Paraguay: Comprising an Account of a Four Years' Residence in that Republic Under the Government of the Dictator Francia,* 2nd ed., 3 vols. (London, 1839), 2:208–11.

38. Juan Bautista Rivarola Paoli is currently working on a study of the hacienda in Paraguay. In his discussion of the late colonial period he sheds light upon the political-economic activities of many of these immigrants. They profited by being members of the Asunción cabildo through participation in the auctions of the "propios de la ciudad." One profited by being the *administrador* of the city's hospital, others by membership in the Junta de Diezmos. By 1795 these peninsulares had a lock on such minor political posts, and they milked them for all they were worth. No wonder that Dr. José Gaspar de Francia, one of the few criollos in a minor position of political power in Asunción, later evidenced as dictator of Paraguay a deep suspicion of the Spanish-born.

39. For the events of independence, see Luis Vittone, *El Paraguay en la lucha por su independencia* (Asunción, 1960). For the often complex relations between Buenos Aires and Paraguay in the early independence era, see Julio César Chaves, *Historia de las relaciones entre Buenos-Ayres y el Paraguay, 1810–1813* (Buenos Aires, 1959).

40. Chavez, *Historia de las relaciones,* 186–214; and Treaty between Buenos Aires and Paraguay, Asunción, 12 October 1811, ANA-SH 214.

41. Still the best survey (though very nationalistic in tenor) of Dr. Francia is Julio César Chaves, *El Supremo Dictador,* 4th ed. (Madrid, 1964). A revisionist view of Francia and early Paraguay that presents the dictator as a popular reformer is

Richard Alan White, *Paraguay's Autonomous Revolution, 1810–1840* (Albuquerque, 1978). Also placing Francia in the perspective of early national Paraguay is John Hoyt Williams, *The Rise and Fall of the Paraguayan Republic, 1800–1870* (Austin, 1979), 19–99.

42. Chaves, *Historia de las relaciones entre Buenos-Ayres y el Paraguay,* 192.

43. Reglamento de Gobierno, Paraguayan Congress of 1813, Asunción, 12 October 1813, ANA-SH 222.

44. White, *Paraguay's Autonomous Revolution,* 227.

45. Ibid.

46. Tulio Halperín-Donghi, *Politics, Economics, and Society in Argentina in the Revolutionary Period* (Cambridge, Eng., 1975), 86. An excellent account of the activities of British merchants in the littoral of the Río de la Plata is given in J. P. and W. P. Robertson, *Letters on South America: Comprising Travels on the Banks of the Parana and Rio de la Plata* 3 vols. (London, 1843).

47. Robertson, *Letters on Paraguay,* 2:283–84.

48. The isolation of Paraguay in the 1820s and 1830s and Francia's control over that republic's society and economy has led some scholars to ascribe to Francia's regime an internal economic development untouched by dependence upon the outside world as well as a popular radicalism that preserved the essence of Paraguayan culture. See White, *Paraguay's Autonomous Revolution,* and E. Bradford Burns, *The Poverty of Progress: Latin America in the Nineteenth Century* (Berkeley, 1980), 128–31. Cooney and Thomas L. Whigham disagree with this revisionist interpretation. They maintain that Francia was actually a conservative nationalist, rather than a popular reformer. They also assert that from the era of independence to the Paraguayan War, the economy of the republic grew, but it did not change. Defense-related state expenditures on telegraph lines, arsenals, shipyards, a foundry, steamboats, and even a railroad in the 1850s had remarkably little impact upon the traditional economy of the republic. The issues of Francia's popular radicalism, dependency, and contribution to internal economic development are explored in greater detail in Whigham, *The Politics of River Trade: Tradition and Development in the Upper Plata, 1780–1870* (Albuquerque, 1991).

49. J. R. Rengger and M. Longchamps, *The Reign of Doctor Joseph Gaspard Roderick de Francia in Paraguay: being an account of a six years' residence in that republic from July, 1819 to May, 1825* (London, 1827), 96. Another source (worthy of mention even though polemically anti-Francia) that deals with the impact of this new isolation is Ramón Gil Navarro, *Veinte años en un calabozo: O sea la desgraciada historia de viente y tantos argentinos muertos o envejecidos en los calabozos del Paraguay,* 3rd ed. (Asunción, n.d.).

50. Agustín de Eyzaguirre to Manuel Yavar (merchant of Buenos Aires), Santiago de Chile, 12 May 1813, in Jaime Eyzaguirre, ed., *Archivo Epistolar de la Familia Eyzaguirre, 1747–1854* (Buenos Aires, 1960), 209–10. Testamento de D.n Josef Coene, José Gregorio Peyeyra and José Tomás Ysasí to Doctor Francia, Asunción, May 1823, ANA-Sección Propiedades y Testamentos, vol. 839.

51. Williams, *Rise and Fall of the Paraguayan Republic,* 40.

52. Francia to Subdelegate of Pilar Torres, Asunción, 16 February 1822, ANA-NE 3106.

53. Miguel Guanes to Francia, Asunción, February 1826, ANA-SJC 2047.

54. Rengger and Longchamps, *The Reign of Doctor Joseph Roderick de Francia in Paraguay,* 172–73.

55. Alexandro García Díez and Juan Pérez Bernal to Francia, Asunción, 1825, ANA-SH 237. By the mid-1830s, however, these two Spaniards had fallen afoul of the dictator. Decree of Francia, Asunción, 30 June 1834, ANA-SH 242.

56. Business Records of Emeterio Velilla, Asunción, 1813–39, in ANA-SJC 2191.

57. The continuity of elites from the late colonial era into the national period deserves more study. It appears that not only did the native and immigrant peninsular merchant class survive the Francia era, but so did most of the traditional landholding elite of Paraguay. This contradicts the common view that Dr. Francia eradicated both groups. Too much evidence exists, however, revealing that such eradication was only partial. The authors currently are studying this continuity and transition of the Paraguayan elites from the colonial era into the national period.

58. Francia to Comandante of Pilar José Tomás Gill, Asunción, 21 December 1825, ANA-SH 708; and same to same, Asunción, 24 January 1827, ANA-SH 3411.

59. Francia to Comandante of Pilar José Tomás Gill, Asunción, 22 December 1825, ANA-SH 708.

60. Francia to Comandante of Pilar José Tomás Gill, Asunción, 26 May 1826, ANA-SH 238. Also see Williams, *Rise and Fall of the Paraguayan Republic,* 73.

61. Lynch, *Spanish Colonial Administration,* 110–15; and Pedro Somellera, "Notas del Doctor Don Pedro Somellera a la introducción que ha puesto el Doctor Rengger a su ensayo histórico sobre la revolución del Paraguay," in Museo Mitre, *Documentos del Archivo de Belgrano,* 7 vols. (Buenos Aires, 1914), 3:314–15.

62. This area across the Paraná is the present site of the Argentine city of Posadas. Alejo Peyret, *Cartas sobre Misiones* (Buenos Aires, 1881), 34–35. Also see V. Martin de Moussey, *Description géographique et statistique de la Confédération Argentine* 3 vols. (Paris, 1860–64), 3:693.

63. Francisco Wisner, *El dictador del Paraguay José Gaspar de Francia* (Buenos Aires, 1957), 118–19; and John Hoyt Williams, "Paraguayan Isolation Under Dr. Francia: A Reevaluation," *Hispanic American Historical Review,* 52:1 (February, 1972): 102–22.

64. Williams, "Paraguayan Isolation Under Francia," 110–12; and R. Antonio Ramos, "Correa de Camara en Asunción," *Boletín del Instituto de Investigaciones Históricas* (Buenos Aires), 30 (1952): 60–71.

65. Cuaderno de derecho de extracción (1830), ANA-NE 2928; Cuaderno de derecho de extracción (1831), ANA-NE 2936; Cuaderno de derecho de extracción (1833), ANA-NE 2951; and White, *Paraguay's Autonomous Revolution,* 246–52.

66. Francia to Delegate of Itapúa. Asunción, 9 October 1832, ANA-SH 241.

67. In May 1838 one inhabitant of Yuty, Roque Romero, attempted to introduce 600 pesos of goods illegally obtained in Itapúa. Contraband passed in the opposite direction as well, many bales (tercios) making their way south *sin guía*. Expediente of Roque Romero, Yuty, 17 May 1838, ANA-SH 243; and Fernando Yturburo (smuggler) to Francia, 9 May 1839, ANA-NE 2611.

68. Jean Etienne Richard de Grandsire, "Briefe aus Paraguay, mitgeheilt von Alexander von Humbolt," *Hertha, Zeitschrift für Erd-, Voelker-, und Staatenkunde*

(Stuttgart and Tübingen, 1825), 702–4. Demand for these items, while limited, remained relatively steady in the period under discussion. See Francia to Delegado of Itapúa, Asunción, 17 March 1832, ANA-SH 241; Francia to Delegado of Itapúa, Asunción 19 and 30 May 1837, ANA-SH 243; and Ramón León to Francia, Itapúa, 4 March 1827, ANA-NE 1894.

69. Genaro Berón de Astrada to Pedro Ferré, 1 February 1833, AGPC, Correspondencia Oficial, legajo 1833.

70. Francia to subdelegate of Itapúa, Asunción, 2 November 1831, ANA-SH 241; and José León Ramírez to Francia, Itapúa, 7 November 1831, ANA-Colección Rio Branco I-30, 22, 96 no. 1.

71. The grief expressed by these merchants on hearing of the death of Francia was reported as far away as Buenos Aires. *British Packet and Argentine News* (Buenos Aires), 19 December 1840.

72. Eucebio Pereyra to Francia, Asunción (?), 1838 (?), ANA-NE 1889; and Francisco Antonio Lescano to Francia, Asunción (?), March 1835, ANA-SJC 2096.

73. Francia to Delegate of Itapúa, Asunción, 15 February 1833, ANA-SH 242.

74. Francia to Comandante of Itapúa, Asunción, 22 December 1831, ANA-SH 241; and Francia to the Comandante of Concepción, Asunción, 18 August 1832, ANA-NE 3412.

75. In a letter to the governor of Santa Fe, Governor Ferré stressed the pernicious effect of the São Borja–Itapúa connection "through which passes all news of our political affairs and through which Francia obtains all manner of armaments and munitions. . . . this can only mean that the Dictator thinks big, that he wishes to take advantage of our domestic quarrels." Ferré to Domingo Cullen, Corrientes, 1 September 1832, in Pedro Ferré, *Memorias del Brigadier General,* 2 vols. (Buenos Aires, 1921), 1:422–23. The porteños initially promised help to the Correntinos; that aid never arrived. José Viamonte and Tomás Guido to Ferré, Buenos Aires, 30 January 1832, AGPC-Expedientes Administrativas 1834, legajo 41.

76. Francia to subdelegate of Itapúa José León Ramírez, Asunción, 8 September 1832, ANA-SH 241.

77. Julio César Chaves, *El Presidente López: vida y gobierno de don Carlos* (Buenos Aires, 1955), 20–26; and Peter A. Schmitt, *Paraguay und Europa: Die diplomatische Beziehungen unter Carlos Antonio Lopez und Francisco Solano Lopez, 1841–1870* (Berlin, 1963), 18–44.

78. Juan E. O'Leary, *La alianza de 1845 con Corrientes: Aparición de Solano López en el escenario del Plata* (Asuncion, 1945).

79. Juan Andrés Gelly to J. A. Gelly y Obes, Säo Borja, 31 August 1847, AGN-Documentos de la Biblioteca Nacional, 15093, legajo 756. López had ordered an extensive reconnaissance of the Misiones the previous year, probably to understand better the military situation in that region. López to Comandante Interino of Encarnación, Asunción, 28 August 1846, ANA-SH 276.

80. López to Wisner, Asunción, 23 January 1849, ANA-SH 286. Also see *El Paraguayo Independiente* (Asunción), 10 June 1848.

81. Francisco Solano López (?) to Colonel Basilio Antonio Ojeda, Paso de la Patria, 15 September 1849, ANA-NE 2003.

82. Manuel Florencio Mantilla, *Crónica histórica de Corrientes,* 2 vols., (Buenos Aires, 1928–29), 2:216–17.

83. Informe of Pedro Virasoro, Santo Tome, 9 June 1849, AGPC-EA 1849, legajo 102; and Marco Tulio Centeno, "San Juan de Hormiguero: Crónica de su orígen y desarrollo, antecedentes de la refundación de Santo Tomé (Corrientes)," *Primer Encuentro de Geohistoria Regional: Exposiciones* (1980): 159–62.

11

Conclusion

KENNETH J. ANDRIEN AND LYMAN L. JOHNSON

As the essays in this volume indicate, the state played an important role in shaping the socioeconomic development of Spanish America. Throughout the late colonial period the state often determined the context for economic growth by allocating labor, providing access to essential raw materials, subsidizing production, and compelling consumption. Crown policies helped to organize and sustain local, regional, and international market relationships. Over the course of the colonial period, producers for both domestic and export markets often depended on politically defined relations of production and exchange. The colonial economy developed in a symbiotic relationship with the state, rather than in competition with it.

Although independence brought profound political and economic changes in Spanish America, the legacy of state intervention in the economy endured. Independence led to a reallocation of economic resources, but it did not lead national elites to abandon an activist state. The diminished national regimes of Spanish America lacked the territorial reach and authority of their colonial predecessor. These fragile new governments lacked the ability, not the desire, to direct economic activity. As several contributors to this volume show, the tradition of an activist, dirigiste state survived the breakup of the empire.

Each essay in this collection provides a tightly focused investigation of an important issue in the political economy of Spanish America during the Age of Revolution. Taken together, however, they raise several broad comparative issues about continuities in the role of the state as an economic actor during this transitional epoch. In the remainder of this chapter, we will identify some of these key historical issues. Our intention is not to provide a synthesis of the authors' opinions or a narrow summary of their findings; instead, we will offer conclusions drawn both from these essays and from our own research in the hope that we will stimulate further research and debate.

The Political Economy of Mexico and South America, 1750–1850

Despite structural similarities in basic economic patterns, the provinces of Mexico and Spanish South America had evolved in different directions by the late Bourbon period. The centrality of the state is clear in both areas, but market forces were much stronger in Mexico. Therefore, the slow collapse of the colonial state between 1809 and 1825 had a more profound impact on the fragile South American regional economies. Although Mexico, too, entered a period of economic crisis and political instability following independence, its regional markets had greater coherence and resilience.

The persistence of colonial policies is most visible in the continued use of state power to appropriate and redistribute the wealth of indigenous communities. Although altered, the system of Amerindian tribute and some form of coerced participation in market exchanges persisted after independence. Brian Hamnett provides in Oaxaca the clearest evidence for the continuity of such colonial policies, but, as Kenneth Andrien suggests, these exploitative mechanisms endured also in Ecuador. As late as 1877 the capitation tax in Oaxaca provided nearly one-third of total state revenues, and the colonial tribute system continued essentially unchanged until 1857 in Ecuador. Jerry Cooney and Thomas Whigham also suggest that similar patterns endured in Paraguay.

The repartimiento de mercancías (the forced distribution of European and domestic wares to Amerindian communities by the corregidor or his agent) provides one important example of how intervention by the colonial state helped to establish the character of local markets. Although the repartimiento was a form of commerce, with profits determined in part by market forces, the system depended on the authority of the state and its agents. It was both a system of forced consumption and an indirect tax on indigenous production. Despite its importance in tying Amerindians to colonial market exchanges, particularly in the Andes, the repartimiento came under intense attack by Spanish reformers and some regional groups, particularly Amerindian communities by the 1770s. In the central Andes, the Tupac Amaru rebellion compelled the formal abolition of this onerous system. Yet a combination of bureaucratic inertia and elite economic self-interest allowed illegal vestiges of the institution to survive beyond independence. Even after the repartimiento de mercancías finally died out, local Spanish American elites tried to create alternative forms of state intervention to maintain their power and privileges over Amerindian producers and consumers.

The repartimiento de mercancías also illustrates some salient differences between the economic histories of Andean South America and Mexico. Both areas were important colonial textile producers distributing cloth to widely dispersed regional markets. In Ecuador, Spanish and creole entrepreneurs controlled the production of woolens to supply repartimiento quotas, relying on state support to recruit forced and wage labor from Amerindian villages. Since the Ecuadorian labor force in the highland obrajes also had to accept some of its compensation in textiles, much of the matrix of production and consumption depended on state power.

In Oaxaca the production and sale of textiles and cochineal relied on the repartimiento system, but there were two important differences from the Andean case. First, the production process remained in the control of indigenous communities throughout the colonial and early national periods. Cottage production and some residual communal autonomy characterized the work regime. This was quite different from the Ecuadorian obrajes, which employed poorly paid wage and *mita* laborers displaced from their communities. Second, the primary markets for Oaxaca's textile products were not as dependent on compelled consumption as were the markets for textiles in the Andes.

The evidence suggests that by the eighteenth century, there was a freer, more mature market in Mexico than in most of Spanish South America. This is not to say that Mexico had a true national market in the colonial period; the limited nature of its exchanges is clear. The subsistence crises that afflicted late colonial Mexico indicate that the local impact of crop failures was exacerbated by poor market intelligence, inadequate transportation systems, and other characteristics of limited market integration. Despite these structural weaknesses, late colonial Mexico clearly had developed an economic momentum that required a less active, interventionist state than in South America.

Similar characteristics were manifest in the political arena. New Spain certainly had a more uniform administrative structure and greater political stability than did the independent nation of Mexico in the 1820s and 1830s. The lack of economic integration suggests there was no colony-wide identity or informed agreement on fundamental political issues that united the citizenry. The viceroyalty of New Spain, with its many discrete microeconomies, had little potential to become a unified, modern nation-state in the early nineteenth century.

State Intervention in the Economy, 1750–1850

In the sixteenth century the colonial state began to connect the fragile regional economies of Spain's American colonies to international markets centered in Europe. The export of bullion, dyes, and other specialized products expanded rapidly because the colonial state concentrated scarce capital, labor, and management resources under its protective umbrella. These government-supported, long-distance relationships simultaneously evolved in an uneasy relationship with the more mundane and less profitable regional markets for grain and other subsistence goods.

Because the state concentrated resources in developing the export sector, little investment capital remained for roads and other forms of infrastructure in the colonies. The resulting high transportation costs and poor quality market intelligence hindered the development of domestic markets for basic consumption goods with low profit margins. Producers for profitable European markets, often located near the coast or tied to ports by the best roads, commonly had more up-to-date economic information than producers supplying local or regional markets.

The institutional structures and fiscal policies of the colonial state also favored the export sector. Spanish efforts to develop rational fiscal structures and maximize revenue from its vast American empire helped to concentrate public-sector institutions and government expenditures in regions connected to the Atlantic trade. Although historians have commonly noted the size of the colonial government—its intrusiveness, costliness, and susceptibility to elite manipulation—the role of the state in concentrating and distributing wealth remains little understood. As shown in Andrien's essay, the state's ability to extract wealth from the regional economies of Ecuador increased dramatically in the late eighteenth century. State fiscal policies compelled the transfer of wealth from the expanding cacao region and the already exploited highland indigenous communities to the creole and peninsular elites of Quito and to the metropolis. These policies promoted consumption at the expense of savings and investment in production.

Other essays provide additional examples of how the state played a role in directing regional economic development. Kendall Brown clearly demonstrates how state policies helped to determine levels of mining production in Mexico and Peru. Because of the close relationship between the supply and price of mercury and the production of silver, the government's position as monopoly mercury supplier influenced silver mining output throughout the Indies and dictated the success or failure of individual mining enterprises. Richard and Linda Salvucci and Aslán Cohen place the state-promoted expansion of the Mexican mining sector in its larger economic context. Mining profits—induced in part by lowered taxes and more abundant, less expensive mercury—boosted textile imports from Europe, which undercut local producers. Over the last decades of the colonial period, state policies led to the redirection of the colony's scarce investment capital away from the textile sector and limited the potential for greater employment in that sector.

The Río de la Plata provides an obvious example of state-induced development in the Bourbon era. The growth of Buenos Aires was heavily subsidized by transfers of wealth from Potosí and by the establishment of large and costly civilian bureaucracies and military garrisons. The government policies that promoted Paraguay's economic expansion in the late-colonial period are less well known. The establishment of the tobacco monopoly stimulated a profitable new agricultural sector in Paraguay. Because the estanco paid for tobacco in silver, the monopoly monetarized an economy whose expansion had been retarded by its reliance on barter and local script. Indeed, much of the integration of Paraguayan products in the widening circuits of the Río de la Plata's market economy depended in some way on the workings of the Bourbon bureaucracy. As Cooney and Whigham indicate, the use of libranzas to facilitate long-distance trade and and the use of the postal service and consulado agents to provide essential commercial intelligence played an important role in Paraguay's economic expansion.

Merchant families, such as the Iturbe e Iraeta, also relied on the international framework of state-supported monopolies and markets to guarantee profits. In the case of this Basque family, John Kicza outlines the components of their trade—Chinese goods, cochineal, indigo, cacao, and local manufactures—arrayed across the large canvas of the Pacific and Caribbean markets. Many of these commodities came from markets that were opened legally to Mexican merchants only with the proclamation of imperial free trade during the period 1765–89. According to the Salvuccis and Cohen, this same system provided colonial Mexican wheat producers with a portion of the Cuban market despite the higher cost and poorer quality of their products relative to foreign competitors. In Peru, similar state interventions prolonged the life of the poorly run Huancavelica mercury mine, even though cheaper mercury was available in Europe. Put directly, colonial state policies and the bureaucrats who enforced them played a central part in the development of Spain's American colonies. The sectoral distribution of government expenditures, combined with subsidies and protectionist legislation, managed to channel economic inputs in a manner analogous to the geographic features such as the Andean cordillera and the Río de la Plata estuary.

The state was also involved directly—and indirectly through monopoly agreements—in the production and sale of goods. Tobacco (and its by-products) and mercury are two obvious examples. In addition, gun powder, playing cards, and military stores were produced under license from the colonial regime. The state had an equally clear-cut impact on colonial labor markets. As Susan Deans-Smith points out, the tobacco monopoly was the single largest manufacturing employer in Mexico City, which was the biggest urban center in colonial Spanish America. The ability of monopoly workers to bring pressure on managers through work stoppages and direct action contributed to inefficiency and overmanning. Throughout the empire the crown employed laborers also for the construction and maintenance of fortifications, offices, courts, warehouses, jetties, docks, and roads. If the government's relatively large bureaucratic and military payrolls are added to the labor force in royal monopolies, construction projects, and the service sector, the impact of the state on employment becomes clear. In Buenos Aires, at least, even wage levels were affected by state involvement.

State policies compelling the labor of Amerindians and African slaves and their American-born descendants also bolstered the colonial mining industry and export agriculture because the exploitation of mineral and land resources required the mobilization of labor. In the first decades of Spanish settlement, colonists directly imposed labor requirements on indigenous peoples and arranged for the transfer of a few slaves from the peninsula or the Atlantic islands. When these private efforts proved inadequate, particularly after sixteenth-century epidemics devastated the Amerindian population, the need for the state to rationalize and augment the labor supply became obvious. Agents of the state organized the distribution of Amerindian corvée laborers among groups such as miners, dye producers, and the owners of textile mills. The state also played a role in regulating the numbers and destinations of African slaves coming to the empire. Such policies often proved central in determining the course of economic development and the character of social hierarchies in regions throughout Indies.

The Costly Legacy of State Intervention

State intervention in the development process proved costly over the long run in Spanish America. The empire's extensive bureaucracy and, after the 1770s, its large military establishment were expensive. Andrien demonstrates clearly that the per-capita tax burden in late colonial Ecuador was considerably greater than in British North America. This burden was even more onerous during the peak of the crisis in the highland textile industry. The crown imposed particularly heavy burdens, through consumption taxes or Amerindian tribute levies, on the poorest classes. Put simply, the distribution of wealth was a function of a political process that victimized the poor, the weak, and the geographically marginal.

Deans-Smith and Brown suggest that institutionalized inefficiencies in mining and the tobacco factory added indirect costs to production. These enterprises had little incentive to invest in new technology or improved efficiency. Despite problems in turning a profit in the tobacco monopoly's Mexico City manufactory, managers invested virtually no money in machinery or new production techniques. Factory workers also resisted efforts to increase productivity. Moreover, the problem of inadequate technology continued to plague tobacco production well into the national period. The decision to sustain the costly and inefficient Huancavelica mercury mine also resulted more from political than economic considerations. The Andean mining sector bore the resulting costs. Low levels of investment, in technology or in production generally, prevailed also in the city and province of Buenos Aires—a pattern that persisted after independence, at least until the fall of Rosas.

The empire's protected markets and redistributive mechanisms permitted favored producers to transfer the costs of inefficiency to consumers or, through the imposition of low wages, to their workers. When confronted by economic crisis, colonial businessmen usually reacted by petitioning the state for additional protection rather than by restructuring their enterprises. They usually sought and received preferential treatment in local markets and in allocations of labor, raw materials, and tax exemptions from the state. Politically well-connected economic interests in the British American colonies, such as Caribbean sugar planters, sometimes gained similar advantages. The use of state power to achieve economic advantage was not unusual in the eighteenth-century European world. What distinguishes the Spanish American from the British colonial experience was the level of the public sector's access to economic resources and the embedded cultural expectation that most enterprises would operate with state support.

Independence had a profound impact on the state's ability to influence the economy. No national government in Spanish America was able to command either the fiscal resources or the regulatory authority of the old colonial regime. Once independent, the nations of Spanish America lost the benefits of a uniform and stable monetary union, well-established credit conventions (such as those noted in Paraguay by Cooney and Whigham), and reliable access to forced Amerindian labor. In addition, chattel slavery had been undermined by the political necessity of enlisting black support for the rebellions against Spain. Although some of these changes were significant humanitarian achievements, in narrowly economic terms they meant that market forces, not the state, would control the allocation of needed labor resources. Marginally competitive industries dependent on access to forced labor had difficulty surviving after independence. Higher labor costs contributed to the collapse of Andean mining and textile industries as well as to the contraction of Oaxacan dye production.

Independence and the rapid appearance of national and provincial tariff and tax structures disrupted long-established commercial patterns. Merchant families, such as the Iturbe e Iraeta, had to restructure their mercantile activities to function in smaller, less profitable domestic markets or in more competitive international markets. Mexico's grain exporters faced direct competition from more efficient North American suppliers in the Cuban market. Peruvian and Mexican silver miners were forced, for the first time, to purchase their own supplies of mercury at market prices. Oaxacan dye producers confronted the expansion of Guatemalan dye exports followed by the appearance of synthetic European products. And Paraguayan ship builders and yerba growers lost their dominant position in the formerly restricted Platine markets.

These structural changes provided new opportunities as well as lost advantages. Often the most vibrant economic sectors following independence were those in which development had been curtailed by the colonial state in order to serve some fiscal or geopolitical purpose. The disappearance of Spanish commercial monopolies, for example, provided new opportunities for producers of agricultural exports, such as coffee, cacao, and hides. The rapid development of the grazing sector in the province of Buenos Aires is just one striking example of this process of transformation. As Lyman Johnson points out, the provincial economy grew impressively, and the distribution of wealth changed profoundly. The grazing-sector elite gained wealth shares relative to the poor and middle classes, and the countryside expanded more rapidly than the city of Buenos Aires.

Independence ended many integrated colonial commercial networks, particularly those centered in the mining zones of Peru and Upper Peru. This transformation of traditional market relations after 1825 was most painful to the regional mining, textile, and agrarian interests in the southern Andes. In the colonial era, the state created compensatory mechanisms to limit the effects of geographic isolation and the resulting high transportation costs. With independence, producers of textiles, livestock, and alcoholic beverages for these markets found themselves disadvantaged both by the loss of protection and by the newly erected tariff barriers of the independent governments. As a result, it was not until the California gold rush and the guano boom—both external stimuli—that economic recovery began in earnest for most of the old viceroyalty of Peru. Although less disruptive, similar losses of intercolonial markets affected Paraguay, Oaxaca, and Buenos Aires.

Regionalism also undermined the process of creating genuine national markets in the early national period. Centrifugal economic forces weakened domestic markets throughout much of Spanish America, especially in Mexico and Argentina. Timothy Anna is convincing when he argues that regionalism was the primary force leading to the overthrow of Iturbide. It was also a major obstacle to economic growth. Anna's statement that there was no such thing as "Mexico" describes more than the inability to agree on a name for the new nation. The Salvuccis and Cohen make clear that there was no "Mexican" market either. This incomplete market structure was inherited, in large part, from the colonial era. At that time weak, unpredictable markets inhibited the production even of basic consumer goods. The regional forces unleashed by independence naturally curtailed any existing momentum towards greater integration. This pattern is exemplified by the breakup of the centralized tobacco monopoly, as the state governments gained control over regional manufactories. The lack of integrated national markets also encouraged the development of the export sector. Environmental obstacles, poor infrastructure, and the rapid proliferation of provincial taxes, customs duties, and destabilizing monetary experiments combined to discourage investment in the internal economy of most new nations. Impediments to profitable enterprise proved less threatening in the export arena, and when they appeared, producers could compensate by relying on superior credit mechanisms, more reliable market intelligence, preferential access to desired imports, and access to hard currency. The movement of capital resources into the grazing sector in the province of Buenos Aires, for example, cannot be explained simply by the pull of the British market and the machinations of British merchants. It occurred also because the weak national market in Argentina failed to compensate for the loss of colonial commerce with Paraguay and Bolivia. Historians still know far too little about important factors—such as labor costs, natural resources, and capital stock—to assess the vitality of domestic markets on the eve of the nineteenth-century export boom. Nevertheless, the flow of both domestic and foreign investment capital into export production throughout Spanish America undoubtedly represented rational allocations based on experience.

Despite the loss of revenue and authority by national governments, the region's new political elites attempted to maintain essential elements of the colonial state's traditional economic role. Paraguay provides a clear example. Whigham has elsewhere emphasized that the political economy of the Francia government often continued the policies enacted by the Bourbon bureaucracy after 1776.[1] Abundant evidence suggests that Francia and his immediate political heirs attempted to use the state as a primary instrument of economic development and management. In the era before 1865, no important area of the Paraguayan economy operated without significant government supervision, protection, or direct participation.

Hamnett describes an activist, if fiscally strapped, Oaxacan state government that promoted unlikely development schemes, such as a transisthmian canal and various plans for Pacific port development. It encouraged the cultivation of new crops, such as coffee, and attempted to reinvigorate residual colonial industries such as cochineal. This state government also actively solicited foreign investment, especially for mining ventures. In addition, the Salvuccis and Cohen find that tariff protection for Mexican textiles was rooted in the widespread opinion that the national government should play a role in managing the economy and allocating wealth shares. In Argentina the Rosas regime even developed provincial tariff, monetary, and land policies aimed at promoting the interests of favored economic sectors. The political economy of the Bourbon administration of the late colonial period benefited urban commercial interests, wheat farmers, and the public sector—not grazing interests. By the mid-1820s, however, new domestic and international market conditions led to the rise of provincial livestock interests, and government policies changed accordingly. Although the recipients of governmental largess changed throughout Spanish America, an important underlying condition continued—the persistent support among elite groups for governmental involvement in the economy.

National governments also played the colonial state's role in allocating scarce labor resources. The African slave trade effectively disappeared following independence in Spanish America. Although slavery persisted until the 1850s in some nations, its economic importance was marginal. The mita or repartimiento also effectively disappeared in this same period. Yet the need to compel labor endured, particularly where the most expansive new economic sectors—such as the Argentine pampa or the guano islands—were isolated from traditional labor supplies. In these cases, the national governments used mechanisms such as vagrancy laws, debt peonage, and immigration to recruit and hold workers, thus alleviating labor shortages.

Few republican governments maintained the colonial state's direct involvement in production. Reduced fiscal resources, managerial inexperience, and altered market realities made such ventures less attractive or impractical. Nevertheless, vestigial elements of the colonial system survived in the Mexican and Ecuadorian estancos. Even the Peruvian government's promotion and supervision of the guano industry mirrored the colonial state's deep involvement in the Huancavelica mercury mine.

Final Remarks

Any effort to study the economic development of Spanish America during the period 1750–1850 must include an analysis of the public sector, a theme that rarely appears in the existing literature. This research agenda must go beyond the analysis of tax, tariff, and monetary policies or the elaboration of efforts by new governments to promote enterprise, secure new markets, or solicit foreign investment. Scholars must examine the impact of all governmental interventions over time in order to assess the long-term, cumulative consequences of public policy on development. This approach would allow for a more sophisticated, dynamic analysis of the relationship between the public and private sectors of the Spanish American economies in the Age of Revolution.

Historians must also recognize the cultural character of economic behavior in Spanish America. Culture translated accumulated economic experience in ways that influenced the decisions of individual producers and consumers. The region's long experience with an interventionist colonial state produced societal expectations that operated dialectically in the early national period with competing liberal programs and the changed institutional and fiscal realities. The essay by the Salvuccis and Cohen illustrates this point concretely. The Mexican debate over tariff protection was fundamentally a contest between vested interests with a long experience of state participation in the economy and intellectuals who were attracted to the utility of free trade. The resolution of this debate, however, was predictable given the colonial culture and the unequal political weight of the contending parties.

The essays presented here suggest obvious continuities with the colonial past in the political economy of the early national period. Yet, they also identify important structural changes in production and exchange. Before scholars are able to assess confidently the comparative economic history of the transitional era, they must undertake more basic research. They will need to ask new questions and pursue answers at the national and regional levels. We believe that this book is a contribution to that end.

Notes

1. Thomas Whigham, *The Politics of the River Trade: Tradition and Development in the Upper Plata, 1780–1870* (Albuquerque, 1991), passim.

Index

Editors and Contributors

Kenneth J. Andrien is professor of history at Ohio State University.

Lyman L. Johnson is professor of history at the University of North Carolina, Charlotte.

Timmothy E. Anna is professor of history at the University of Manitoba.

Brian R. Hamnett is professor of history at the University of Essex.

Susan Deans-Smith is professor of history at the University of Texas, Austin.

Richard J. Slavucci is professor of history at the University of California, Berkeley.

Linda K. Salvucci is professor of history at Trinity University, San Antonio.

Aslán Cohen is an official in the Oficina de Negociación del Tratado de Libre Comercio in Mexico.

John E. Kicza is professor of history at Washington State University.

Kendall W. Brown is professor of history at Hillsdale College.

Jerry W. Cooney is professor of history at the University of Louisville.

Thomas L. Whigham is professor of history at the University of Georgia.